THE

EVERYTHING®

FAMILY GUIDE TO

WASHINGTON D.C.

SECOND EDITION

All the best hotels, restaurants, sites, and
attractions in the nation's capital

Lori Perkins

Adams Media
Avon, Massachusetts

To my son, Max Jimenez, who put up with countless trips to the nation's capital and served as my guide, giving me "inside" information about the things he loved about D.C.

Publishing Director: Gary M. Krebs
Managing Editor: Kate McBride
Copy Chief: Laura MacLaughlin
Acquisitions Editor: Eric M. Hall
Development Editor: Julie Gutin
Production Editor: Jamie Wielgus

Production Director: Susan Beale
Production Manager: Michelle Roy Kelly
Series Designer: Daria Perreault
Cover Design: Paul Beatrice, Matt LeBlanc
Layout and Graphics: Colleen Cunningham, Rachael Eiben, Michelle Roy Kelly, John Paulhus, Daria Perreault, Erin Ring

An Everything® Series Book.
Everything® and everything.com® are registered trademarks of F+W Publications, Inc.

Published by Adams Media, an F+W Publications Company
57 Littlefield Street, Avon, MA 02322 U.S.A.
www.adamsmedia.com

ISBN: 1-59337-137-3
Printed in the Canada.

J I H G F E D C B A

Library of Congress Cataloging-in-Publication Data
Perkins, Lori.
The everything family guide to Washington, D.C. / Lori Perkins.– 2nd ed.
p.   cm.
An everything series book
ISBN 1-59337-137-3
1. Washington (D.C.)–Guidebooks. 2. Family recreation–Washington (D.C.)–Guidebooks.
3. Children–Travel–Washington (D.C.)–Guidebooks. I. Title. II. Series: Everything series.
F192.3.P47 2004
917.5304'41–dc22
2004009168

This publication is designed to provide accurate and authoritative information with regard to the subject matter covered. It is sold with the understanding that the publisher is not engaged in rendering legal, accounting, or other professional advice. If legal advice or other expert assistance is required, the services of a competent professional person should be sought.
—From a *Declaration of Principles* jointly adopted by a Committee of the American Bar Association and a Committee of Publishers and Associations

Many of the designations used by manufacturers and sellers to distinguish their products are claimed as trademarks. Where those designations appear in this book and Adams Media was aware of a trademark claim, the designations have been printed with initial capital letters.

Although the author has taken care to ensure that this book accurately sets forth information as of the time it was prepared, prices, practices, and polices at attractions may change at any time, and may be different from the information provided here.

Cover illustrations by Barry Littmann
Mall map © Map Resources

D.C. neighborhood map used with permission of the D.C. Office of Planning, the National Park Service, the D.C. Department of Parks and Recreation, and the District Department of Transportation.

Metrorail System map used with permission of the Washington Metropolitan Area Transit Authority (WMATA).

This book is available at quantity discounts for bulk purchases. For information, call 1-800-872-5627.

Visit the entire Everything® series at www.everything.com

Contents

Top Ten Things to Do in D.C.

1. Watch fireworks over the Mall on the Fourth of July as you join thousands of Americans in celebration of your country's birthday, and then go and read the Declaration of Independence to your kids at the National Archives and see that actual star-spangled banner at the Museum of American History.

2. Shake the hand of your congressperson or senator.

3. See all that money being printed at the mint.

4. Visit the Tomb of the Unknown Soldier and the eternal flame at the Kennedy gravesite.

5. Stand in front of the Vietnam Veterans Memorial long enough to see someone rub a name from the wall.

6. Climb inside the space shuttle, try on astronaut gloves and helmets, and join your kids on a ride on the flight simulator at the awesome Air and Space Museum.

7. In the wintertime, ice-skate in the outdoor sculpture garden of the National Gallery of Art.

8. In the springtime, push a baby stroller through the cherry orchard in full bloom.

9. Take the D.C. Duck Tour with the kids, and let them blow those duck bills until you hear them in your sleep.

10. Eat as many of Ben's chili dogs as you can and then go to Love Café for chocolate cupcakes.

Introduction

Washington, D.C., is the travel destination for more than 30 million visitors a year and one of the top three national family vacation sites. It truly has something for everyone, from the youngest to the oldest. No matter how many times you visit, there will always be something new and exciting, as well as familiar and rewarding, to see.

It is a great city. I have been there as a young girl with my parents, as a teenager on a school trip, as a young woman traveling on business, and as both the mother of young children and, later, the mother of jaded preteens. I must have visited the city more than twenty times in my lifetime, and each time has been memorable and full of surprises.

Most families come to Washington because it is the seat of our government, a city rich in American history and full of museums—the fifteen museums under Smithsonian Institution management are free of charge. But D.C. is much more than a living history lesson. It is one of the top art centers in the nation and the world, offering major art exhibitions and fascinating architecture. On top of that, it is a college town, with eight universities.

Because there is so much to see and do (and so many new museums and attractions opening every year), many people make Washington a rotating spot on a variable list of vacation places and see a different side of the city each time they visit.

D.C. is one of the most fun and educational places you can visit with your kids, from toddlers to teenagers. The city is like an interactive American history lesson and playground. Aside from the most obvious kid-pleasing attractions (the National Zoo, the Air and Space Museum, and the Museum of Natural History), there are many other one-of-a-kind kid-pleasing experiences, from the new International Spy Museum to the Mint—and what kid doesn't love seeing money printed and shredded? The National Geographic Explorer's Hall has interactive exhibits and a giant dinosaur-egg fossil, and the National Museum of Health and Medicine has the most astounding display of gross medical artifacts in the country.

For those interested in American history and how our government works, the city offers the White House; the Capitol; the Pentagon; the National Archives; the Supreme Court; and the Jefferson, Lincoln, Roosevelt, Vietnam, Korean, and World War II War memorials, as well as a treasure trove of historic homes and monuments.

The Smithsonian Institution itself is like an American theme park. Its most popular museums are the National Air and Space Museum (featuring the Wright brothers' 1903 *Flyer* and the Apollo 11 Space Museum) and now the new Udvar-Hazy Center (with the *Enola Gay* and the space shuttle *Enterprise*), the Museum of Natural History (with the cursed Hope diamond and the new Hall of Mammals, as well as all those dinosaur fossils and bones) and the National Museum of American History (featuring the ruby slippers Judy Garland wore in *The Wizard of Oz* and the gowns worn by the various first ladies at their inaugural balls). The Smithsonian collection also features museums on arts and industries, African and Asian art, decorative arts, American art, great portraits, and modern art.

The Smithsonian also runs the National Zoo (where you can see the pandas and a white tiger), the National Postal Museum (a surprisingly kid-pleasing experience), the Museum of the American Indian, and the Anacostia Museum, which highlights African-American art and culture.

For the history buff, no visit to Washington, D.C., would be complete without a visit to Ford's Theatre, where President Lincoln was shot, and to the Petersen House across the street, where he died. Arlington Cemetery is the site of John F. Kennedy's grave, the Tomb of the Unknown Soldier, and General Robert E. Lee's home, which is part of one of the more fascinating Civil War stories in the city.

And that's not all! There's plenty of shopping to do in the museum shops, specialty stores, and even outlet centers outside of town! Now is your time to start planning your family vacation to one of the most entertaining cities in the nation. And you'll probably be back again and again.

CHAPTER 1

Welcome to Washington, D.C.

WASHINGTON, D.C., the capital of the United States, is one of the leading vacation destinations for American and foreign tourists every year. It is a city full of attractions and rich with history. From its birth as a compromise between the northern and southern states and up to the present day, this city has remained the symbolic center of our country and the center of our federal government. In this chapter, you'll get an introduction to D.C.'s history and the details about traveling there.

A City Is Born

Most students of American history know that D.C. was chosen as the nation's capital after both New York and Philadelphia were given tryouts. It was chosen for its then-central location, perched between the North and the South.

When the decision was made, the city did not yet exist. Maryland and Virginia donated some of their land around the Potomac River to form the federal district, the District of Columbia (D.C.). George Washington played an important role in planning the city, and he entrusted Charles L'Enfant, a French engineer, with designing many of the city's major structures and monuments. A year after George Washington's death in 1799, Congress passed the law that formally moved the U.S. capital from Philadelphia to

Washington, D.C. Naming the city after our first president was Congress's way of honoring George Washington for all that he had done for our country.

Burning of the White House

Just over a decade later, D.C. came under attack. During the War of 1812, the Americans fought the British, who were bent on recapturing their former colonies. It is the only international war fought on American soil after the Revolution.

In the summer of 1814, the British defeated American troops at the Battle of Bladensburg and entered the American capital. Their goal was to burn it, a symbolic act to show their victory. In addition to burning the White House, the British also torched the Capitol, the Library of Congress, and several military sites. Fortunately, because of heavy rains, the fire subsided without harming much of the city.

≡FAST FACT

Dolley Madison, who was the first lady at that time, is remembered for rescuing the life-sized Gilbert Stuart portrait of George Washington and other artifacts of the presidential building before evacuation. After the fire subsided and the building was renovated with white paint, it became known as the White House.

Washington During the Civil War

The city recovered from the War of 1812 and thrived again, but it soon found itself in the middle of another war—the Civil War. Although no battles were fought in Washington, D.C., it became a virtual military camp, with armed troops housed everywhere from the White House to the alleys of the Foggy Bottom neighborhood, which was referred to as "camptown." D.C. was the main storage area for military supplies for the Union Army, as well as a medical center. Many of the city's buildings, such as the U.S. Patent Building (now the National Museum of American Art and the National Portrait Gallery), were transformed into makeshift hospitals.

As a result, the population of the city swelled from 60,000 to 120,000 almost overnight. Many of the new residents were freed slaves who came to the city for protection; a lot of them made their home on the grounds of the Arlington House, where they formed their own town, known as the Freedman's Village.

Assassination of President Lincoln

Five days after the city began celebrating the end of the Civil War, President Lincoln was assassinated while at a performance at Ford's Theatre, and the country went into mourning. The city itself was in chaos, both from the overburdening of its resources with so many new residents and the political upheaval. Many of the city's slums were created during this time, and those neighborhoods remained in that condition until well into the twentieth century.

Moving On

Nevertheless, the government pulled through, and it made rebuilding the city one of the first orders of business. Washington, D.C., became a mecca for freed slaves and a true seat of government. Federal funding literally rebuilt the city in the nineteenth and early twentieth centuries, giving us the marvelous monuments, museums, and parks we have today.

≡FAST FACT

The tradition of rallies and protests that make our capital the political entity it is today started after the Civil War and crescendoed through the 1960s, when anti–Vietnam War protests and civil rights demonstrations we held almost daily on the Mall. It was there that Martin Luther King Jr. made his "I Have a Dream" speech, written at the nearby Willard Hotel.

D.C. Today

Today, Washington, D.C., is a beautiful city with fine dining, excellent art, theater, music, and entertainment that rivals the world's leading hotspots. It's a great place to visit year-round, with many wonderful seasonal attractions such as the famous cherry trees circling the Tidal Basin that blossom in the early spring or the candlelight tours of the White House during the holiday season. Many people come annually for the solemn and touching Memorial Day ceremonies at the Vietnam Veterans Memorial and Arlington National Cemetery, for the fabulous fireworks display over the National Mall for the Fourth of July, or for the annual black family reunion weekend on the Mall the first weekend of September.

Because the climate is relatively mild for three seasons out of four, there is never a bad time to visit the nation's capital, which means that it is a city that regularly receives and accommodates tourists. However, this also means that the many sites and attractions are often crowded, which can translate into long lines to get into popular sites or no entry at all.

🧳 TRAVEL TIP

Before you go, do some research online. Even if you don't have a computer, most public libraries offer free Internet access and can help you take advantage of it. Once you are on the Internet, you can use a search engine such as Google to surf the Web by typing in the words "Washington, D.C." This will bring hundreds of listings, everything from event calendars to sports listings. Your search will be more successful if you know where to look.

The Four Seasons

If you're not sure what the best time is for you to visit D.C., there's a lot to consider. If you're worried about the crowds, fall and winter are preferable, but in these seasons Congress is in session, so hotel rates are higher than in the summer.

In the Fall

Washington, D.C., and the adjacent states of Virginia and Maryland are beautiful in the fall. The city and the surrounding countryside are filled with trees and parklands that offer a wonderful display of fall foliage. Mount Vernon is especially scenic this time of year. The tourist crowds are sparse, except over three-day weekends that mark national holidays like Columbus Day and Veterans Day.

Wintertime

Winter is also a good time to visit the capital. There are many special events planned around the holidays, and most of the museums and historic houses offer special Christmas displays. While the winter in D.C. is milder than in the Northeast, it still snows in the capital.

TRAVEL TIP

Christmas in Washington is delightful. The White House features its tree-lighting ceremony; Ford's Theatre has an annual performance of Dickens's *A Christmas Carol*; and Mount Vernon and the Pope-Leighey House are festooned with seasonal ornaments.

Spring in D.C.

Spring in the capital city is spectacular. D.C. has a wealth of public gardens and greenery, as well as the annual Easter-egg roll on the White House lawn. When the cherry trees along the Tidal Basin near the Jefferson Memorial are in bloom in the early spring, D.C. is at its finest in a sea of pink. For this two-week period in late March or early April, there are constant festivities, marked by a parade at the end of the cherry blossom season. The 3,700 cherry trees were a gift to the United States from Japan in 1912. The first two trees were planted by First Lady Mrs. William Howard Taft and Viscountess Chinda of Japan, the Japanese ambassador's wife. Those two trees are still standing today, near the statue of John Paul Jones on 17th Street.

As the weather grows warmer, more and more tourists arrive to tour the capital. Many schools plan organized trips for this time of the year, so museums and historical sites are generally crowded in the later part of the spring.

TRAVEL TIP

The two busiest tourist weekends in D.C. are the Fourth of July and Memorial Day. So if you are planning on visiting then, make your hotel, transportation, and touring arrangements as early as possible.

Summertime

Summer is the city's busiest tourist season, with tourists out-numbering residents by twelve to one. The National Air and Space Museum and the National Museum of Natural History receive at least a million visitors each during the months of July and August. From Memorial Day through Labor Day all the sites are crowded, and you will need tickets for all major attractions this time of year.

But the good news is that the city is well aware of the volume of visitors it receives, so many of the nation's leading attractions are open late during the summer. You can pack more into a summer visit than any other time of the year. There are also free concerts and outdoor activities throughout the city all summer long.

Summer in D.C. can be brutally hot, but everything is well air-conditioned, from the museums to the Metro to the lobbies of buildings.

What to Pack

Washington, D.C., is a fairly laid-back city. If you plan on visiting the tourist sites, comfort should be your priority: jeans (or shorts in the summer) and sneakers or comfortable walking shoes. If you're visiting a lot of museums and plan to shop, bring an empty knapsack, or you'll be carrying around shopping bags loaded with souvenirs all day. Be prepared to check your knapsack at the door of every attraction and to have your belongings screened.

If you know you will be attending an arena event, an outdoor concert, or parade, you might want to pack binoculars. Also, don't forget your camera and/or video camera.

Spring and late summer are often rainy, so pack a collapsible umbrella or a rain poncho and put it in that knapsack. In the summer, pack a bathing suit. Many of the hotels have pools, and you'll want to cool off.

JUST FOR PARENTS

If you are planning on going to the theater, the Kennedy Center, or some of the better restaurants, plan to dress up a bit—jackets and ties for men, nice dresses for women. Some of the better restaurants will not allow men to dine without proper attire. Besides, dressing up is part of the fun of an elegant night on the town!

Plan Ahead

It is possible to visit Washington, D.C., and wing it, but there are so many must-see things to do that require tickets (both free and paid) that it is really in your interest to plan ahead, especially if you are going for a short visit or vacationing during the holidays or the peak travel season.

Almost all the government tours require tickets, and some of these tours have very limited windows of opportunity, especially after the terrorist attack of September 11. For instance, the White House was closed to tours by the general public for over two years and has just reopened to much more limited public touring. It is now only possible to have a guided tour through your member of congress. These self-guided tours of ten people may visit the national residence between 7:30 A.M. and 11:30 A.M., Tuesday through Saturday. However, this is an ongoing process of opening the White House to more access, so call the White House information line at ☎ 202-456-7041 or check its Web site at ✎*www.white house.gov* to see if any more tickets have been added or the hours have been expanded.

To plan a trip through your member of congress, it is now suggested that you call your representative's or senator's local office six months before your trip. You can look up the numbers in your local phone book or by calling information or searching on the Web for his or her Web site. You can also write to him or her at the following address:

Name of Representative	Name of Senator
House of Representatives	U.S. Senate
Washington, D.C. 20515	Washington, D.C. 20510

Write the words "Advance Tickets" on the envelope. If you're short on time, it might be worth your while to call the Washington office and fax your letter. You may also be able to apply for tickets online through your representative's office.

In addition to the White House tour, government tours and sites that require tickets are the following:

- The Washington Monument
- The Bureau of Engraving and Printing
- The Capitol
- The Supreme Court
- The Kennedy Center

Getting Your Tickets Online

Some of the more popular attractions also require tickets. Waiting in line for a ticket can eat up a lot of your day, but you can call a ticket service and get advance tickets for a small service charge. Tickets.com will supply you with up to four tickets for a nominal service charge of $3 per ticket and a $1 processing charge on the whole order.

Tickets.com
☎1-800-400-9373 (10 A.M. to 9 P.M.)
✍*www.tickets.com*

For instance, Tickets.com offers tickets to the Holocaust Museum—if you purchase them online or by phone, tickets will be waiting for you inside the museum at the pass desk. If you use Tickets.com to book a Ford's Theatre tour, tickets can be picked up at the will-call desk.

💼 TRAVEL TIP

The National Parks Service offers tickets to the Washington Monument for a charge of $1.50, plus an overall order charge of $1.50. To contact the service, call ☎1-800-967-2283, or visit its Web site at ✍*http://reservations.nps.gov*.

Events and Performances

Washington, D.C., has a number of terrific theatrical and musical venues, some of which are free. Before your trip, it might be a good idea to find out what events and performances are coming up while you are in town. The *Washington Post* publishes an excellent weekend guide every Friday, so if you have a friend in the city, make sure he or she saves a copy for you. If you don't, visit the Post's Web site at ✍*www.washingtonpost.com* and go to the entertainment listings of your choice. The following are major cultural venues in Washington.

John F. Kennedy Center for the Performing Arts

The Center hosts free concerts most evenings at 6:00 P.M., as well as paid performances of theater, dance, music, and more. Call ☎1-800-444-1324 for information or visit the Web site at ✍*www.kennedy-center.org*.

MCI Center

The MCI Center is *the* venue for sports and concerts in D.C. For more information and to order tickets, call ☎1-800-551-SEAT or visit their Web site at ✍*www.mcicenter.com*.

Wolf Trap Theatre

This is an outdoor venue where you can catch wonderful performances—operas, classical music concerts, and more. Call ☎703-255-1868 or visit their site at ✍*www.wolftrap.org*.

National Shakespeare Company

The National Shakespeare Company presents classical theater productions. Call ☎202-393-2700 or visit them online at ✍*www.shakespearedc.org*.

Ford's Theatre

The theater where President Lincoln was assassinated is still an active theater. Call ☎202-347-4833 for information about performances.

☂ RAINY DAY FUN

If you decide you want to see a performance the day of the show, you might be able to get half-price tickets. You can call TICKETplace at ☎202-TICKETS the night before or the day of the show. Tickets can be purchased over the phone or bought directly at the TICKETplace sales booth in the Old Post Office Pavilion. Full-price tickets to most D.C. events can be purchased over the phone through TicketMaster by calling ☎202-432-SEAT.

CHAPTER 2

Must-See Attractions

THERE IS SO MUCH TO DO in Washington, D.C., that you could spend a month in the city and still not have seen the whole town. There are more than seventy museums, regular concerts, and performances (some of which are free). There are also many events every weekend, on top of incredible restaurants offering high cuisine and one-of-a-kind dining experiences. But there are some D.C.-based attractions and events that define a trip to the nation's capital, and these should be on every first-time visitor's agenda.

The Smithsonian Institution

The Smithsonian is composed of fifteen museums and galleries dedicated to preserving our nation's history, art, and culture, as well as the art and culture of other countries. There is nothing else like this museum collection in the world, a true one-of-a-kind gem that we, as a nation, should be very proud of. (The individual museums are covered in detail in Chapters 5 and 6.)

It would be impossible to see all of the Smithsonian museums in one day or even a few days. Some of them are simply too large, and others don't enjoy a convenient location, but most visitors to the city make time for the impressive and fun National Air and

Space Museum, as well as the National Museum of Natural History and the National Museum of American History. Visiting these three museums in one day is a tough accomplishment, really only possible during the summer months, when the museums are often open late. Along with six others, these museums are all located on the Mall, between 4th and 14th Streets between Constitution and Independence Avenues.

The National Air and Space Museum

This is the most popular of the Smithsonian museums, getting close to 8 million visitors a year. That means it is often crowded. Get there early, and plan on spending at least three hours once there.

⚓ RAINY DAY FUN

Catch one of the wonderful IMAX movies or let the kids explore the new flight-simulator rides at the Air and Space Museum. Many of these rides are replicas of the planes and spaceships on display.

The museum is huge. It now has a sister, the Steven F. Udvar-Hazy Center, in the D.C. suburbs (the *Enola Gay* is there), because the airplanes and spacecraft themselves are so large.

Some of the wonderful objects and exhibits in the main museum include the following:

- The Wright brothers' *Flyer*
- Charles Lindbergh's *Spirit of St. Louis*
- Amelia Earhart's airplane
- The airplane in which Chuck Yeager broke the speed of sound
- Apollo II, with space suits
- A lunar rock
- The Hubble space telescope
- Space shuttle *Columbia*

In addition, there's an IMAX theater with some wonderful films about space exploration and the history of flight, as well as interactive games in which you can pilot a plane or spacecraft, some of which are on display in the museum. When you've had enough, there's an expansive remodeled food court that offers fast food from McDonald's, Boston Market, and Donato's Pizza.

The National Museum of Natural History

This museum has something for everyone in the family. Women love the exhibit of gems—especially the legendary cursed Hope diamond (a replica of which can be purchased in the Smithsonian gift shop). And kids love the dinosaurs and the brand-new Hall of Mammals. There's also one of the few preserved specimens of the giant squid and a wonderfully creepy Orkin Insect Zoo, where some of the live specimens can be touched. In the spring and summer, the museum also hosts a butterfly garden.

The IMAX theater on the premises has wonderful 3D films about dinosaurs, fossils, and bugs, and special movies that are often linked to an exhibit. The Albert Einstein Planetarium features new technology that actually makes you feel the sensation of flying through the universe. The completely remodeled cafeteria is airy and offers a full selection of salads, sandwiches, and hot dishes.

There is a lot to do and see at the National Museum of Natural History. Plan on spending at least two to three hours here.

FAST FACT

The newly renovated mammal wing of the National Museum of Natural History has a number of hands-on sites for kids, where tiny hands can touch fossilized bones and examine the skull of an extinct bear up close to get a real "feel" for how familiar animals have evolved.

The National Museum of American History

The Museum of American History is an absolute must-see on any visit to D.C. It is a smorgasbord of American history starting with the Revolution. No woman can leave the city without looking at the exhibit of the first ladies' inaugural gowns or Judy Garland's ruby slippers from *The Wizard of Oz*.

Among the many must-see items on display at this museum are the original star-spangled banner (the one that inspired the national anthem), and various exhibits on the development of technology, featuring such artifacts as Foucault's pendulum, Edison's light bulb, and an early Model T Ford, as well as a very interactive exhibit on transportation. This exhibit is located in the recently opened wing on the history of transportation, which features compelling looks into the making of the New York City subway system and Route 66. If this is not your first trip to this museum, go to this exhibit first and stay a while. There's plenty for kids to explore.

There's an old-fashioned replica of an ice cream parlor on the first floor that serves wonderful pastries, coffee, and ice cream. This museum takes about two and a half hours to see properly.

The White House

This is a truly American experience but one you will really have to plan. After the terrorist attacks of September 11, the White House was closed to public touring, and it has only recently reopened for very limited touring. You have to request a tour through your congressperson, and it is suggested that you do this six months before your trip. Tours are only given Tuesdays through Saturdays, 7:30 to 11:30 A.M.

Should you be lucky enough to tour the White House, seven rooms and the public halls are open to viewing, including the China Room, where pieces of China from every presidency are on display, as well as the library and the Map Room.

There is a White House Visitors' Center on the southeast corner of 15th and E Streets, where there is an exhibit of White House history, furniture, architecture, and first family artifacts. There are no bathrooms or phones available to the public.

📁 TRAVEL TIP

There are no bathrooms open to the public in the White House, so make sure you stop at the visitors' center before you go through the security check. There are also no public phones, and all cell phones must be turned off.

The International Spy Museum

This is a relatively new museum to the city (opened in 2003), but it is utterly charming and entertaining. It takes somewhere between two and three hours to see and is like no other museum. You are given an alias when you enter the museum as you tour through the history of spying, with an emphasis on American spying activities during the twentieth century. James Bond's Aston Martin is here, as well as an extensive display on female spies, a duct tunnel your children can crawl through, and some good exhibits on famous spies of World War II and the infamous Cold War. In short, the International Spy Museum is wonderfully interactive.

The museum also hosts a great gift shop and a nice cafeteria where you can buy "killer sandwiches."

═FAST FACT

Chef Julia Child, director John Ford, actress Marlene Dietrich, and dancer Josephine Baker all merit write-ups in the celebrity section of the International Spy Museum. Find out why when you visit the museum.

Washington Monument

Due to the terrorist attacks of September 11, access to the Washington Monument has changed. The monument itself is open, but the grounds are closed for security reasons.

To visit the monument, you'll need to get tickets through the National Park Reservation Service (NPRS). You can do it over the phone by calling ☎1-800-967-2283. You can also go online to their Web site at ✍*http://reservations.nps.gov* (at a $1.50 fee per ticket). Free tickets are given out at the kiosk on the grounds of the monument from 8:00 A.M. until 4:30 P.M, but in the summer months they are often gone by 9:00 A.M.

Purchasing the tickets in advance is definitely worth it. A restoration of the monument was completed in 2000, and as a result the observation deck now has air conditioning along with its unparalleled vistas of the city. There is also a newly revised interpretive exhibit area and a new elevator with glass doors so you can view the commemorative stones in the stairwell.

Vietnam Veterans Memorial

How could something so simple have such power? The Vietnam Veterans Memorial is one of those brilliant pieces of public art that captures the right emotions and serves its purpose of commemorating the American soldiers who lost their lives in the conflict. The big black granite wall of the memorial is etched with the names of 58,226 who died and/or went missing in action. The effect is solemn and powerful. Every day, friends and family of the deceased can be seen rubbing the names from the wall or leaving letters or mementos.

💼 TRAVEL TIP

If possible, try to visit the Vietnam Veterans Memorial in the daytime and again at night—the effect is very different. It is open from 8:00 A.M. until midnight. If you go just before dusk, you can experience both at one time.

Lincoln and Jefferson Memorials

Both the Lincoln and the Jefferson Memorials are open until midnight and are brilliantly lit up in the evening. If you have a car or can take an evening tour of the memorials by bus or trolley, that is the time to visit as their stature is at its best.

The Lincoln Memorial was designed to resemble a Greek temple, with the seated president overlooking a reflecting pool. His writings appear on the wall behind him. There's an exhibit area where you will find excerpts from his speeches, as well as a changing display of photographs.

The Jefferson Memorial with its domed rotunda overlooks the Tidal Basin. The memorial features a bronzed statue of Jefferson, as well as a sampling of his writing. Though the two presidents lived almost a century apart, their two memorials were completed within thirty years of each other, and Lincoln's was erected first.

The National Zoo

No trip to the nation's capital is complete without a trip to the zoo, where you can see the pair of pandas on loan from China, the tropical rain forest, a white tiger, and one of the few Komodo dragons bred in captivity. There are two restaurants and a number of gift shops, as well as some terrific spots for family photos.

CHAPTER 3

Getting There

WASHINGTON, D.C., IS A FULL-ACCESS CITY, with many routes of transportation available. It has three airports, a very comfortable and safe combination train and bus station that was recently remodeled, and highways that are fairly easy to navigate.

Most visitors to the city drive in, but you do not need a car once you are there. The city's Metro system is as good as Paris or New York's—actually better, because it's newer and completely air-conditioned—and taxis are affordable, whereas parking downtown is hard to come by and very expensive. Because of the number of rallies, demonstrations, and political activities, as well as a fair amount of tourist traffic, it is often impossible to reach the downtown streets close to tourist attractions, let alone to find nearby parking.

Take an Airplane

The three airports serving Washington, D.C., have all been recently modernized. Two of them are accessible by Metro, and you can get to and from the third via Amtrak, making it very easy and affordable to get from the airport to your hotel.

Ronald Reagan Washington National Airport

Known until 1998 as National Airport, Reagan National (RNA) is the airport closest to downtown Washington. Situated just across the Potomac River from D.C., it is a short cab ride (about twenty minutes) or an easy Metro ride from the heart of the city. The Metro system's Blue and Yellow lines can take you to or from Reagan National.

The airport is served by eleven airlines, none of which flies international flights (except to and from Canada), as it is required by law that no Reagan National flight can exceed 12,500 miles. Even with this restriction, it is one of the busiest airports in the nation.

📑 TRAVEL TIP

If you're looking to save money on your airfare and have some flexibility in your travel schedule, try bidding on a ticket at Priceline.com. What's great about this service is that you decide how much you want to pay for your tickets. Priceline will try to locate an airline that has seats available and that will accept your offer. Tickets can be purchased hours, days, weeks, or even months in advance. For more information (and to check the restrictions), call ☎1-800-PRICELINE or visit ✎*www.priceline.com.*

With the recent name change came a rehab and a new terminal. If you have some free time to waste at the airport, look for the artwork displayed there. The various concourses also feature a Smithsonian shop (just in case you forgot to buy something during your visit), a National Zoo store, a National Geographic store, and a selection of fast-food and restaurant establishments as well as coffee shops.

Washington Dulles International Airport (IAD)

One of two international airports serving the city, Dulles is twenty-six miles from downtown in Chantilly, Virginia. By car, it is a thirty-five- to forty-minute ride without rush-hour traffic. Most travelers take a cab from the airport, which runs about $40 to $50. However, there is a Metrobus that serves the airport, which will connect you with the Orange line of the Metro system. The bus ride takes thirty minutes, and then it's another ten to twenty minutes by subway.

The various concourses feature a wealth of news and bookstores, as well as coffee shops, gift shops, and restaurants. The airport is undergoing a ten-year expansion that will double its capacity by the year 2010.

Baltimore-Washington International Airport (BWI)

This is a smaller airport than either Reagan National or Dulles. It is easier to book because most people go for the large airports. It is forty-five minutes from downtown by car, just a few miles outside of Baltimore.

Its main terminal also sports a Smithsonian shop, as well as the ubiquitous Starbucks. There is also a full-service café and a kid's playground, and you can catch Amtrak here and be in Union Station in 30 minutes. Or you can take a new Metrobus service from BWI that takes about 20 minutes to get to D.C.'s Green Line.

Domestic and International Carriers

Almost every major airline flies into Washington, D.C. Sixteen domestic airlines and twenty foreign ones serve the capital.

DOMESTIC CARRIERS	
AirTran Airways (Dulles)	☏1-800-247-8726
	✐www.airtran.com
Alaska Airlines (RNA, Dulles)	☏1-800-252-7522
	✐www.alaskaair.com
American Airlines (RNA, Dulles, BWI)	☏1-800-433-7300
	✐www.aa.com
America West (Dulles, BWI)	☏1-800-235-9292
	✐www.americawest.com
ATA (RNA)	☏1-800-435-9282
	✐www.ata.com

(continued)

DOMESTIC CARRIERS *(continued)*	
Continental (RNA, Dulles, BWI)	✆1-800-525-0280 ✐www.continental.com
Delta (RNA, Dulles, BWI)	✆1-800-241-1212 ✐www.delta.com
Frontier Airlines (BWI, RNA)	✆1-800-432-1359 ✐www.frontierairlines.com
JetBlue (Dulles)	✆1-800-538-2583 ✐www.jetblue.com
Midwest Express (RNA)	✆1-800-452-2022 ✐www.midwestexpress.com
Northwest Airlines (RNA, Dulles, BWI)	✆1-800-225-2525 ✐www.nwa.com
Song (Dulles)	✆1-800-359-7664 ✐www.flysong.com
Southwest Airlines (BWI)	✆1-800-435-9792 ✐www.southwest.com
Spirit Airlines (RNA)	✆1-800-772-7117 ✐www.spiritair.com
United Airlines (RNA, Dulles, BWI)	✆1-800-241-6522 ✐www.ual.com
US Airways (RNA, Dulles, BWI)	✆1-800-428-4322 ✐www.usairways.com

 JUST FOR PARENTS

If you are flying a distance, you can call ahead and request a "child's meal" on the flight. You can also ask if they have any special features for kids. Some airlines still give out wings.

Shuttle Services from New York City

If you live in New York City or the surrounding areas, you can take a Delta, U.S. Airways, or American Eagle shuttle to D.C.'s Reagan National Airport.

Delta runs an hourly shuttle flight between New York's LaGuardia Airport and Reagan National Airport on the half-hour from 6:30 A.M. until 8:30 P.M. on weeknights, with a last flight at 9:00 P.M. The shuttle flies from 7:30 A.M. to 8:30 P.M. on Saturday and from 8:30 A.M. till 9:00 P.M. on Sunday.

U.S. Airways' shuttle service also flies from New York's LaGuardia Airport to Reagan National, with hourly flights from 7:00 A.M. to 9:00 P.M. on weekdays and Saturday, and service from 9:00 A.M. to 9:00 P.M. on Sunday.

Your final option is an American Eagle shuttle. American Airlines added its shuttle service to D.C. from LaGuardia in October 2003, and the airline offers ten daily flights to Reagan National on the hour.

If you're flying into Washington, D.C., from overseas, you might take one of the following international carriers.

INTERNATIONAL CARRIERS	
Aeroflot (Dulles)	☎1-888-340-6400
	✎www.aeroflot.org
Air Canada (RNA, Dulles, BWI)	☎1-888-247-2262
	✎www.aircanada.ca
Air France (Dulles)	☎1-800-321-8726
	✎www.airfrance.com
Air India (Dulles)	☎1-800-255-3191
	✎www.airindia.com
Air Jamaica (BWI)	☎1-800-523-5585
	✎www.airjamaica.com
All Nippon Airways (Dulles)	☎1-800-235-9262
	✎www.fly-ana.com
Austrian Airlines (Dulles)	☎1-800-843-0002
	✎www.aua.com
British Airways (Dulles, BWI)	☎1-800-247-9297
	✎www.britishairways.com

(continued)

INTERNATIONAL CARRIERS (continued)	
El-Al Israel Airlines (BWI)	✆1-800-223-6700 ✉www.elal.co.il
Ethiopian Airlines (Dulles)	✆1-800-445-2733 ✉www.flyethiopian.com
Grupo TACA International Airlines (Dulles)	✆1-800-535-8780 ✉www.grupotaca.com
Icelandair (BWI)	✆1-800-223-5500 ✉www.icelandair.com
KLM Royal Dutch Airlines (Dulles)	✆1-800-374-7747 ✉www.klm.com
Korean Air (Dulles)	✆1-800-438-5000 ✉www.koreanair.com
Lufthansa (Dulles)	✆1-800-645-3880 ✉www.lufthansa.com
Qantas Airways (Dulles)	✆1-800-227-4500 ✉www.qantas.com.au
Scandinavian Airlines (Dulles)	✆1-800-221-2350 ✉www.sas.se
Saudi Arabian Airlines (Dulles)	✆1-800-472-8342 ✉www.saudiairlines.com
Spanair (Dulles)	✆1-800-545-5757 ✉www.spanair.es
Virgin Atlantic (Dulles)	✆1-800-862-8621 ✉www.virgin-atlantic.com

In and out of the Airport

Travel to and from any of the D.C. airports is easy. Your best options are to take the Metro or a taxi.

Reagan National Airport

If you arrive at the Ronald Reagan National Airport and you don't have a lot of luggage, the fastest and cheapest way to get to your hotel is the Metro system. Reagan National Airport connects directly with the Blue and Yellow Metro lines. The cost of a ride is $1.20 during non-rush hours and $1.70 during rush hour (if you arrive during rush hours, you might want to take an alternate method of transportation because the trains get very crowded at this time). You can also take a Metrobus from the airport.

A taxi from Reagan National Airport to downtown should cost you between $12 and $15. D.C. cabs are run on a zone and passenger number system, so it should be straightforward and affordable, but some cab drivers try to gouge tourists (especially if they think you don't know the city), so ask about the price before you get going.

Dulles International Airport

A Metrobus takes passengers to an Orange line Metro station (with a bus transfer, the two rides cost only an additional twenty-five cents). The Washington Flyer bus will take you to the Metro station for $8.00. It takes about an hour to get downtown. A cab ride from Dulles to downtown Washington will run you between $35 and $45.

Baltimore-Washington International Airport

There are two shuttle-type services from BWI. The Montgomery Airport Shuttle goes to Union Station and other locations, and the Airport Connection II will take you downtown in a shared van. Amtrak also runs train service to Union Station from BWI. If you prefer to take a cab, the fare would be about $45 to downtown D.C. You can now take the B30 Metrobus express from the BWI to the Greenbelt Station, which will run into D.C.'s Green Metro line, for $2.00 per trip.

TRAVEL TIP

If you'd like to take Amtrak between BWI and Union Station, fares run from $9 to $17 per person. You can pay on the train, and the trip takes about half an hour. Another option is the Maryland Rural Commuter System (MARC). During the week, commuter trains will take you from the BWI train station to Union Station for $5 per person.

Private Transportation Services

There are also private transportation services that will pick you up and drive you to your hotel (and vice versa on the way back).

Super Shuttle

☎ 1-800-258-3826

☎ 703-416-6661

This is a seven-passenger shared-ride van service that is easily recognizable by its blue color. It provides service from 5:30 A.M. to 12:30 P.M. and serves all three airports. Fares are based on Zip Code. A ride from Reagan National runs about $9, from Dulles about $22, and from BWI about $30. There are reduced rates for an additional person traveling to the same destination.

Washington Flyer

☎ 1-888-WASHFLY

This bus service runs between Dulles and Reagan National airports, as well as to Union Station downtown and to the Metro station at West Church Falls. The ride to the Metro station is $8 one-way or $14 roundtrip to Reagan National, and they offer a family fare for up to three members. Children under 6 ride free.

Washington Flyer Limousine

☎ 703-685-1400

Stretch limos and sedans are available from Dulles to downtown Washington, D.C., with prices starting at $45.

The Montgomery Airport Shuttle

☎ 301-230-4000

This twenty-four-hour shuttle service serves all three airports and runs to Union Station and a number of other locations. Fares start at $16, with a reduced price for the second person traveling to the same destination. Reservations are strongly recommended. Credit cards accepted.

The Airport Connection II

✎ 1-800-284-6066

This is a shared-ride van service between BWI and downtown D.C., with fares running between $20 and $30, depending upon your destination.

World Airport Shuttle

✎ 1-800-734-5566

This shuttle offers van service from BWI and Dulles. Sample fares are $35 from BWI to downtown, $28 from Dulles to downtown.

Getting to D.C. by Train

Amtrak goes directly into D.C.'s remodeled Union Station with daily service from Boston, Chicago, New York, and Los Angeles, and many stops in between. From New York to Washington, D.C., there are Metroliner trains that make the trip in less than three hours, which competes with the airline shuttle services given that you now have to get to the airport earlier due to security measures.

👥 JUST FOR PARENTS

Amtrak often has a half-price program for children traveling with adults, so check before you buy your tickets to see if they are running that promotion. Amtrak also offers American Automobile Association (AAA) discounts.

It is a pleasure to disembark at Union Station. The station has three levels of shops, good upscale restaurants, and an entire food court offering a wide variety of fast food from sushi to sauerbraten. It also features a nine-screen movie theater, which means it is bustling with locals, as well as travelers, at all times.

Union Station is a stop on the Red line of the Metro system, so if you pack light, this is a quick and convenient way to get to your hotel. Outside the station is a taxi stand where you will never have to wait for a cab. Most cab rides to downtown hotels cost only $5 (one zone fare) but will charge an additional fee per person.

Amtrak fares to the same destination vary depending on what day and what time of the day you leave. Discounts for students and senior citizens are available, and other discounts may apply. For more information, call ✆1-800-USA-RAIL, or log on to ✍www.amtrak.com.

≡FAST FACT

Greyhound (✆1-800-231-2222, ✍www.greyhound.com) serves Washington, D.C., from almost anywhere in the country. Buses arrive at a station four blocks from Union Station (which is the closest Metro station), so if you arrive after dark, plan to take a cab to your destination because the neighborhood is often desolate. Greyhound offers a student and senior citizen discount club, and children between the ages of 3 and 11 ride for half-price.

Make It a Roadtrip

Washington, D.C., is accessible from a number of major highways, and the ride is straightforward. From the north you can take I-270, I-95, or I-295; from the south, you can take Route 1 or Route 301; from the east you can take Route 50/301 or Route 450; and from the west, you can take Route 50/I-66 or Route 29/211.

Once you hit the city proper, you will have to navigate the fabled beltway (I-95 and I-495). This sixty-six-mile highway circles the city and is usually crowded, especially during the morning and evening rush hours.

Signage is not perfect in the city, so make sure you consult your map and know exactly where you are going. The city also has an enormous number of one-way streets and traffic circles, so go to ✍www.mapquest.com and print out directions before you leave home (as well as reverse directions, although most hotel staff are gifted at getting you onto the highways). Otherwise you could lose half an hour going in circles on one-way streets. If you are traveling during rush hour, you might want to tune your car radio to one of the city's all-news stations, which offer periodic traffic reports. WTOP-FM is at 1500 AM and 107.7 FM.

Renting a Car

Although you don't need a car in D.C. itself, if you have business or vacation plans in the surrounding areas of Virginia and Maryland (for instance, you plan to visit Mount Vernon), having a car is your best bet.

Car rentals are available at all three airports, as well as at Union Station. Many major car-rental chains offer services in D.C.

Alamo Rent a Car	✆1-800-GO-ALAMO
	✎www.alamo.com
Dollar Rent a Car	✆1-800-800-3665
	✎www.dollar.com
Enterprise Rent-a-Car	✆1-800-RENT-A-CAR
	✎www.enterprise.com
Hertz	✆1-800-654-3131
	✎www.hertz.com
Thrifty Car Rental	✆1-800-THRIFTY
	✎www.thrifty.com

Car rentals at the airports are often more expensive than at other locations, so be sure you price your package. Also ask about local taxes and surcharges.

💼 TRAVEL TIP

If you are flying or taking Amtrak, inquire about fly/drive packages with your airline at the time of your plane ticket purchase because often they can give you a good package deal.

Parking in D.C.

Whether you arrive in your car or rent one during some part of your stay at D.C., you should consider leaving your car at a parking garage as you go and see the sights inside city limits. Most visitors park their cars in the hotel's parking lot for an additional fee of up to $25 a day. Or you may choose to take advantage of the services provided by the twenty-four-hour parking lot at Union Station (✆202-289-1908, ✍*www.unionstationdc.com*), since it offers cheaper rates than hotel parking.

There is metered parking downtown (free after 6:30 P.M., and on weekends), but over-meter tickets run $25. If your car is towed, it will be taken to a tow pound in Maryland (✉4800 Addison Rd., ✆202-727-1000). You can take the Metro to get there—get off at the Dearwood Metro stop on the Orange line.

CHAPTER 4

Discover the City

WASHINGTON, D.C., is a city that's perfect for the tourist. Its layout is planned according to an easily grasped system of letters and numbers; its neighborhoods are easily accessible; and you've got lots of options for public transportation to go from one place to the next. To familiarize yourself with D.C., review this chapter, then take a tour that will give you an overview of the city and its major attractions before you move on to more specific plans.

The D.C. Street System

Because Washington, D.C., was designed before building ever began on land carved out of Maryland and Virginia, its layout makes perfect sense. East-west streets use the letters of the alphabet (A Street, B Street, and so on) and north-south streets are numbered (First Street, Second Street). When all the letters have been used, the east-west streets continue alphabetically with two-syllable names—Adams, Belmont—and then move on to three-syllable ones. Diagonal avenues named after various states intersect the grid and form several traffic circles.

The city is divided into four quadrants—northwest, northeast, southwest, and southeast—with the U.S. Capitol more or less at the center. These quadrant locators are important when writing to someone in the city or when you give cab drivers the address of your destination.

While this design is quite wonderful, it is meaningless when you are trying to find a movie theater in the Adams Morgan neighborhood using only a subway map, which has no street names— just Metro station names and routes in bright colors. Therefore, one of the first things you need to do when you get to your hotel room (or on your way to the city) is orient yourself with the dozen or so neighborhoods that make up the city, as well as the distance from your hotel to your destination. This will help you in planning Metro trips, as well as judging how expensive a cab ride will be.

≡FAST FACT

Here are a few terms that will help you get around D.C. The Hill (Capitol Hill) is the area immediately surrounding the U.S. Capitol. The Mall is the downtown area where you will find most of the Smithsonian museums and several of the city's major sightseeing attractions; it is a two-and-a-half-mile strip between Constitution and Independence Avenues that starts at the Lincoln Memorial and ends at the U.S. Capitol. The Metro is the city's underground mass transit system (subway).

Overview of the Neighborhoods

The following sections should suffice as a good introduction to D.C.'s neighborhoods. We'll begin with the three most frequented areas (downtown, the Mall, and Capitol Hill) and then go on to other neighborhoods in alphabetical order.

Most of the hotels in Washington, D.C., both upscale and budget, are located in what is called the downtown area, so this will most likely be your first stop from the airport. Downtown is also the location of many of the city's finest tourist sites that lie outside of the Mall.

Downtown

This is a fifteen-block area between 7th and 22nd Streets along Pennsylvania Avenue. The downtown area has undergone a major renovation in the past decade. Almost every block has already been renewed or is scheduled to be undergoing construction.

Many of the city's tourist attractions are located in this neighborhood, including the following:

- National Aquarium
- Ford's Theatre
- Petersen House
- MCI Center
- Old Post Office Pavilion
- National Museum of Women in the Arts
- National Museum of American Art
- International Spy Museum
- Washington, D.C., Convention Center
- The White House
- National Archives

These are only the standouts in a very concentrated area of things to see. If you have comfortable walking shoes, you can walk throughout the downtown area, but you don't have to because there are frequent Metro stops along the way. Most of them are not named after the nearest street—for instance, they include Federal Triangle, Metro Center, National Archives/Navy Memorial, and the far exit of the Gallery Place/Chinatown station. This means you have to carry two maps with you at all times—a street map and a Metro map.

The downtown neighborhood offers plenty to do. There are many fabulous restaurants for every budget and occasion. A strip on 7th Street that's lined with art galleries has become one of the best places to view local art. There's plenty of nightlife in the downtown area, too.

💼 TRAVEL TIP

When you exit the Gallery Place/Chinatown Metro station at 7th and H Streets, you will see a gilded arch of gold and red that marks the entrance to Washington's small Chinatown (about two blocks). This, the world's widest Chinese arch, was given to D.C. by its sister city, Beijing, in 1984, and is referred to as the Chinese Friendship archway. During the Chinese New Year celebration, generally held in January or February, the twenty-meter archway (about sixty-five feet) is lit up and topped by 300 painted dragons.

The National Mall

Everyone who comes to D.C. heads to the Mall at some point during his or her stay. Nine of the fifteen Smithsonian museums are here, as are most of the monuments and memorials. It is easy to find on most street maps, as it is defined by two-and-a-half miles of parkland between Constitution and Independence Avenues from the Capitol to the Lincoln Memorial. Popular sites in this area include these:

- Smithsonian Castle
- National Air and Space Museum
- National Museum of Natural History
- National Museum of American History
- Hirshhorn Museum and Sculpture Garden
- National Gallery of Art
- Freer Gallery of Art and the Arthur M. Sackler Gallery
- National Museum of African Art
- Arts and Industries Building
- Washington Monument
- U.S. Holocaust Museum
- Korean War Veterans Memorial

- Vietnam Veterans Memorial
- Lincoln Memorial

There are few restaurants in this area other than those in the museums. The Smithsonian Metro stop will leave you in the middle of the Mall.

Capitol Hill

Even though the Capitol and a number of heavily visited sites are in this neighborhood, Capitol Hill is mainly residential, with many apartment buildings and neighborhood restaurants. Consequently, the food is good and less expensive than in other parts of the city. It is also the location of the city's famed Eastern Market (at 7th and C Streets, SE), which has been a site of free-for-all commerce since the Victorian days, with vendors selling everything from crafts to produce on a daily basis. It's especially bustling on weekends.

Other sites in the Capitol Hill area include the following:

- Library of Congress
- Folger Shakespeare Library
- National Postal Museum
- Union Station
- United States Botanic Garden
- Supreme Court Building

Metro stops in this area are Eastern Market, Capital South, Judiciary Square, and Union Station.

Adams Morgan and Kalorama

Centered upon 18th Street and Columbia Road (NW), Adams Morgan is a slightly off-the-beaten-track neighborhood that features a wealth of ethnic restaurants, cafes, nightclubs, bookstores, and the National Zoo. The Kalorama district ("Kalorama" is a Greek word for "beautiful view") runs from Adams Morgan to North Dupont Circle and showcases beautiful homes and apartment buildings. To get to Adams Morgan and Kalorama, take the Metro to Woodley Park Zoo, or walk up from Dupont Circle.

Dupont Circle

You just might find yourself returning to Dupont Circle over and over again, though it is a relatively small part of the city. It has wonderful restaurants of all varieties, bookstores, art galleries, movie theaters, and a thriving nightlife. The Circle is also the center of D.C.'s gay nightlife, with several gay bars within walking distance of one another. Tourist sites in this area include the Heurich and Woodrow Wilson Houses, the Textile Museum, and the Phillips Collection. The Metro stop is Dupont Circle.

≡FAST FACT

Dupont Circle is named after Samuel F. Dupont, of New Jersey, a commander of the navy during the Civil War who captured the confederate site of Port Royal, South Carolina. A statue of Dupont stands in the center of the circle.

Foggy Bottom

This neighborhood was the industrial area of the city in the late eighteenth and early nineteenth centuries. In the summertime, the area was marshy and infested with mosquitoes, which is where it got its name. Before that nickname, it had been known as Funkstown, named after Jacob Funk, the owner of a particularly nasty local factory. Of course, Foggy Bottom has been drained and spiffed up.

Foggy Bottom lies just southwest of the downtown tourist district and northwest of Georgetown. Tourist sites in this neighborhood include the U.S. State Department, The John F. Kennedy Center for the Performing Arts, and the luxurious (and notorious)

Watergate complex. The closest Metro stops are Foggy Bottom and Farragut North.

≡FAST FACT

Foggy Bottom was the industrial center of the city even before the American revolution. In 1765, Jacob Funk, a German immigrant, bought 130 acres of land, where he placed his factories. The first brewery is said to have opened in 1796. The neighborhood also became the home to two universities by the early 1800s—a theological seminary and The Columbian College, which later became George Washington University. After the Civil War, Catholic University was added to the mix.

Georgetown

Georgetown is one of the oldest Colonial townships in the country and has some of the oldest homes in the city. One of its prime tourist sites is the Old Stone House, which was built before the Revolutionary War.

Georgetown was already an independent town when Washington, D.C., was in the process of being designed. While it is now part of the city, Georgetown does keep its distance from the heart of downtown by being nearly inaccessible without a car and by having some of the highest-priced homes in the region.

Despite the inconvenience of getting there, Georgetown is definitely worth visiting. It's one of the most charming parts of the city; many visitors enjoy strolling about to see its historic homes, such as Dumbarton Oaks. Because Georgetown is home to Georgetown University, it is packed with interesting, youth-oriented shops, as well as many restaurants and pubs and a co-op of art galleries. It is also one of the city's nightlife centers, especially on weekends. To reach Georgetown, you can take the Metro to the Foggy Bottom stop, but it's a long walk. A cab ride from downtown may be a better option—the fare should be around $5—and Georgetown is always full of cabs.

Glover Park

This is the residential neighborhood bordering the Washington National Cathedral. There are a number of good restaurants and movie theaters in this area. The former mansions and now embassies that make up Embassy Row (a must-see walk or drive) are located between Glover Park and Woodley Park.

In the midst of Embassy Row lies the Naval Observatory, where the nation's master clocks are set. Next door is the vice president's mansion, which is so far off the road that it can hardly be seen from the street. Across from the British Embassy, you'll find an idyllic park featuring a statue of the Persian poet Kahlil Gibran.

The nearest Metro station is Tenleytown, but it's a ten-minute walk to the National Cathedral, so take a bus transfer when you exit the train station and you can hop on any bus for thirty-five cents.

≡FAST FACT

Washington's Embassy Row is an entire neighborhood devoted to the city's diplomatic community. It houses more than 160 different embassies and the homes of ambassadors along Massachusetts Avenue. Many of the embassies and ambassadors' residences are restored mansions. For instance, General Patton's home is now the home of the Australian ambassador. Other ambassadors have commissioned fabulous (and quirky) buildings and homes.

Woodley Park

This is a beautiful residential neighborhood that grew up around Martin Van Buren's and Grover Cleveland's summer homes. It borders the Adams Morgan neighborhood and starts at the National Zoo. There are a number of good restaurants in the area. Its largest landmark is the Washington Marriot Wardman Park, and it is also home to the Omni Shorehawk, another large hotel. Cleveland Park and Woodley Park-Zoo are the closest Metro stops.

U Street Corridor

This stretch of the city between 12th and 16th streets on U Street NW was once the center of African-American nightlife in the city (known as "Black Broadway") where such luminaries as Duke Ellington and Cab Calloway performed when they were in town. It still retains its reputation for nightlife, with a number of jazz and rock nightclubs, and now features the recently restored Lincoln Theater, where the annual D.C. movie festival is held. Metro stops include U Street/Cardozo and Shaw-Howard University.

RAINY DAY FUN

Pay a visit to the U Street Corridor for some culinary treasures. Ben's Chili Bowl, a neighborhood institution for more than seventy-five years, is world renowned after being featured on the *Cosby Show* in the 1990s. Oprah's raves about the Love Café, where you can get great homemade $2 cupcakes, has put this restaurant on the map.

Tyson's Corner, Virginia

Though not technically a D.C. neighborhood, Tyson's Corner is a shopping hotspot and a bargain-shopping mecca for tourists and residents alike. It is one of the largest U.S. retail centers outside of New York City.

The name comes from two of the malls—Tyson's Corner Center and Tyson's Galleria—which together feature a total of eight major department stores, including Bloomingdale's and Nordstrom's, as well as more than 400 shops and restaurants. Tyson's Corner isn't on the Metro. If you have a car available, take Route 7.

Getting Around Town

Once you know where you are and where you want to go, Washington, D.C., is a very easy city to navigate. The Metro system is safe, convenient, affordable, and fairly extensive throughout downtown. If the Metro doesn't go somewhere, the Metrobus system probably does, but it takes much longer and buses do not run as frequently. Taxis are abundant and usually quite affordable.

Take the Metro

The Metro system is run by Washington Metropolitan Area Transit Authority, which celebrated its thirtieth anniversary in 2003. The Metro system now includes eighty-three stops and 103 miles of track.

The system runs efficiently throughout the downtown area (where most of the tourist sites are located) and to specific destinations in suburban Maryland and northern Virginia. If the Metro system can get you where you need to go, it is the best way to travel in the nation's capital.

Kids love the Metro system; it's often an attraction in itself for them. Many of the stations (such as Dupont Circle) are deep below the ground, with long escalators and high, domed ceilings.

≡FAST FACT

The deepest station is at Forest Glen on the Red line, which is 196 feet below ground (twenty-one stories). The longest escalator is at Wheaton Station (also on the Red line), which at 230 feet is also the longest escalator in the Western hemisphere.

Stations are marked by a brown obelisk with the capital letter M at the top. Each station has a station-manager kiosk on the premises, and you can usually ask them questions and for directions. Note that eating and drinking on the Metro system is strictly prohibited.

Purchasing Tickets

Once you enter a station, you have to buy a ticket at an automated machine. A chart shows you how much the fare is from your starting station to your destination. The Metro Area Transit Authority has pledged that fares will not rise between the years 2004 and 2006. Currently, most rides are $1.20 except during rush hour, when fares are $1.70. (The system is very crowded during those times.) The machines take coins as well as bills of up to $20, but they will only give you up to $5 in change.

You can buy a roundtrip ticket or a $6 one-day fare. If you plan your trips around a central location and use a combination of the Metro system, the bus system, and walking, it's unlikely that you'll spend $6 on the Metro in one day. A roundtrip ticket is probably all you'll need.

There are special discount passes as well. A full week's worth of Metro riding can be purchased for $20, which could certainly be a wise choice if you will be visiting the different neighborhoods of the city. However, there's a slight catch. Should any individual trip cost more than $2, you will be required to pay the additional amount before exiting the station. There is also a $30 seven-day card, if you know you'll be visiting the stations that require additional fees.

You can buy $20 worth of trips and receive a 10 percent discount on your rides. Children ages 6 and older must have a ticket, and there is no discount for them. Senior citizens pay half price with identification.

Once you have walked through the entrance turnstile, your ticket will pop back out at you. You must retain it and put it in the exit turnstile at your destination station. If you lose your ticket, you can buy another one inside the station to exit.

FAST FACT

My son says the gray, vaulted, honeycombed ceilings of the Metro system remind him of the Space Mountain ride at Disneyland, and it is a popular urban myth that the system was designed by Disney architects. The Metro's media department wouldn't corroborate this story, but it's been around ever since the Metro was operational in 1976, so you be the judge.

The Metro Network

There are five lines in the D.C. Metro system: Red, Orange, Green, Yellow, and Blue. The Metro Center Station (in downtown Washington) connects three of them (Red, Blue, and Orange) and the next stop, Gallery Place/Chinatown, links the other two (Yellow and Green), so it is very easy to change trains. There are pocket Metro maps available in six languages outside most of these kiosks.

If you know you are going to take a bus later on in the day (or you think you may get tired walking from one tourist site to another), look for the bus-ticket machine on the inside of the station (before you exit) and take a transfer ticket. This will enable you to take a Metrobus for a 35-cent fee—otherwise, you would have to pay $1.20. There is no transfer from the bus to the train.

Hours of Operation

The Metro system is open from 5:30 A.M. to midnight on Monday, Tuesday, Wednesday, Thursday, and Sunday; from 5:30 A.M. to 3:00 A.M. on Friday; and from 7:00 A.M. to 3:00 A.M. on Saturday. Every train station lists the time of the last train at that station for the evening.

For more information on the Metro system call ☎202-962-1234, or visit their Web site at ✐*www.wmata.com*. There is a search engine on the Web site that will plot your route for you if you type in your start and destination.

≡FAST FACT

It took four decades of planning to create the Washington, D.C., mass transit system. Congress authorized the creation of a planning commission to study mass transit in 1952, but the first Metro station didn't open until 1976, just in time for the masses who descended upon the city for the bicentennial. On the first day of service in March 1976, there were 19,913 passengers. In August of 1988, the Metrorail carried its billionth rider.

Take the Bus

The city's surface transit system is also extensive (over 15,000 stops) and works wonderfully, either in conjunction with the Metro system or for short rides when your feet just give out on you. You can usually catch a bus within five to ten minutes of waiting, and most stops include a bus shelter where you can wait for the next bus.

You will need a Metrobus card or exact change for the bus, as the driver cannot give change, but the bus does take dollar bills. Rides are $1.20, and transfers are free. If you have a transfer from the Metro, the fare is only 35 cents.

Ride the Taxi

Instead of a meter system, taxis in D.C. run on a zone system, which is posted in every cab. Most rides in the downtown area, or from downtown to Georgetown, are one fare zone, which should be $5 for one person and $2 extra for each additional person. There is a dollar surcharge for rush-hour traffic. Of course, you have to tip the driver—usually a dollar or two—depending on how expensive the ride was.

If you ask a cab to take you outside of the city, you will be charged by the mile, which is how the airport fares are calculated. This fare system starts at $2.25 for the first half mile and adds $.75 for each half mile after that.

The *Washington Post* Web site has a taxi fare calculator, which you can use to get a specific idea of how much your trip should cost. You can also call ☎202-331-1671 to find out the fare between a location in D.C. and a destination in Maryland or Virginia. For fares within the city, call ☎202-645-6018.

You can hail a cab on the street or call a cab service, which will cost you an additional $1.50. Cab companies available for radio service include Capital Cab, ☎202-546-2400, and Yellow Cab, ☎202-544-1212. All cab drivers will give you a receipt when asked.

Make sure you pay attention to the driver's license number and the cab number when you get in the taxi. If you have a complaint about a driver, you can call ☎202-645-6005 to report the problem.

Guided Tours

Washington, D.C., offers a number of options to touring the city, from faux trolley cars to buses to boat tours. These tours offer an easy way for you to get oriented in the city. Be aware, though, that many of these tours are closed during the winter months, so call ahead to confirm availability.

Walking Tours

Washington, D.C., has a large variety of walking tours that you can take, some of which last an entire day and others that are just a few hours long. There is a lot to choose from here, from the off-beat (such as the scandal tours) to more traditional historic tours.

City Tours

✆ 301-294-9514

✐ *www.dcsightseeing.com*

Washington author and tour guide Anthony S. Pitch offers five different anecdotal history tours of Washington, D.C., on such topics and areas as Georgetown, the Adams Morgan neighborhood, homes of the presidents, around the White House, and the White House to the Capitol. Tours are given on Sundays from 11:00 A.M. to 1:00 P.M. for $10 per person.

Celebrity Tours

✆ 301-762-3049

Of course, many rich and famous people live in Washington, D.C., or at least have residences here; for instance, Arnold Schwarzenegger and Elizabeth Taylor both own homes in Georgetown. If you enjoy seeing how celebrities live, you can join author Jan Pottker, author of *Celebrity Washington,* on a guided tour of the city's famous past and present residences, watering holes, and movie locations. Tours cost $15 and last about two hours.

African-American Heritage Tour
☎ 202-636-9203

Visit the Frederick Douglass National Historic Site, Lincoln Park, the Supreme Court, the "From Field to Factory" exhibit in the Smithsonian's National Museum of American History, and more. Tickets are $15 for adults and $8 for children ages 3 to 11.

☂ RAINY DAY FUN

The embassies and mansions of Embassy Row house some incredible art and culture from the various countries represented, but you can't just go up to a door and go in to view it. Two times a year (in the fall and spring), there is an all-day Embassy Row guided tour, so check the *Washington Post* calendar listings for this event. Proceeds usually go to charity.

Duke Ellington's D.C. Neighborhood Tour
☎ 202-636-9203

See Duke Ellington's D.C. by bus and by foot. On the tour, you'll visit the Shaw neighborhood where Ellington grew up, as well as the Lincoln Theater, the Mary McLeod Bethune House, Whitelaw Hotel, and more. The tour includes lunch with a theater performance. Tickets are $39.95 for adults and $29.95 for children.

Scandal Tours
☎ 202-783-7212

Costumed members of the Washington comedy group Gross National Product impersonate political figures and offer a humor-filled tour of the city's most notorious history, from the Watergate to the Tidal Basin to Gary Hart's townhouse and the White House itself. Tickets are $30; tours run from March through October (call for exact dates).

Georgetown Walking Tour
&301-588-8999

Mary Kay Ricks offers a variety of tours of Georgetown, as well as a tour of Oak Hill Cemetery and a ride on the Underground Railroad with a look at Georgetown during the Civil War. The tour will cost you $15 per person; children under 18 can join free of charge, if accompanied by an adult.

Washington Walks
&202-484-1565

www.washingtonwalks.com

A new touring company with some terrific off-the-beaten-path routes, including the "White House Un-Tour" every Tuesday through Saturday, and a tour of Haunted Washington every Wednesday. Recommended family walks are "Good Night, Mr. Lincoln" and the White House Un-Tour. Tickets are $10 per person and $5 for children under 12. Walks last approximately two hours; groups meet outside a Metro station.

Old Town Trolley

This is a narrated two-hour tour on an orange-and-green open-air trolley. Its eighteen stops include most of the downtown sites, as well as Arlington National Cemetery, Georgetown, Embassy Row, and the National Cathedral. You can get off and on throughout the day by showing the bus driver your ticket stub or a sticker they give you to wear (trolleys come around every thirty minutes). They also have printed flyers of walking tours of Georgetown and the Mall. There's a map of tour stops, which also features a number of discounts on food and shopping if you show the establishment your ticket.

Tours start at 9:00 A.M. and end at 4:00 P.M. You may be able to buy a ticket at your hotel (and therefore charge it to your room) or you can pay on the trolley or buy a ticket at the counter in Union Station (which is the first stop). Tickets are $26 for adults, $13 for children.

Old Town Trolley also offers a Washington After-Hours tour. This two-and-a-half-hour narrated night tour features ghost stories and views of the city's monuments. Tickets are $26 for adults and $13 for children. These tours are often sold out before noon during the busy season, so call early for reservations, ☎202-832-9800. You can also buy your tickets online for a 10 percent savings at ⌕*www.historictours.com*.

Tourmobile

The blue-and-white Tourmobile travels to many of the same locations as the Old Town Trolley, but it does not go to Georgetown or the National Cathedral. It is the only vehicle allowed to tour inside Arlington National Cemetery (authorized to do so by the National Park Service). Instead of trudging up the green hills on foot, you can sit as the trolley takes you by the Kennedy graves, the Tomb of the Unknown Soldier, Arlington House, and the Women in Service Memorial on the cemetery grounds. This is a definite consideration if you have young children or visitors who have a hard time walking long distances. You can buy Tourmobile tickets to tour just the cemetery, which cost $6 for adults and $3 for children and can be purchased at the cemetery's visitors' center. Tourmobile, by the way, offers the only guided tour of the cemetery—vehicle-driven or otherwise.

You can board the Tourmobile at any of its twenty-five stops and pay the driver when you get on. As with Old Town Trolley, you can get on and off the Tourmobile at any stop and reboard later (with ticket). Tourmobiles come around every twenty minutes.

The cost of the Tourmobile is $20 for adults and $10 for children. The Tourmobile operates from 9:00 A.M. to 6:30 P.M. from Memorial Day through Labor Day, and until 4:30 P.M. during the winter and spring months. It is available all year long, except Christmas Day, when most national and government sites are also closed.

Tourmobile also offers a Washington by Night tour, which is a four-hour narrated tour of the Jefferson, Franklin Delano Roosevelt, and Lincoln Memorials (where you can disembark for visits), with stops outside the White House and the Capitol building. It departs from Union Station and is $20 for adults and $10 for children.

There are combination two-day packages for various tours such as Arlington Cemetery, Washington, D.C., Mount Vernon, and/or Cedar Hill. Call or visit the Tourmobile Web site at ⌕*www.tourmobile.com*

for prices and more information, as these tours are not always available.

Reservations are suggested for Washington by Night tours, which you can call for at ☎202-554-5100 or make at the Web site. There's a quiz on the Web site where you can attempt to win free tour tickets by answering Washington, D.C., trivia. You can also purchase tickets at TicketMaster by calling ☎1-800-832-9800, but there is a small fee for this service.

🧳 TRAVEL TIP

Looking for something a little different? How about a minibus tour? The Washington Area Minibus Tours offers daily four-hour tours leaving at 9:00 A.M. and 1:00 P.M. for a tour of the city in air-conditioned coaches. Tickets are $25 for adults and $13 for children. A three-hour night tour is also available at a cost of $28 for adults and $14 for children. For more information, call ☎202-526-2049.

Motorcoach Tours

If you're more interested in motorcoach tours, you have several options as well.

Gold Line/Gray Line
☎1-800-862-1400
☎301-386-8300

This tour company offers full (nine-hour) and half-day (four-hour) narrated tours of the city. The motorcoach will leave from Union Station or pick you up and drop you off at your hotel. If you would like to hear a tour of the city in a language other than English, they offer tours in Spanish, French, Italian, German, and Japanese, but you must call for information and reservations. You can pay for this tour by credit card. There is also a Twilight Tour of five memorials (Jefferson, Lincoln, Franklin Delano Roosevelt, Vietnam, and Korean War), as well as the Statue of Iwo Jima at

Arlington National Cemetery and the John F. Kennedy Center. The Twilight Tour leaves Union Station at 7:30 P.M. and drops you off at your hotel about four hours later. If the other night tours are booked, you can usually get a seat on one of these. The cost is $25 for adults and $12 for children—again, you can pay by credit card.

All About Town
📞 301-856-5566

All About Town is a bus-tour operation that offers guided all-day tours as well as half-day tours in the city's only glass-topped sightseeing coaches, along with evening tours on buses to major sites throughout the city and to Mount Vernon, with pickup and drop-off at your hotel.

Water Tours

If you and your family are feeling adventurous, you might consider seeing Washington, D.C., on a water tour. There are lots of activities to choose from—kayaking, canoeing, river cruising, and much more

Atlantic Kayak
📞 703-838-9072
🖰 www.atlantickayak.com

This aquatic tour leads you through Georgetown's C&O Canal and focuses on the city's architecture and history. Guides paddle alongside tourists in small groups of boats. No children under 10 years of age can take this tour, but for everyone else, the tour operators state that no experience is necessary. Tickets are $39 and $49.

Capital River Cruises
📞 301-460-7447

This fifty-minute, narrated tour of the Potomac on a sixty-five-foot riverboat departs from the Georgetown waterfront and circles the city, offering views of the Kennedy Center, the various monuments, and the Capitol building. Tours leave daily from noon until 7:00 P.M. Tickets are $10 for adults and $5 for children.

D.C. Ducks

☎ 202-832-9800

This is a terrific tour for families. This famous tour uses white amphibious vehicles (boats on wheels)—which were built for the U.S. Army during World War II to transport troops—to provide tourists a one-hour tour of the city on the ground followed by a half-hour tour ride on the Potomac. Tours leave from Union Station beginning at 10:00 A.M. from April through October (perhaps longer, depending upon the weather). Tickets are $26 for adults and $13 for children.

Spirit of Washington/Potomac Spirit

☎ 202-554-8000

✐ *www.spiritofwashington.com*

This climate-controlled riverboat tours the Potomac River and offers a tour of Mount Vernon, as well as lunch, dinner, and moonlight cruises. The boat departs Pier 4, at 6th and Water Street SW, at 9:00 A.M. and returns at 2:30 P.M., Tuesday through Sunday. You can purchase breakfast and lunch on board. There is also a forty-minute cruise to Mount Vernon. Roundtrip fares include the admission to Mount Vernon and are $26.50 for adults and $17 for children. Reservations are recommended.

☂ RAINY DAY FUN

Right Hand Sun Limousines offers a three-hour tour in either a sedan ($135 for three people) or a stretch ($165 for up to eight people) during the week, and slightly higher on Thursday through Sunday. For more information, call ☎ 1-866-808-9702 (toll free) or visit ✐ *www.righthandsun.com*.

Shore Shot Cruises

☎ 202-554-6500

This narrated tour of the Potomac departs from Georgetown Harbor, 31st and K Streets NW. The cost is $10 for adults, $5 for children.

Washington Water Bus
☎ 1-800-288-7925

Water buses make a number of regular stops along the Potomac so that tourists can have the option of disembarking at locations such as the Jefferson, Franklin Delano Roosevelt, and Lincoln Memorials. One fare allows you to hop on and off all day.

C&O Canal Barge Rides
☎ 301-739-4200

This tour offers mule-drawn canal rides along the C&O Canal; tour-guide commentary is also included. The barges depart from Georgetown and operate from April through October, so be sure to call and get the current prices and days of operation.

Bike the Sites Tour

For the athletically inclined, Bike the Sites tour group offers a three-hour guided bicycle tour on eight miles of paths and trails that pass fifty-five landmarks and monuments. The tour is recommended for ages 9 and up and includes bicycle rental, as well as gear, a licensed guide, and a snack. Tickets are $40 per adult and $15 for children.

👥 JUST FOR PARENTS

Bike the Sites offers a longer tour for the truly athletic (that is, for older teens or adults) that takes you from Old Town to Mount Vernon on a nine-mile bike path along the Potomac River. Tickets are $55 per person, which includes lunch and admission fees. There are also evening tours ending in Georgetown.

Call ☎ 202-842-2453 for more information or visit their Web site at ✉ *www.bikethesites.com*.

CHAPTER 5

Introduction to the Smithsonian

YOU CAN'T VISIT WASHINGTON, D.C., without seeing some of the Smithsonian Institution's fifteen museums and galleries. They are the jewels of the crown in this town. If you have the luxury of being able to explore all or most of the Smithsonian branches in D.C., you will see a breadth of art, history, science, and culture unparalleled anywhere in the world. (If you only have time for the top three Smithsonians, they are covered in the next chapter.)

The museums are open every day except Christmas, and they are all free—and that's not chump change that you'll be saving. Visiting a similar number of museums in any other city would run at least $150 per person.

The History of the Smithsonian Institution

The story of the Smithsonian Institution is fascinating. The Smithsonian exists because James Smithson, a wealthy English scientist, thought the principles of our nation and the scientific discoveries that were being produced here in the nineteenth century were so amazing that he wanted to found "an establishment for the increase and diffusion of knowledge among men" in the United States.

Upon his death in Italy in 1829, he willed his fortune to his nephew and stipulated that should his nephew die without heirs, the entire Smithson fortune, which was worth about half a million dollars (an enormous amount of money in those days, which eventually came to the United States in bags of gold sovereigns) would be given to the United States to fund such an institution.

≡FAST FACT

Who was the man behind this great gift? He was born James Lewis Macie in France in 1765, but later learned that his father was Hugh Smithson, Duke of North Cumberland. He changed his name to Smithson while a student at Oxford, where he studied science, and later became a noted mineralogist. He discovered a zinc carbonite, Smithsonite, which was named after him, and was invited to become a fellow of the Royal Society, a British group dedicated to scientific research, at the age of twenty-two.

Smithsonian Made into Law

It took eight years of discussion in Congress before the Smithson gift was accepted and then another nine years before the Smithsonian Institution became a reality, with President Andrew Polk signing an act of Congress that established the Smithsonian Institution.

Since then, a trust has been established to oversee the Institution; this trust receives private funds and donations, as well as more than $250 million in government funding a year. This is how the museums are able to function without charging entrance fees.

Smithsonian Today

In the century and a half since the Smithsonian was founded, it has grown from a one-building science center to a seventeen-building Institution—one museum is in New York—that contains more than 200 million objects. And it is still growing today.

In 1999, the Smithsonian received two major donations. A noted collector of Asian art, Dr. Paul Singer, donated art to complement the existing collection in the Arthur M. Sackler Gallery. And billionaire Steven F. Udvar-Hazy donated $60 million to create a newly opened sister museum of the Air and Space Museum at Dulles Airport, which displays 180 airplanes and spacecraft, including the space shuttle *Enterprise.*

In 2004, the Smithsonian also saw the addition of a new building that houses a new museum—the National Museum of the American Indian, located on the Mall. There are also plans to move the Anacostia Museum, which features the art, history, and culture of D.C.-area African-Americans, to a larger building closer to public transportation by the year 2006. In addition, the renovated and restored National Museum of American Art and the National Portrait Gallery are due to reopen in 2006, and the National Museum of American History is to undergo an extensive renovation to make the star-spangled banner the Museum's central icon.

The Castle

✉1000 Jefferson Dr. SW
✆202-357-2700
✐*www.si.edu*

The Smithsonian Institution Building, also known as the Castle, is home to the Information Center and the offices of the Smithsonian Institution. When you get to the Mall, you'll be sure to spot it—look for the red sandstone building that looks like a castle. Though not a museum itself, this is the headquarters of the Institution, where all its main offices are located.

The Norman-style castle (a combination of twelfth-century Romanesque and Gothic architectural styles) was designed in 1855 by noted architect James Renwick, who also designed St. Patrick's Cathedral in New York and the Renwick Gallery, which is named after him. It has become the symbol of the Smithsonian over the years; you can find it on key chains and Christmas ornaments in any of the museum's shops.

Think of the Castle as your gateway to the Smithsonian theme park. There is a visitor's information desk where you can ask questions and get directions. You can also see models of the museums on the Mall and watch interactive videos. There is a twenty-four-minute film on the history of the Institution, as well as an overview of the museums and galleries that runs continuously throughout the day. Information on special exhibits and events is also available at the Castle.

RAINY DAY FUN

The sumptuous Sunday brunch known as "the noble feast" is also presented here in the Castle Common Room from 11:00 A.M. until 3:00 P.M., ☎202-357-2957. (See restaurant listings in Chapter 15.) The Smithsonian cafeteria is closed to the public during the rest of the week.

A Haunting at the Smithsonian?

The marble sarcophagus of James Smithson, the founder of the Institution, is also housed in this building in its own room behind the information desk, and to the right (in a former guardroom) you will find a piece of Smithsonite, a zinc carbonite he discovered that was named after him.

Smithson never actually visited the United States when he was alive (and never even corresponded with any Americans that we know of). His bones were brought over to the United States at the turn of the twentieth century when an Italian marble drilling company bought the cemetery in Genoa where Smithson was buried. His crypt was set up in a former guardroom in the Smithsonian Castle.

In the 1970s, guards and Castle workers started to comment on weird occurrences in the Castle, such as alarms going off without cause and the ancient elevator jamming for no reason. Books were being pulled out and abandoned in the Woodrow Wilson Library, and many late-night workers complained of feeling that someone was watching them. This went on for about a decade. Then, in the late 1970s, Smithson's sarcophagus was opened during a renovation. Inside was a tin box with Smithson's bones inside, haphazardly mixed together with fragments of his original coffin. After the bones were realigned properly and the sarcophagus resealed, the Castle has remained quiet.

Location and Hours
The Castle is located on the Mall, accessible from the Smithsonian Metro station. The Castle is open from 9:00 A.M. to 5:30 P.M. daily, but the Information Center is open from 10:00 A.M. until 4:00 P.M., sometimes later in the summer (call for hours). Castle tours are available every day in the mornings.

Freer Gallery of Art

Jefferson Dr. at 12th St. SW
202-633-4880
www.asia.si.edu

This museum, admittedly smaller than some of the giants like the National Air and Space Museum, is a real find. Its home is an Italian Renaissance–style building originally designed to hold the National Museum of Fine Arts.

The Freer Gallery is named after its donor, Charles Lang Freer, a Chicago industrialist who collected Asian art and nineteenth- and twentieth-century American works. He donated 7,500 pieces of art to the gallery, as well as the money to build the gallery; another 20,000 pieces have been donated or acquired since 1923, making it one of the world's most extensive collections of ancient and modern Asian and Asian-inspired art.

Since the collection is so extensive, pieces are shown on a rotating schedule, but there are some permanent features on view.

These include the largest collection of Whistler's paintings; a wing on Japanese art that features some incredible painted wooden screens; Korean ceramics; Chinese paintings and ancient art; Buddhist art; South Asian art; Islamic art—Freer was especially fond of Persian painting from the sixteenth century; Egyptian glass; and the "Luxury Arts of the Silk Route Empires" exhibit. The Silk Route exhibit is on view in the underground corridor connecting the Freer Gallery with the Sackler Gallery, and it combines some holdings of both museums. The Freer Gallery's museum shop offers many beautiful Japanese tea items, as well as books about Asian art that are unique to this gift shop.

The Peacock Room

The epitome of the Freer's vision is the restored Peacock Room, designed and painted by James McNeill Whistler. This room is a one-of-a-kind visual experience that is spectacular to behold more than 100 years after it was painted. When the museum is open late on summer evenings, or in the early morning hours, you may be able to sit alone here for a while and take in the all-encompassing splendor of it.

The Peacock Room was once the dining room of one of Whistler's London patrons, who had an interior architect design a room to hold his Chinese porcelain collection and his prized Whistler painting, *The Princess from the Land of Porcelain*, which was displayed above the fireplace. The architect consulted Whistler on the color of the room, and while the patron was away on a business trip Whistler took over the design of the room, having the ceiling covered in gold leaf over which he painted a pattern of peacock feathers. He echoed that pattern in four painted wooden panels of peacocks on wooden shutters.

Whistler had done all this interior design without his patron's permission, and when the patron was presented with the bill, he was not amused and refused to pay the full price. Whistler got back at him by painting a confrontational scene of two peacocks fighting, which he titled *Art and Money; or The Story of the Room*.

The room was purchased by Freer in 1904 and dismantled and brought to his home. It was willed to the gallery in 1919. The Peacock Room has been restored twice since it was installed in the Freer, the most recent installation having revealed the blue, green, and gold peacock feather pattern on the ceiling and the gold paint on the wainscoting. It is indeed an inspired home for *The Princess from the Land of Porcelain.*

👥 JUST FOR PARENTS

The Peacock Room is so serene and peaceful that you might want to ask your spouse to take the kids for a run through the nearby Enid Haupt garden outside the Smithsonian Castle while you sit for a few quiet minutes, contemplating how this fabulous piece of art history made it intact into our national heritage.

Location and Hours

The Freer Gallery is located on the Mall, accessible from the Smithsonian Metro station. It is open from 10 A.M. to 5:30 P.M., later on some summer evenings.

The Arthur M. Sackler Gallery

✉ 1050 Independence Ave. SW
☏ 202-633-4880
🖱 *www.asia.si.edu*

This gallery, housed underground, is dedicated to the history of the artistic development of Asian and Near Eastern art from ancient times to the present. Shows of contemporary Asian artists are often on view here, as well as traveling exhibits from major museums. Some exhibits offer the visitor the chance to touch objects to feel their weight and texture. In the Japanese porcelain exhibit, there are shards of porcelain for viewers to handle.

Like the Freer Gallery, the Sackler has an extensive collection shown on a rotating schedule. Permanent exhibits include:

- "Art of China" (from Dr. Sackler's own collection)
- "Contemporary Japanese Porcelain"
- "Metalwork and Ceramics from Ancient Iran"
- "Puja: Expressions of Hindu Devotion"
- "Sculpture of Southeast Asia"

Guided tours are conducted daily. The museum gift shops mirrors the collection with a wide variety of prints, books, and porcelain available for purchase.

📼 TRAVEL TIP

If you plan to make purchases at any of the Smithsonian gift shops, you might be interested to know that the merchandise is tax free. That's because the Smithsonian Institution is run by the government.

Location and Hours

The Arthur M. Sackler Gallery is adjacent to the Freer Gallery. It is located on the Mall and is accessible from the Smithsonian Metro station. Hours of operation are from 10 A.M. to 5:30 P.M., later on some summer evenings.

The Hirshhorn Museum and Sculpture Garden

✉Independence Ave. at 7th St. SW
☎202-633-HMSG
🖥*www.hirshhorn.si.edu*

The Hirshhorn is one of the leading museums of contemporary art in America, right up there with New York's Museum of Modern Art and the Guggenheim, and it's something no visitor interested in modern art should miss. It has an extensive collection of twentieth-century art, from a room full of Picassos to the latest controversial works by the likes of Britain's bad-boy artist Damian Hirst (the only one of his works on permanent display in the United States). Popular favorites include the Calder mobiles, Nam June Pak's video American flag made out of television screens, and the various icons from the 1960s Pop Art movement.

The sunken outdoor sculpture garden reveals a marvelous collection of important modern sculpture, from pivotal works by Rodin to unusual three-dimensional work by de Kooning.

≡FAST FACT

The Hirshhorn is named after Latvian-born art collector Joseph Hirshhorn. Hirshhorn gave the Smithsonian more than 12,000 pieces of modern art, and these formed the nucleus of this museum's collection, which opened in the 1970s.

The museum itself is a work of art, echoing the spiraling interior design of New York's Guggenheim so that each floor is a self-contained circle around a courtyard with floor-to-ceiling windows that make use of natural light. Some have commented that the museum, designed by Gordon Bunshaft, looks like a giant doughnut or drum.

Lay of the Land

On the first floor, you have the option to view a continuously shown twenty-minute film that discusses the art on display in the museum, as well as an overview of modern art and suggestions on how to experience the works. The first floor also houses special exhibitions and the museum's gift store, which has a quirky collection of art knickknacks, from Picasso plates to a Red Grooms clock, as well as a good selection of books and posters.

The works on display are arranged chronologically from the turn of the twentieth century to the present, moving from the third floor to the ground floor, where the new acquisitions are located. Major movements in twentieth-century art are represented here, from Picasso's early Cubist painting and sculpture (the Picasso Room chronicles the artist's entire career) to the surrealism of Magritte and Miró, as well as a sizable collection of American realists such as Edward Hopper, George Bellows, Thomas Hart Benton, and various members of the Ashcan School.

The second floor focuses on modern art of the second half of the century, with an impressive display of abstract expressionist works by Jackson Pollock, Barnett Newman's *Stations of the Cross,* and 1960s pop icons such as Claes Oldenburg's *7-UP* and Warhol's *Marilyn Monroe's Lips.*

On the lower level there is a hall that displays recent acquisitions and contemporary works where you can find the Hirst and a Cindy Sherman print, as well as a work by Sam Gilliam, a noted abstract colorist whose studio is located in D.C.

Sculptures are located on the interior galleries of the first three floors, overlooking the courtyard, and these galleries chronicle the spatial developments of the last century with works by Degas, Picasso, Giacometti, and Matisse. You'll find a rare wooden sculpture by Gauguin, as well as a clever piece by Man Ray, all of which culminates in the powerful Robert Arneson giant bust called *General Nuke.*

Circling the museum are a number of recent sculpture acquisitions. You can sit in a tree-lined area while eating self-service from the Full Circle Cafe, which is open from May until September.

Location and Hours

The Hirshhorn Museum and Sculpture Garden is located on the Mall, accessible from the L'Enfant Plaza Metro station. The museum is open from 10 A.M. to 5:30 P.M., and it's often open later in the summer; the sculpture garden is open from 7:30 A.M. til dusk. Guided tours are available at 10:30 A.M., noon, and 1:30 P.M., and there's an additional tour at 2:30 P.M. on Sundays.

National Museum of African Art

✉950 Independence Ave. SW
📞202-633-4600
✑*www.nmafa.si.edu*

This museum, with its ground-floor and underground galleries, is one of the country's few museums dedicated solely to African art, with more than 7,000 pieces in the collection. Included in its holdings are traditional pieces as well as contemporary works.

The museum has special exhibits on the ground floor, where you enter, and its permanent collection includes a marvelous show on the art of the personal object, with more than 100 objects on view, such as baskets, bowls, cups, and so on. Another permanent exhibit on African ceramics has more than 140 bowls and figures. Also on permanent view are an exhibit entitled "Images of a Power and Identity," which features a selection of masks and figures; an exhibit on the African city of Benin from C.E. 1300 to the end of British colonial rule, and an exhibit on the Ancient Nubian city of Kerma, an Egyptian city, from 2500 to 1500 B.C.E.

The gift shop is on the first level and offers a selection of African crafts and jewelry, as well as books and posters.

Location and Hours

The National Museum of African Art is located on the Mall, accessible from the Smithsonian or L'Enfant Plaza Metro station. It is open from 10 A.M. to 5:30 P.M.

National Postal Museum

✉2 Massachusetts Ave. at First St. NE
✑*www.postalmuseum.si.edu*

This surprisingly entertaining museum is dedicated to the history of postal service and stamps in this country. The exhibits on the

Pony Express and airmail are particularly interesting, especially to children. Visitors also get a chance to sort the mail, create their own mail routes over land and sea, ride a stagecoach, land an airmail biplane via a computer game (it's quite difficult), and create their own postal imprint on a postcard, which they can mail to friends and family.

In addition, there is an extensive exhibit on the printing and history of stamps, as well as a complete master collection of the entire history of American stamps (copies are on view in plastic pull-out displays). The museum also features a gallery on the art of letter writing, using examples from wartime correspondence from World War I to Operation Desert Storm. There are a number of vehicles used to deliver the mail on view, from 1911 biplanes based on the designs of the Wright Brothers to a 1931 Ford Model A mail truck.

RAINY DAY FUN

What a surprisingly engaging museum the National Postal Museum is! The museum began with a donation of a sheet of ten-cent Confederate stamps and now contains more than 13 million items. Geared toward children and stamp collectors, this museum offers a very interactive history of postal service in America. If it starts raining downtown, hop in here.

There are two gift shops on the premises. One offers posters, T-shirts, and various items from the general Smithsonian collection. In the stamp store across the hall, you can buy stamps for the postcards you create in the museum, as well as rare and special-edition stamps.

Location and Hours

The National Postal Museum is located in the Washington City Post Office Building, next to Union Station. It is open from 10 A.M. to 5:30 P.M. Guided tours are at 11:00 A.M. and 1:00 P.M. every day, with an extra tour at 2:00 P.M. on weekdays.

Renwick Gallery of the National Museum of American Art

✉Pennsylvania Ave. at 17th St. NW
✆202-357-2700
✎*www.americanart.si.edu*

This museum is situated in an Empire-style mansion (designed by James Renwick) near the White House and not far from the Corcoran Gallery. The building itself was once the site of the Corcoran Gallery, and the exterior features the inscription "Dedicated to Art" and an etched portrait of Corcoran. Later, it was used as a courthouse until Jackie Kennedy convinced the Smithsonian Institution to take it over. The museum is a branch of the National Museum of American Art, and it highlights craft and design.

When you enter its lush interior, restored in late nineteenth-century grandeur, you'll find yourself in the Grand Salon, which features mauve walls, carved wainscoting, and a large skylight that makes you feel like you've stepped back in time to the Victorian era. The Grand Salon is home to a number of paintings by minor nineteenth- and twentieth-century painters and two colossal Centennial urns on top of the plush velvet banquettes.

Across the hall from the Grand Salon is an archway that was built to showcase Hiram Powers's highly controversial sculpture *Greek Slave,* a nude woman in chains considered so scandalous in the nineteenth century that it was shown to groups of men and women on different days of the week. Now Wendal Castle's trompe l'oeil *Ghost Clock* is displayed in this space (with the *Greek Slave* on display in the Corcoran Gallery of Art) and it too is a masterpiece, its brilliantly carved wood painted white to resemble a sheet draped over a grandfather clock.

Other rooms in the museum feature outstandingly quirky pieces of American craft and design such as Larry Fuente's *Game Fish*, made from bright pieces of beads, buttons, coins, game pieces, blocks, magnetized letters, light bulbs, paintbrushes, and even a yo-yo.

The Renwick Gallery is a surprisingly fun museum in an exqui-site setting. Its gift shop features a rich selection of scarves and glass pieces, as well as unique jewelry.

Location and Hours

The Renwick Gallery is located one block west of the White House. It is accessible from the Farragut West Metro station. Hours of operation are from 10 A.M. to 5:30 P.M.

The National Zoological Park

✉3001 Connecticut Ave. NW
✆202-673-4821
✐*www.natzoo.si.edu*

This 163-acre zoo features what seems like almost every creature known to man, with 3,600 animals representing 475 species. The zoo was designed by Frederick Law Olmsted, the ingenious land-scape architect who also designed New York's Central Park and Boston's Public Gardens.

Highlights include the Amazonian tropical rain forest; orang-utans that use a computer-based language system; American bison; and our beloved giant pandas. There are also lions, a white tiger, elephants, rhinos, and a wonderful aviary. Children find the exhibit of mole rats in the small-mammals building particularly fascinating. The National Zoo is also the home of one of the few Komodo dragons ever bred in captivity. To see everything, you'll have to walk around, so be sure everyone wears comfortable shoes! It will take you a minimum of four hours to do the zoo justice.

Exhibits at a Glance

During the summer months, four exhibits are often crowded: Amazonia, the invertebrate exhibit, the Reptile Discovery Center, and the giant panda exhibit. Amazonia, the new tropical rain forest and the zoo's largest exhibit, features a steamy habitat for free-roaming amphibians, small mammals, and birds, as well as an aquarium to hold tropical fish. The Reptile Discovery Center has a number of interactive exhibit areas for children to learn about the biology of reptiles and amphibians. The invertebrate exhibit features a giant octopus, which is fed several times a day. The museum director claims that the octopus has been able to open a screw-top jar with a shrimp inside all by itself! The Pollinarium, a glass-enclosed addition, illustrates the mechanics of pollination and the role insects play.

The giant panda exhibit features Mei Xiang and Tian Tian. They are here on a ten-year loan from China, where there are only about 1,000 giant pandas left. Only twenty of those live outside of China, which is why this couple is so popular with American visitors and often has a line waiting to see them. In the winter months the pandas may be indoors, but in the summer they can be seen through glass walls strolling through their outdoor yard.

≡FAST FACT

When President Nixon opened diplomatic relations with China in 1971, the nations exchanged gifts. China gave the United States two giant pandas, Ling-Ling ("Darling Little Girl") and Hsing-Hsing ("Shining Star"), two of the four giant pandas living outside of China at that time. Ling-Ling died at age 23 in 1992, and Hsing-Hsing died in 1999.

The recently renovated monkey house features the Think Tank, where orangutans play on computers. In addition to housing giraffes, rhinos, and hippos, the elephant house has a wonderful indoor exhibit on the anatomy of the elephant in comparison to dinosaurs that will leave any child fascinated. The small-mammal house features everything from small cats to mongooses. The Great Flight Cage, a wonderful aviary with 150 species of birds, is particularly well done, as is the neighboring exhibit on the wetlands, which contains five wading pools featuring waterfowl and wading birds. The lion and tiger exhibit is also quite interactive, with many displays for children to learn about these animals' jungle instincts and preservation of the species.

Other exhibits include Otters in the Valley, a fun-to-watch habitat when the animals are active—there's a glass wall in their den, so you can even see them sleeping—and the American Prairie, where descendants of the zoo's famous bison still roam.

Food and Shops

There are two restaurants on the premises—a full-scale main restaurant and an outdoor cafe. A fabulous indoor gift shop features all sorts of zoo-related toys, books, plates, scarves, and jewelry with an animal motif. If you forget to buy something here, there are smaller zoo stores at Union Station and Reagan National Airport.

Location and Hours

The National Zoo is located on the 3000 block of Connecticut Avenue, between Cathedral Avenue and Devonshire Place, and is accessible from the Woodley Park/Zoo Metro station—a ten-minute walk will get you from the station to the zoo. Grounds are open from 8:00 A.M. until 6:00 P.M.; from April 15 to October 15, the zoo stays open until 8:00 P.M. There is limited pay parking on the zoo grounds, which fills up in the summer by 10:00 A.M. Stroller rentals are available.

Other Galleries and Museums

The following offers brief reviews of the rest of the museums and galleries of the Smithsonian currently located in the nation's capital.

The Anacostia Museum
✉ 1901 Fort Place SE
✆ 202-287-3306
✍ *www.anacostia.si.edu*

This museum of African-American social and cultural history focuses on Washington, D.C., Maryland, Virginia, North Carolina,

South Carolina, and Georgia. Established in 1967, the Anacostia was the first federally funded neighborhood museum. Exhibitions have highlighted the work of local Southern artists, as well as the African-American culture and heritage in all walks of life, including music, religion, and more. This museum is scheduled for a relocation to another building in the near future.

Arts and Industries Building
✉900 Jefferson Drive SW
☞www.si.edu

This was the building where the Smithsonian collection was first shown, and it is a beautiful example of Victorian architecture. The museum houses collections of American Victoriana, as well as crafts and special sociological exhibits of various peoples in America (Japanese-Americans in Hawaii, for instance). It is currently closed for renovations, so check before you make plans to visit.

👫 JUST FOR PARENTS

Need to bring back a souvenir for your coworkers or your boss? The gift shop in the Museum of Arts and Industries is considered one of the best places to buy office gifts in Washington, D.C. They have a fabulous display of paperweights and letter openers. As the museum is currently closed for renovations, check that the gift shop is open before you visit.

The National Museum of the American Indian
✉4th St. and Independence Ave. SW
☎202-633-1000
☞www.nmai.si.edu

This museum, opened in the fall of 2004, houses the impressive George Gustave Heye collection, which features thousands of

North American Indian masterpieces such as baskets, blankets, clothing, pottery, stone carvings, and masks. There are also artifacts from Mexico, the Caribbean, and Central and South American Indians. The museum is located the Mall, next to the National Air and Space Museum.

National Portrait Gallery

&202-275-1738

www.npg.si.edu

This incredible museum features paintings and sculptures of Americans of note, from portraits of all the presidents to paintings of this country's leading scientists, artists, writers, and historical figures. This museum and its sister museum, the National Museum of American Art, will be closed as they undergo an extensive six-year renovation. The two are scheduled to reopen in 2006.

The National Museum of American Art

&202-357-2700

www.americanart.si.edu

One of the few museums in the world dedicated solely to American art, this permanent collection houses some great Colonial masterpieces, as well as the paintings that tell the story of our country. This museum and its sister museum, the National Portrait Gallery, share the former home of the Old Patent Office Building, the site of Lincoln's second inaugural ball. The National Portrait Gallery will be closed until 2006 for an extensive renovation, but traveling exhibits will be shown in art museums throughout the country.

CHAPTER 6

The Top Three Smithsonian Museums

VISITING ALL OR EVEN MOST of the Smithsonian museums and galleries might be too much for you, especially if you are only in town for a long weekend. In this case, you might wish to concentrate on the three must-see Smithsonian attractions—the National Air and Space Museum (the only one of its kind in the world), the National Museum of Natural History, and the National Museum of American History. Plan on dedicating at least three hours to fully explore each one of these museums.

This chapter includes detailed descriptions of the top three museums. At the end of the chapter, you'll find visitor information, including directions and hours of operation.

National Air and Space Museum

This is the most-visited museum in the Smithsonian complex, and some say the world, hosting more than 8 million museum-goers annually. It is a vast museum that chronicles the history of flight and aviation in twenty-three galleries, each devoted to a subject or theme, as well as 300 authentic spacecraft and rockets, space suits, a touchable moon rock, propellers, engines, and many interactive exhibits.

⬛ TRAVEL TIP

Put aside at least three hours (four if you have children with you or if you are really interested in flight) to see the National Air and Space Museum. This time is necessary because there is no way you can rush through this incredible museum, especially in the summer months when it's quite crowded.

Milestones of Flight

This is the most popular exhibit in the museum; you can see it from the street through the glass wall of the museum. Here you will find:

- The Wright Brothers' 1903 *Flyer,* the first human-propelled flying machine
- *The Spirit of St. Louis,* the aircraft in which twenty-five-year-old Charles Lindbergh made the first transatlantic flight, from New York to Paris, in thirty-three hours, thirty minutes, in 1927
- The Bell X-1 *Glamorous Glennis,* in which Chuck Yaeger became the first pilot to fly faster than the speed of sound, in 1947
- Gemini IV, which carried astronauts Edward White and James A. McDivitt on the first manned space walk (exhibited with their space suits, too)
- The Apollo 11 command module, which was the first spacecraft to land on the moon (with astronaut Michael Collins's space suit on display as well)

Other highlights include the world's only touchable moon rock, which was collected by Apollo 17 astronauts; the Viking Lander, the test vehicle for the first spacecraft to explore the surface of Mars; Goddard rockets from 1926 and 1941; and the United States's Pershing II and USSR's SS-20 missiles, which are nuclear missiles banned by the INF treaty of 1987.

First-Floor Galleries

Galleries on the first floor include permanent exhibits on air transportation, the black experience in aviation, and the golden age of flight, which chronicles aviation history between the two world wars and features many classic planes, such as the Beechcraft Staggerwing. There is also a gallery on the history of jet aviation, where you will find an explanation of how the commercial jetliner came into being and can watch a film on technological developments.

≡FAST FACT

In the fall of 1999, the museum added its newest addition to the Milestones Gallery—the Breitling Orbiter 3 gondola, which was the first balloon to successfully circle the earth nonstop, in 1998.

The first floor also has an exhibit on the history of early flight, from gliders that inspired the Wright Brothers to the first seaplanes and a Bleroit IX, the most popular pre–World War I monoplane. In the "How Things Fly" exhibit, there are hands-on demonstrations of the scientific principles that enable airplanes to fly. You can also crawl into the cockpit of a Cessna 150 and manipulate the controls (a very popular experience for kids of all ages).

The first floor also features a gallery on exploring the earth from above for mapping, weather, and spying purposes, and another gallery on the stars that explains how satellites are used to map and examine radiant energy from the sun and the stars, with a host of solar instruments on display, as well as a film on the history of telescopes and our current knowledge of our galaxy and those beyond.

The Space Race gallery is one of the most popular exhibits on the first floor, with various models of American spacecraft, rocketry, missiles, space suits, and an overview of the space race. Here you will find a full-size test model of the Hubble Space Telescope, the

Apollo-Soyuz spacecraft (the first manned international space mission), a model of the space shuttle *Columbia* on its launch pad, and the Skylab orbital workshop, which visitors can walk through (another very popular exhibit).

IMAX Theater

The Samuel P. Langley IMAX Theater features an IMAX screen that is five stories high and seven stories wide. Films on the history of flight and space exploration are shown daily. This is a unique experience, and children love films on this giant screen, especially the ever-popular *To Fly*. Tickets sell out quickly in the summer months, so purchase them early in the day even if you want to see a show in the afternoon (the 10:00 A.M. shows are usually not sold out). You can also purchase tickets at the box office up to two weeks in advance, so you might want to stop in the museum when you get to town and buy tickets for later on in the week. Tickets are $8.00 for adults and $6.50 for children and seniors.

The Rest of the First Floor

You can enter the museum shop on the first floor, but it is a three-story, 12,000-square-foot emporium. It is also the largest of the Smithsonian museum stores, where almost every kid who ventures in walks out with the freeze-dried "astronaut" ice cream (at about two bucks, a bargain as far as purchasers of kids' souvenirs are concerned).

At the west end of the first floor is the very popular arcade with the fancier name of "At the Controls," where almost every child who enters the museum will want to pilot a flight simulator. There are dozens of aircraft to choose from, many of which are on display in the museum. The four-minute ride is $6.50 per person but worth every penny.

The Second Floor

Galleries on the second floor include exhibits on air and sea exploration from 1911 to present and also display biplanes, World

War I carriers, and navy fighters. There are two separate exhibit halls featuring aviation during World War I and World War II. The second is an extremely popular hall, displaying aircraft from five countries including a Messerschmitt and a P-51D Mustang.

Another hall on this floor features an exhibit on exploring the planets, where you can see a full-scale replica of *Voyager*, the spacecraft that explored Jupiter, Saturn, Uranus, and Neptune, as well as a meteorite collected in Antarctica that scientists believe may be a piece of Mars.

≡FAST FACT

The first successful powered, controlled, sustained flight by humans took place on December 17, 1903, in Kitty Hawk, North Carolina, using a plane designed and constructed by Orville and Wilbur Wright. You'll find the 1903 *Flyer* at the Air and Space Museum.

The Pioneers of Flight exhibit houses many record-holding airplanes. The most popular is Amelia Earhart's Lockheed Vega. In this plane, Earhart became the first woman to make a transatlantic solo flight, in 1932 from Newfoundland to Northern Ireland in fourteen hours and fifty-two minutes.

Other galleries on the second floor include a look at space exploration in the future, including a realistic Martian landscape; an overview of the Apollo program, with examples of moon soil and space food and suits; and an exhibit of art about flight and space exploration. The final gallery looks at computers and space exploration featuring the world's fastest computer, the brain of the Minuteman missile, and interactive displays for designing spacecraft.

The Albert Einstein Planetarium is located on the second floor, where there are various shows on the night sky, astronomy, and space projected onto a domed interior. Tickets for the planetarium shows can be purchased at the Langley Theater box office at $5.50 per person.

If You Get Hungry

The Air and Space Museum has redesigned its Wright Place into a wonderful food court featuring a host of fast-food options, including McDonald's (with a space-related trinket in the Happy Meal), Boston Market, and Donato's Pizza. It is really perfect for this very busy museum.

Steven F. Udvar-Hazy Center

If you have been inspired by the Air and Space Museum and/or you just can't get enough of aviation history, there is a new sister museum near Dulles Airport that houses some of the larger aircraft that the museum just couldn't cram into its two stories.

The Udvar-Hazy Center opened to the public in 2003 on a 176.5-acre lot and features exhibit hangars, an observation tower where visitors can watch plane traffic, an IMAX theater, and restaurants. Noted exhibits include the fully restored *Enola Gay,* the space shuttle *Enterprise,* an F-40 Phantom Fighter, an SR-71 Blackbird, and one of the surviving Concorde planes that flew between France and England. Another feature of the Center is the Wall of Honor, a permanent memorial to the tens of thousands of people who have contributed to air and space science. In total, the Udvar-Hazy Center showcases an additional 200 aircraft and 100 major space artifacts.

The National Museum of Natural History

The green-domed National Museum of Natural History is the second most visited museum in the Smithsonian complex, with more than 6 million annual visitors (with about a million during each of the summer months). To do this museum justice, you should expect to spend at least three or four hours in it.

Highlights of the museum include the fabled Hope diamond, which always draws a huge crowd. The nearby Hall of Minerals is a favorite among children, with re-creations of a copper mine, many touchable geodes and rocks, and a good display of meteorites. Kids also love the insect zoo, where they can see inside termites' nests and a beehive and see a display of Madagascar cockroaches.

☂ RAINY DAY FUN

One of the many highlights of the National Museum of Natural History is the Orkin Insect Zoo, where children can examine a tarantula, electronically match bugs that infest a home to the places they like to nest (with this being a very popular kid activity), and explore the interior of an ant hill (especially popular with children after the movies *ANTZ* and *A Bug's Life*). Scientists on hand allow children to "pet" some resident insects.

The Hall of Bones is a great learning display on how mammal skeletons have evolved, and the replica of a giant blue whale and two preserved squid carcasses (two of only three architeuthis—giant squid—bodies in the country) are displayed and explained very well.

The Curse of the Hope Diamond

Many people say that the reason the Hope diamond lies behind glass in the Smithsonian is because the curse on the diamond can't harm anyone from there.

According to legend, the diamond was once the eye of an Indian idol, which was stolen, smuggled into Paris, and later turned up as the Blue diamond, part of the French royal jewels. Everyone who came in contact with the jewel was said to have met with tragedy, from Louis XIV's oldest son to his oldest grandson and his great-grandson. There's even a rumor that the stone was used as a bribe to get Louis XVI and Marie Antoinette out of France, and we know what happened to them.

The diamond disappeared for a while—some think it appears around the neck of Queen Maria Louisa of Spain in a Goya painting—and resurfaced in Amsterdam, where it was recut. The jeweler died penniless because his son stole the gem, and the jeweler's son committed suicide after his father's death. It was purchased by Harry Hope in London in 1830 (from whom we get the name), whose son and daughter-in-law inherited the stone but also died penniless.

An Eastern European prince bought the stone and gave it to a Follies Bergere actress, whom he later shot. A Greek owner and his family were killed in a horrible car accident. The stone is also said to have then turned up in Russia in the hands of Catherine the Great, who did not have a happy ending to her life.

A wealthy Turkish sultan bought the diamond and gave it to his favorite wife, who was later murdered after he was dethroned. Evelyn Walsh McLean, wife to the heir of the *Washington Post* fortune, had seen the blue stone while on her honeymoon in Turkey. She bought it, and, knowing about its history and the accompanying legend, supposedly had a priest bless it before she wore it. However, that did her no good because her only son was killed in a bizarre car accident right outside his home; her husband was committed to a mental institution after his involvement with the Teapot Dome scandal was revealed; and her daughter committed suicide.

New York jeweler Harry Winston bought the stone in the early 1950s and gave it to the Smithsonian on permanent loan, some say because his wife kept begging him to let her wear it. Winston sent the diamond to the museum by registered mail, and there's a story that after the mailman handled the package, his life was cursed: his leg was mangled in a car accident, his wife died of a heart attack, his dog died, and his house burned down.

Ground Floor

The ground-floor entrance on Constitution Avenue opens with highlights from the collection, including geodes and crystals, a 700,000-year-old hand ax, totem poles from the Pacific Northwest, a gigantic fossilized shark tooth, meteorites, and butterflies from

South America. A collection of 300 bird specimens is also on this floor.

The totally remodeled Atrium Cafeteria is here too, offering many child-pleasing meals (hamburgers, pizza), as well as hot food and personally prepared sandwiches.

The museum's gift shop is also on this level and has two wings—one exclusively for children. Museum artifacts, such as a lead coffin, are on display throughout the shop. The museum shop is extensive, and you could spend an hour in it as well. You can also buy a replica of the Hope diamond—with matching earrings!

📖 TRAVEL TIP

All the Smithsonian gift shops are worth exploring, but the one in the American Museum of Natural History is one of the best in the entire city. There's an entire floor for your kids, as well as replicas of some of the most beautiful jewelry and art and American arts and crafts. You can buy Christmas ornaments in the shape of Dorothy's ruby slippers, earrings made out of pennies, or even potholders and kitchen towels with the image of Rosie the Riveter on them.

First Floor

If you enter the museum from the Mall, you will walk into the museum's rotunda, where you will be greeted by a giant display of an African bush elephant with his trunk extended. This mighty creature has been a constant feature of childhood visits to Washington, D.C., since before the baby-boomers were kids.

There are eight exhibit halls on this floor, some of which have banners over their entrances from the rotunda.

Fossils: The History of Life

This display exhibits the oldest known fossil—of microorganisms—from 3.5 billion years ago, with a film explaining the theory of evolution and various exhibits and fossils tracing the emergence of life from the ancient sea to the conquest of land. Some of the highlights of this exhibit include rare 530-year-old fossilized soft-bodied animals in shale, which were discovered by the fourth secretary of the Smithsonian in 1910, and the fossilized skeleton of an early whale.

The exhibit charts the evolution of ancient amphibians and plants and concludes with the dinosaur exhibit, where the skeletal remains of a diplodocus, an eighty-foot sauropod and the largest land-based dinosaur, is on display with a comptosaurus, stegosaurus, and an allosaurus. Informative, hands-on exhibits on dinosaur limbs, jaws, and teeth accompany this exhibit.

Ice Age Mammals

The next hall is dedicated to Ice Age mammals, where there are skeletons of saber-tooth tigers (one from the La Brea Tar Pits in California) and a woolly mammoth skeleton and tusk, as well as some preserved mammoth skin! Also on view is an Ice Age bison, freeze-dried by nature and recovered by Alaskan gold miners. This hall also features life-sized tableaus of Neanderthal man and Ice Age mammals.

Asian and Pacific Cultures

The next series of exhibits on this floor features the people of Asia and the Pacific, displaying crafts, objects, clothing, and religious artifacts of the history and culture of the region. Highlights include a re-creation of a Chinese opera, Confucian and Shinto shrines, and an iron Buddha from Korea. In the Pacific exhibition, highlights include two huge stone disks used as money and one of the huge stone heads from Easter Island.

African History and Culture

The recently renovated exhibit hall on African culture features exhibits on African peoples from the Strait of Gibraltar to the Cape of Good Hope and the historical experience of the African diaspora. Highlights include a seventeenth-century Nigerian cast brass head and African headdresses from the nineteenth and twentieth centuries.

Eskimo and Indian Cultures

This is an exhibit on the various American Indian cultures, from the Eskimo to the North American and South American Indians. Highlights include displays on seal hunting, ice fishing, and igloo construction in the Arctic region; a teepee and buffalo hides in the North American section; and an impressive 1880 Sioux headdress with seventy-seven eagle feathers.

Birds of the World

On display are all kinds of birds, from the penguins of the Arctic to passenger pigeons, the most common American bird in the eighteenth century. The passenger pigeon became extinct by 1914, when the last bird of the species died in captivity. Other extinct species on display include the penguinlike great auk and the Carolina parakeet.

Birds are displayed in re-creations of their natural habitats. The exhibit also features displays on birds' feeding habits, migration, reproduction, and importance to people.

Sea Life: Exploring Marine Ecosystems

This is one of the highlights of the museum's collection. Here you can find a ninety-two-foot model of the great blue whale, which was actually modeled after a real whale carcass, and a stellar exhibit on the giant squid, where there are two preserved specimens of two different species of squid. The films accompanying this exhibit are fascinating and informative, as are the displays that explain how squids capture their prey (with clawlike hooks) and how one species stuns prey with strobelike flash organs.

Other exhibits in this area include re-creations of a Maine sea coast and a Caribbean coral reef, as well as mounted specimens of walrus and sea otters.

The Behring Family of Mammals

The Mammal Hall has been completely renovated and was newly opened to the public in 2003. It contains 274 specimens, such as a sloth hanging upside down in a South American rain forest; a giraffe drinking from an African watering hole; and a pair of African lions bringing down a water buffalo. The renovation reorganizes the material so that visitors can see the evolution of the various mammal species and their traits. It includes an eight-minute video as well as fossils that can be touched by tiny human hands, such as the skull of an extinct bear.

Second Floor

The second floor is home to the Janet Hooker Hall of Geology, Gems, and Minerals, which is always packed because the legendary blue Hope diamond is on display here.

👥 JUST FOR PARENTS

In addition to the Hope diamond, the Janet Hooker Hall also displays Marie Antoinette's diamond earrings and Empress Josephine's emerald necklace. Copies of these jewels are all available for purchase in the museum gift shop.

This exhibit hall also has a re-creation of a copper mine, a display of meteorites (including a fascinating story about meteorites that have dropped into people's homes), a moon rock, displays of ores and geodes to touch and examine, and many interactive displays on how minerals are formed.

South America: Continent and Culture

Like the exhibits on the first floor, this hall presents the peoples and cultures of South America in life-size dioramas, such as a Patagonian grassland in the nineteenth century; a re-creation of a tropical rain forest; the arid Pacific coastlands; and Andean mountain valleys. Highlights include objects from the Inca civilization.

Origins of Western Culture

This is one of the most interesting exhibits in the museum. Its goal is to explain the history of Western civilization from the end of the Ice Age to A.D. 500, when the basic patterns of human existence were set.

The exhibit includes a diorama of the cave paintings of Lascaux, France, as well as excellent displays and informative short films about the ancient Egyptians and their burial and embalming processes. The Egyptian exhibits will hold even a seven-year-old spellbound! Additional exhibits on Mesopotamian, ancient Greek, and Roman cultures are also on view here.

The Hall of Bones

Floor-to-ceiling displays of hundreds of animal skeletons, grouped by order and species, dramatically show the theory of evolution. Informative displays illustrate how bone structure adapted to the environment.

The Hall of Reptiles

This is an exhibit of alligators, frogs, turtles, and snakes in dioramas that duplicate their natural settings. Informative displays explain feeding habits, movement, and reptiles' influence on humans.

The Orkin Insect Zoo

This zoo is a relatively small but very entertaining exhibit on the world of insects. Here, you can see a live beehive—put your hand on the glass and you can feel their heat—along with an African termite mound and thrice-daily tarantula feedings (at 10:30 and 11:30 A.M. and 1:30 P.M. on weekdays). There are re-creations of rain forests and caves and swamps, all full of live bugs. The more docile members of the insect world can be held or touched by children (under supervision), including the ever-popular Madagascar cockroach. There's also an insect lab where kids can see butterflies cocooning.

Butterfly Garden

In the warmer months, there's an outdoor butterfly garden on the 9th Street side of the museum building where visitors can see the interaction between butterflies and plants. This is a nice follow-up to the insect zoo.

Discovery Room

This is a hands-on, interactive room for children (and their parents) to touch and explore the many natural objects in the museum's collection. Kids can handle items like fossils, shells, bones, feathers, and so on.

≡FAST FACT

In the Discovery Room, some of the kid-pleasing favorites include the opportunity to peer into a crocodile's mouth; the examination of "Discovery Boxes," which feature a variety of shells, fossils, plants, and bones; and the chance to touch an elephant tusk and a porcupine's spines.

Samuel Johnson Theater

The museum has a brand-new IMAX theater, where visitors can see *Africa's Elephant Kingdom* and the Smithsonian's own *Galapagos* on a six-story screen in 3D. Theater admission is $8.50 for adults and $5.50 for children and seniors.

The National Museum of American History

This is another four-floor museum where you can expect to spend at least three hours (and perhaps an additional hour in the exhaustive gift shop). The exhibit about the first ladies is very popular, especially the section where you can see their inaugural gowns, and Foucault's pendulum never fails to fascinate the visitors. The pop-culture touchstones on view include Archie Bunker's chair,

Mr. Spock's phaser, and Dorothy's ruby slippers. There are a number of exhibits on the scientific innovations and technological advances that have made the United States a world leader, such as Thomas Edison's light bulb and Ford's Model T. There are also halls on the historical events and sociological experiences that define our country.

First Floor

If you enter from Constitution Avenue, you will arrive on the first floor, which houses more than fifteen exhibit halls. These exhibits highlight the history and impact of science and technology on modern society.

Country Store and Post Office

The first hall you will see displays an actual country store and post office that was transported in its entirety from Headsville, West Virginia. The post office continues to operate from within the museum—you can get your postcards stamped "Smithsonian Station."

FAST FACT

The legendary lunch counter from the F.W. Woolworth store in Greensboro, North Carolina, considered by many to be where the 1960s civil rights movement began, is on display on the main floor. Here, four African-American college students sat down, despite the "Whites Only" prohibition, and ordered lunch. When asked to leave, they remained in their seats. Their nonviolent refusal to yield to the Jim Crow laws began a movement to challenge segregation practices throughout the South.

Material World

The purpose of this exhibit is to explain how things are made and how those elements have changed since the beginning of our country. There's a central section on new materials and reusing existing products (such as plywood and plastic) in new ways.

Technological Innovations

The next section of the first floor highlights technological innovations ranging from farm machines (harvesters and tractors) to ships (more than 100 models, including one of the *Mayflower*). On display is the engine room of a Coast Guard ship from the 1920s. There are also displays dealing with a sailor's life—kids find the re-creation of a 1940s tattoo parlor fascinating—including luxury liners, whaling, and disasters at sea (very popular since the movie *Titanic*).

A new permanent exhibit was added in 2003 that highlights developments in transportation and how they influenced American society from horses to trains to cars and public transportation. Especially fun and insightful pieces of this exhibit include the building of the famous Route 66 and the construction of the New York City subway system, complete with reproductions of the water pipes running beneath the city. There are cars and buses and trains for kids to entertain themselves in and with. For a child who loves cars and trucks, this is a dream come true.

Cars and Trains

The same exhibit wing also includes a hall on the development of the automobile, with more than forty antique cars on display (including the 1913 Model T), as well as the automobile's predecessors, the horse-drawn carriage, and alternate wheeled transportation such as bicycles and motorcycles. A hall on railroad innovations includes the Pacific-type steam locomotive 1401 used between 1926 and 1941, a stagecoach from 1836, and a Seattle cable car from 1888. There are additional exhibit rooms on bridge technology and engine design for power machinery.

Electric Power

The exhibit hall on electricity starts with the work of Benjamin Franklin and traces the development of electrical power through the nineteenth century, ending with the work of Thomas Edison and his light bulb. Other technological innovations highlighted on this floor include the development of the typewriter, the phonograph (with a display of one of Edison's first phonographs, from 1877), clocks, and locks.

≡FAST FACT

When most people think of Thomas Edison, they think of only the light bulb, but Edison registered more than 1,000 patents for inventions in his lifetime. Other Edison inventions and improvements include the printing telegraph, phonograph, vote recorder, electric motor, talking doll, and storage battery.

American Industrial Revolution

The exhibit on the American Industrial Revolution is vast, tying together industrial innovations and their effect on the population. It begins with a re-creation of the Crystal Palace, the site of the 1851 World's Fair in London, where American technological innovations were first heralded by Europe, and goes on to examine the impact of machinery and the factory system. On display is the world's oldest operable locomotive, the John Bull, as well as the Colt revolver and another 250 objects.

Science in American Life

This exhibit chronicles scientific innovations over the past 125 years, such as nylon, the atomic bomb, and emerging technologies of bioscience. The hands-on science center is fascinating for children interested in science. Among other experiments, kids can put the four proteins of DNA together in varying patterns to create musical sounds or use a Geiger counter to test for radioactivity.

Information Age

The final exhibit hall on the first floor is on the Information Age, which begins with the Morse telegraph and continues through the developments of the telephone, early computers, radio, and television. This exhibit is designed to be very interactive and offers visitors opportunities to have their fingerprints taken, decipher a German World War I code, and even produce an evening news program.

Second Floor

The emphasis on the second floor is the political and social history of our country, from the times of the Revolutionary War to the present.

The Star-Spangled Banner

One of the first exhibits you'll find on the second floor is the display of the flag, now restored, that Francis Scott Key saw by "the dawn's early light" was "still there," flying over Fort McKinley after a battle of the War of 1812. (After that sight, he wrote the poem "The Star-Spangled Banner," which became the national anthem.) The huge (nine- by ten-foot) historic star-spangled banner is displayed under a protective cover.

TRAVEL TIP

On the second floor, be sure to visit Foucault's pendulum, an example of the nineteenth-century experiment that proved that the earth rotates. The pendulum dominates a second-floor gallery, where the hollow brass ball swings back and forth, periodically knocking down red markers set in a circle. It is somewhat mesmerizing and always surrounded by visitors.

After the Revolution

This exhibit looks at life in the United States in the 1780s and 1790s through the eyes of Native Americans, Europeans, and African-Americans, both slaves and freedmen, re-creating living spaces and the tools used during those times. It also re-creates the harrowing experience of coming to America on a slave ship.

Presidential Exhibits

As a hint that you are approaching the ever-popular exhibit featuring the first ladies, the next gallery displays a reproduction of the Ceremonial Court of the Cross Hall of the White House at the turn of the century, with original furnishings from Teddy Roosevelt's tenure in the White House. Adjoining galleries display presidential memorabilia, such as Thomas Jefferson's portable writing desk and the toys of the children who grew up in the White House.

The first ladies exhibit centers on the presidential wives of the twentieth century and gives a brief biographical and political background on each one. But it's the inaugural gowns that people really come to look at, especially those of Jackie Kennedy, Hillary Clinton, and Laura Bush.

The Suffragette Movement

A nearby exhibit focuses on the role of women in politics from 1890 to 1925, from the middle-class home to the tenement, and also includes some important memorabilia of the suffragette movement, such as Susan B. Anthony's desk.

Exhibits on Migration

This floor also has two exhibits examining the effect of migration on Americans. The first looks at African-American migration from the South to the North in the early part of this century, and the second hall, titled "American Encounters," looks at the effect migration had on the western Native American populations.

Another Hands-on Exhibit

The second of two hands-on exhibits is also located here, and visitors can operate machines featured on the floor, from sending a message by telegraph to turning the handle of a cotton gin.

Third Floor

The third floor features exhibits on the objects and innovations that have had an impact on the country, from coins to firearms.

The section on the history of the armed forces features George Washington's field headquarters tent and a Revolutionary War vessel—the gunboat *Philadelphia*—from 1776, as well as many models of warships from the Revolution to World War I.

═FAST FACT

The Hall of Armed Forces features the display of the stuffed and preserved horse ridden by General Philip Sheridan in the closing months of the Civil War. Displayed intact inside a glass case, the horse is decked in all its Union regalia. The horse was originally named Rienzi but was rechristened Winchester, in honor of the Virginia town where a potential defeat for the Union forces turned into a victory.

There is also a hall on the internment of Japanese-Americans during World War II that includes the executive order signed by Franklin Delano Roosevelt, a barracks room from the internment camp, and audio interviews with people who were kept in the camps.

Other galleries present collections of musical instruments, ceramics, textiles (magnificent quilts are on display), money, and medals. There's a permanent exhibit on the life and music of Ella Fitzgerald, with wonderful clips. The third floor also features a dollhouse from the turn of the century that has more than twenty rooms and is infinitely fascinating in both detail and content.

In addition to the previously mentioned pop-culture icons, cases filled to the brim with television memorabilia are on view around the escalators of both the second and third floor. These include Jim Henson's Muppets Elmo and Oscar the Grouch; Fonzie's jacket from *Happy Days*; and Howdy Doody, the talking, dancing puppet himself.

Ground Floor

The three restaurants and the gift shop are located on the ground floor. (There's a first-floor gift shop entrance as well.) The gift shop features a ton of fabulous knickknacks and Americana ranging from earrings made out of pennies ($2.50) to bags of old-fashioned candy and replicas of some of the White House china.

There is an old-fashioned ice cream parlor facing the Constitution Avenue entrance that offers a full lunch menu as well as wonderful ice cream desserts. The Palm Court Coffee Bar re-creates a turn-of-the-century restaurant, with wooden screens and ceiling fans, and features coffee and snacks such as brownies and scones. The Main Street Cafe is a large cafeteria with a full array of breakfast and lunch items. All the restaurants close by 4:30 P.M., even in the summer when the museum is open later.

🌂 RAINY DAY FUN

The "Hands on History Room" is an interactive exhibit that lets kids climb on a highwheel bicycle and pedal, or explore the techniques and storytelling employed in buffalo hide painting.

Visitors' Information

Here are addresses, phone numbers, Web addresses, directions, and hours of operation for the National Air and Space Museum, the Steven F. Udvar-Hazy Center, the National Museum of Natural History, and the National Museum of American History.

National Air and Space Museum
✉Independence Ave. at 4th Street, SW
☎202-357-2700
✍*www.nasm.si.edu*

The museum is located on the south side of the Mall, with entrances on Jefferson Drive and Independence Avenue. Take the Metro to the L'Enfant Plaza station. The museum is generally open from 10 A.M. to 5:30 P.M., but it may open earlier and close later in the summer, so call for hours. Free daily guided tours are offered at 10:00 A.M. and 1:15 P.M.; science demonstrations are conducted throughout the day.

Steven F. Udvar-Hazy Center
✉ 14390 Air and Space Museum Parkway
✆ 202-357-2700
✎ *www.nasm.si.edu*

The Udvar-Hazy Center is located south of the main terminal at Dulles Airport in Chantilly, Virginia (near the intersection of Routes 28 and 50, about a half-hour drive from downtown D.C.). Parking is provided, but there is a parking fee. Hours of operation are from 10 A.M. to 5:30 P.M.

National Museum of Natural History
✉ 10th St. and Constitution Ave. NW
✆ 202-357-2700
✎ *www.mnh.si.edu*

The museum can be accessed from the Mall, with entrances on both Constitution Avenue and Madison Drive. You can take the Metro to the Federal Triangle stop. General hours are from 10 A.M. to 5:30 P.M. Summer hours (from May 23 to September 1) are 10 A.M. to 7:30 P.M., or later, so it's best to call and inquire. Guided tours are offered at 10:00 A.M. and 1:00 P.M.

National Museum of American History
✉ 14th St. and Constitution Ave. NW
✆ 202-633-1000
✎ *www.americanhistory.si.edu*

The museum is located on the Mall, accessible from the Federal Triangle and Smithsonian Metro stations. Hours are from 10 A.M. to 5:30 P.M. (later during the summer). The museum also offers daily tours and demonstrations; times vary seasonally.

CHAPTER 7

Memorials and Monuments

WASHINGTON IS FULL OF statues, parks, and buildings erected in tribute to many of the country's presidents, and the most important are the four commemorative presidential memorials. Each of these presidential sites is awe-inspiring at any time, but the best way to see them is one right after the other during the nighttime, when they are illuminated. It's also interesting to see them together so you can put their history into perspective.

The various war memorials are near those of the presidents, so a bus tour often includes nine sites in a single four-hour period. Seeing these together also gives a different perspective to our nation's battle history and makes the Lincoln Memorial both a presidential and Civil War memorial.

While probably not for young children, Arlington National Cemetery can be a surprisingly educational and somber experience, with its acres of symmetrically arranged white crosses on the green hills and the various gravesites and memorials on the property.

The United States Holocaust Memorial Museum is a powerful educational experience that brings the horror of this twentieth-century crime directly in front of you with both sensory and visual stimulus. However, it is definitely not for children under 12, unless they have sought out this history. It is so thorough—you need four hours to see this site—and stirs such a strong reaction, that you should plan on visiting it in the afternoon, because it will be very difficult to view anything else that day.

Washington Monument

✆ 202-426-6841

✑*www.nps.gov*

✑*http://reservations.nps.gov* (online reservations)

The Washington Monument was the first memorial to be constructed in the nation's capital, and it's located at the center of the National Mall (between 15th and 17th Streets). The idea for the monument was around early in the city's history, and L'Enfant originally planned to erect a grand statue of George Washington on horseback. However, Congress failed to appropriate the necessary funds for the monument, and by the 1832 centennial of Washington's birth, a private society had been formed to raise funds for a national monument to the first president and Revolutionary War general.

The plans for an equestrian statue seemed too meager for this great man, and in 1845 a competition was sponsored to create something different. Robert Mills won the competition with his design for a Greco-Roman rotunda topped with an obelisk. It included a statuary group with Washington atop a chariot. Fortunately for posterity, they couldn't raise enough money for this grand scheme, and only the obelisk was constructed. The cornerstone was laid in 1848, but the Civil War interfered and the monument wasn't dedicated until 1885, with various descendants of Washington present.

The monument is 555 feet and $5^1/8$ inches high and is the tallest masonry structure in the world. There is a federal law on the books that restricts any building in D.C. from being higher than this monument. Years ago, you could climb the 897 steps to the top, but now you have to take the elevator up. However, you can still walk down with a park ranger guide at 10:00 A.M. and 2:00 P.M.

The view from the top is spectacular, and the whole upper tier and the observation tower were recently renovated. There is a visitors' center inside, which offers videos and displays on the life of the president. The monument receives close to a million visitors a year and underwent a major exterior restoration in 2000.

🧳 TRAVEL TIP

You can also visit the National Law Enforcement Officers Memorial, between 4th and 5th Streets and E and F Streets ☎202-737-3400. It has a visitors' center at ✉605 E Street NW, which is open Monday through Friday from 9:00 A.M. to 5:00 P.M., on Saturday from 10:00 A.M. to 5:00 P.M., and Sunday from noon to 5:00 P.M. The memorial is accessible from the Judiciary Square Metro station. This memorial commemorates federal, state, and local officers who have died in the line of duty.

Location and Hours

The Washington Monument is located on the Mall, accessible from the Smithsonian Metro station. Open hours are from 8:00 A.M. til 5:00 P.M.; the monument stays open until midnight in the summertime (from April through September). The monument is also closed on Christmas Day and closes at noon on July 4.

You must have a ticket to get in, but tickets are free and you can get them at the ticket booth on 15th Street, at the bottom of the hill. Note that the booth opens at 8:00 A.M. and is often out of tickets by noon during the summer; also, there's a limit of six tickets per person. You can also purchase tickets in advance through TicketMaster (☎202-432-7328) for $1.50 per person, with a $.50 one-time processing fee. Online reservations can be made as well.

The Lincoln Memorial

☎202-426-6841
✍www.nps.gov

Lincoln's assassination in 1865 so affected the country that his memorial became the second presidential commemorative site to be built in the nation's capital. It is the second-most-visited of the presidential memorials, with 1.5 million viewers annually. The memorial's design, which we see every day on the back of the penny, is Henry Bacon's neoclassical interpretation of the Parthenon from ancient Greece. Thirty-six Doric columns represent the states of the Union at the time of Lincoln's assassination. In addition, there are two more at the entrance. Forty-eight decorative, wreathlike festoons above the columns symbolize the number of states at the time of the memorial's completion in 1922. Hawaii and Alaska are included on a terrace inscription.

The limestone walls of the memorial chamber feature the carved words of the Gettysburg Address and Lincoln's second inaugural address. There are also two murals by Jules Guerin depicting allegorical interpretations of Lincoln's achievements and beliefs on the north and south walls.

While the view of the Washington Monument across the Reflecting Pool from the front steps is serene, the power of the nineteen-foot-high seated white marble statue of Lincoln looking out onto the city makes you very aware of the loss that was the Civil War. The statue, designed by Daniel Chester French from a death mask, was carved over four years.

Daniel Chester French

Many art historians consider Daniel Chester French to be one of America's greatest sculptors of the nineteenth century, but outside of Washington, D.C., his work is virtually unknown.

It was French's intention to depict Lincoln as "the war president" in the seated statue at the Lincoln Memorial. Lincoln sits in a curule chair like those used by Roman leaders, with his arms resting on the chair arms adorned with faces that are classical symbols of authority. The Union flag is draped over the back of the chair. Lincoln has one hand clenched in a fist and the other open. Some interpret this to suggest both his determination to preserve the Union and his compassion.

Legend also has it that the position of Lincoln's hands spell out "A" and "L" in American Sign Language fingerspelling. While many think this is coincidental, French did later sculpt Thomas Gallaudet, founder of Gallaudet University for the deaf in D.C., in which French did incorporate American Sign Language.

Other works by French in Washington, D.C., include the statue of Samuel F. Dupont at Dupont Circle; the Butt-Millet Memorial (at 17th and E Streets), and the First Infantry Division Memorial (State Place near 17th Street).

An Inspiration to Many

The Lincoln Memorial has become a shrine to civil rights in the twentieth century. While many know that Martin Luther King Jr.'s famous "I Have a Dream" speech was delivered here in 1963, few are aware that as far back as 1939, the Lincoln Memorial was the site of a civil rights protest instigated by Eleanor Roosevelt. The first lady offered the memorial as the location for a recital by Marian Anderson when she was refused the stage of the Daughters of the American Revolution Constitution Hall because she was black. Roosevelt resigned her DAR membership over this snub.

Location and Hours

The Lincoln Memorial is located on 23rd Street between Constitution and Independence Avenues, at the western edge of the Reflecting Pool in Potomac Park. You can reach the memorial from the Foggy Bottom or Smithsonian Metro station, but expect to do some walking.

You can enter the Lincoln Memorial from 8:00 A.M. until midnight any day but Christmas Day. Park rangers offer lectures every thirty minutes. There is also a gift shop and a small bookstore. (The bookstore closes at 10:30 P.M.)

Thomas Jefferson Memorial

✆ 202-426-0682

✍ www.nps.gov

Although the concept of a memorial to the author of the Declaration of Independence and third president of the United

States was planned in the L'Enfant city design, the actual location for the memorial was never laid out, so the cornerstone for this commemorative site was not broken until 1939, after land was purchased on what is now the Tidal Basin. The memorial was dedicated in 1943, the bicentennial anniversary of Jefferson's birth.

≡FAST FACT

The white marble memorial's colonnaded and domed design was created by John Russell Pope, who also designed the National Gallery of Art and the National Archives. The structure is neoclassic in tribute to Jefferson's influences.

The hollow bronze statue by Rudolph Evans, coated in wax to prevent ionization, depicts Jefferson (in a pose intended to represent the Age of Enlightenment) holding a document symbolic of his role as one of the authors of America's founding democratic principles. In this vein, the surrounding marble walls of the memorial are inscribed with the words of the Declaration of Independence, as well as of excerpts of various letters and bills Jefferson authored that articulate his belief in the American citizenry's ability to govern itself. The committee that drafted the Declaration of Independence is sculpted in bas relief above the entrance to the memorial.

The memorial also includes a gallery on Jefferson's life and works. He was also the founder of the University of Virginia, an amateur scientist, and an architect. The gallery is located on the lower level.

Location and Hours

The memorial is located on the south side of the Tidal Basin on Ohio Drive, accessible from the Smithsonian Metro station (expect a long walk). Doors are open from 8:00 A.M. to midnight, but the memorial does not open on Christmas Day. Park rangers give talks every half hour. There is limited one-hour parking on the site.

▣ TRAVEL TIP

During April and May, when the Japanese cherry blossoms are in bloom, the Jefferson Memorial is one of the most beautiful and inspirational sights in the city. It is said that President Roosevelt, who was the guiding force behind the construction of this memorial, had a number of trees removed so that his view of the Jefferson Memorial would be unobstructed.

The Franklin Delano Roosevelt Memorial

☏ 202-426-6841

✐ *www.nps.gov*

The newest of the presidential memorials, this four-room, open-air memorial to President Roosevelt sits on a seven-and-a-half-acre site and is the most visited of the presidential memorial sites, with more than 3 million tourists a year. It is also the only presidential memorial that includes a tribute to a first lady, Eleanor Roosevelt, who was also the first U.S. representative at the United Nations.

The four "rooms" of the memorial represent Roosevelt's four terms in office, from 1933 to 1945, the years spanning the Great Depression through World War II. The first gallery represents his first term with a life-size statue of a poor Appalachian couple, the second room a bread line, the third a person listening to Roosevelt's fireside chats, and the fourth a statue of Eleanor Roosevelt.

There are also numerous fountains and green granite walls inscribed with Roosevelt's words, which are particularly moving when illuminated at night. A Social Programs mural depicts in images, writing, and Braille the fifty-four government programs implemented during Roosevelt's New Deal.

As with all commemorative works, there was some controversy associated with the Franklin Delano Roosevelt Memorial in that the images of Roosevelt do not portray him in a wheelchair, which he used from the age of thirty-nine until his death at age sixty-three as a result of polio. However, a statue of Roosevelt in a wheelchair was commissioned by President Clinton, and it is to be displayed at the entrance to the memorial. A replica of Roosevelt's wheelchair is also on view in the memorial's gift shop.

≡FAST FACT

The Franklin Delano Roosevelt Memorial features many quotations from the president. While Roosevelt is best known for his statement that "We have nothing to fear but fear itself," his thoughts on war should also be remembered: "I have seen war. I have seen war on land and sea. I have seen blood running from the wounded . . . I have seen the dead in the mud. I have seen cities destroyed . . . I have seen children starving. I have seen the agony of mothers and wives. I hate war."

Although the memorial was in the works for more than fifty years, Roosevelt himself had said that he never wanted one. He told his close friend, U.S. Supreme Court Justice Felix Frankfurter, that should posterity decide to erect a memorial to him, it should be no bigger than his White House desk. Until 1997, when the Franklin Delano Roosevelt Memorial was built, the only Roosevelt commemorative marker was a desktop-sized granite stone outside the National Archives building.

Location and Hours

You'll find the Franklin Delano Roosevelt Memorial between the Lincoln and Jefferson Memorials, in West Potomac Park on the west shore of the Tidal Basin. The closest Metro stop is the Smithsonian, but expect a fairly long walk from the station.

The memorial is open from 8:00 A.M. until midnight, and the bookshop that's located on the premises closes at 10:00 P.M. Audiotape guides are available for $5.

Vietnam Veterans Memorial

☏ 202-426-6841

✏ *www.nps.gov*

Known as "the Wall," this is the most visited of the war memorials in Washington, D.C., and certainly one of the most powerful war images ever created. It is impossible to walk by the sloped black granite 492-foot wall and not feel overwhelmed by the loss of lives. The wall is carved with the 58,196 names of those who were killed during the Vietnam War. The earliest recorded casualty dates from 1959, the last from 1975, and each is marked with either a diamond to denote a confirmed death or a cross to indicate that the remains were not found. There is a black bound book at the start of the memorial that lists the names of the dead. It is the size of the Manhattan telephone book.

This memorial is usually crowded, as viewers pass by the reflective wall in a single file. Relatives and friends of those whose names are inscribed on the wall often leave flowers, flags, and tokens or make a charcoal rubbing of the loved one's name. Park rangers collect the offerings at the end of each day and a small sample of them is on display in the National Museum of American History. Park rangers will also provide a printout on the information for a specific name, as well as paper for rubbing.

Vietnam Veterans Memorial Controversy

The design for the Wall was considered highly controversial in 1982, when it was erected. Yale architecture student Maya Ying Lin, then only twenty-two, won the competition sponsored by a private organization, and many were disturbed that the memorial did not follow more traditional war motifs.

Lin's stark design of a simple black granite wall bearing the names of the American soldiers who died in Vietnam was so different from all the war memorials in Washington that it immediately received criticism from just about every veterans' group, as well as special-interest groups and some politicians.

Critics cast aspersions on her vision, her ability, her talent, her age, and her gender. Some called it "dishonorable" and "a scar." But Maya Lin stayed firm to her vision for "the Wall" and refused to change her design. "I believed that this was going to help people," she said of her work.

Her entry described her vision for the Wall as follows:

> . . . Walking through this park, the memorial appears as a rift in the earth. A long, polished, black stone, emerging from and receding into the earth. Approaching the memorial, the ground slopes gently downward and the low walls emerging on either side, growing out of the earth, extend and converge at a point below and ahead. Walking into this grassy site contained by the walls of the memorial, we can barely make out the carved names upon the memorial's walls. These names, seemingly infinite in number, convey the overwhelming numbers, while unifying these individuals into a whole. The memorial is composed not as an unchanging monument, but as a moving composition to be understood as we move into and out of it.

In the nearly twenty years since the memorial was erected, it has been accepted as a brilliant memorial to the sorrow and loss that most Americans feel when looking back on this war.

≡FAST FACT

In the neighboring Constitution Gardens, there are two traditional sculptures dedicated to the soldiers of Vietnam and the female Vietnam veterans. Frederick Hart designed *Three Servicemen,* and Gloria Goodacre designed the Vietnam Women's Memorial.

Location and Hours

To reach the Vietnam Veterans Memorial, take the Metro to Foggy Bottom. The Memorial is located on Constitution Avenue and 23rd Street NW, in Constitution Gardens, just northeast of the Lincoln Memorial. The memorial is open year-round from 8 A.M. to 11:45 P.M.

Korean War Veterans Memorial

📞 202-426-6841
✍ www.nps.gov

This memorial is located within walking distance from the Vietnam Veterans Memorial and across from the Lincoln Memorial. This privately funded commemorative space in honor of the soldiers who fought in the Korean War of the 1950s is more traditional (as were the Cold War politics of that war), and it serves as a powerful counterpoint to the Wall. Like life-size chess pieces, nineteen statues of American servicemen, some wearing ponchos, are posed in various stages of advancement toward an imaginary hill where an American flag and a reflecting pool wait.

Like the Vietnam Veterans Memorial, the Korean War Veterans Memorial also has a black granite reflective wall, at the top of which are the words, "Freedom Is Not Free." Etched on the surface of this wall are the faces of soldiers, chaplains, and war personnel, and around the perimeter of the memorial is a raised gray-granite curb that lists the twenty-two nations that sent men to this conflict. Though much shorter in duration (1950 to 1953), this war had almost as many casualties as the Vietnam War.

Location and Hours

The memorial is located between 21st and 23rd Streets, directly across the street from the Lincoln Memorial. If you don't mind a fairly long walk, you can reach the memorial from the Foggy Bottom Metro station. The memorial is open from 8:00 A.M. until midnight.

U.S. Navy Memorial and Naval Heritage Center

✉701 Pennsylvania Ave. NW
✆202-737-2300

The U.S. Navy Memorial, dedicated to the men and women who served in the U.S. Navy, is an outdoor circular plaza on an etched map of the world, with fountains and waterfalls flowing with the collected waters from the seven seas.

A bronze statue, *The Lone Sailor,* with a signature navy-blue coat, flared jeans, and a duffel bag, stands watching over the map on the plaza. The statue was cast from the remains of eight navy ships (and even a nuclear submarine) in service from the Revolutionary War through World War II.

Nearby is the Naval Heritage Center, which is a database, research center, and museum for the navy. There are informative displays on the history of the navy, its personnel, and ships, as well as the President's Room, which profiles the six presidents who were navy officers. There is also a Navy Memorial Room, which houses the computerized record of navy personnel, both past and present (with more than 200,000 entries, including a young Tony Curtis in Hawaii in 1943 when he was still named Bernie Schwartz) and the showing of the film *At Sea*, which tells the story of today's navy. There is also a ship's store, which sells navy and nautical memorabilia.

🧳 TRAVEL TIP

Free concerts are held in the plaza in the summer months, and dramatic wreath-laying ceremonies are staged on Memorial Day and on Veterans Day. Call for more information.

Location and Hours

The memorial and center are located on Pennsylvania Avenue, near the National Archives Metro station. The U.S. Navy Memorial is open twenty-four hours. The heritage center is open Monday through Saturday, from 9:30 A.M. to 5:00 P.M. The center is closed Thanksgiving Day, Christmas Day, and New Year's Day. Admission is free.

Arlington National Cemetery and Arlington House

☏ 703-697-2131

☏ 703-607-8052 (visitors' center)

✍ *www.arlingtoncemetery.org*

✍ *www.nps.gov* (Arlington House)

Every year, 4.5 million people visit the 614 acres of the Arlington National Cemetery, a cemetery for the military. The many important sites on the grounds include the Kennedy gravesites, the former home of General Lee, the Tomb of the Unknown Soldier, the mast of the USS *Maine*, and the statue commemorating Iwo Jima. You should expect to spend at least two, if not three, hours here.

Women in Military Service Memorial

When you enter the gates of the cemetery grounds, you will pass the newest war memorial in D.C.—the Women in Military Service Memorial—which honors the nearly 2 million women who have served in the armed forces. This memorial, which was designed by a husband-and-wife architect team and dedicated in October of 1987, features a round reflecting pool within a semicircle of a curved granite wall. Arched entries in this granite wall lead to an upper terrace, which offers a sweeping view of the cemetery and the city of Washington.

Etched glass panels within the memorial include quotes about women's experiences in the military. Beneath the memorial is an education center, where the Hall of Honor traces the history of women in the military, as well as a computerized database of personnel and a shop.

💼 TRAVEL TIP

Refer to Chapter 4 if you don't want to do lots of walking and would prefer to take the Tourmobile. But if you do prefer to walk around the cemetery, make sure you wear comfortable shoes because there are a lot of hills.

Visitors' Center

Here you can watch a video on the history of the Arlington cemetery and stop at the gift shop. Bathroom facilities are also available. If you plan to take the Tourmobile, tickets are available here, along with free maps of the grounds and information on specific graves.

Curtis-Lee Mansion

Once out the door of the visitors' center, you should head to the grounds of the Curtis-Lee Mansion, where the history of the cemetery begins. The property was owned by the adopted grandson of George Washington (George Washington Parke Curtis, who is buried on the property). Curtis built the mansion to house his Washington memorabilia and left it to his daughter. She eventually married the man who would later lead the South against the North in the Civil War.

When the Lees left Virginia during the war, the Union took over the grounds and, some say out of spite, began burying the war dead on the property (1,800 casualties of the Battle of Bull Run are buried in front of the house). Their son did try to retain the property after the war, but the many graves on the grounds made it an unattractive home, and he eventually sold it back to the government.

Today, this property is known as the Arlington House. In front of the house is the sarcophagus of Pierre Charles L'Enfant, the man who designed Washington, D.C. His marble tomb sits on a hill overlooking the city.

Kennedy Gravesites

The Kennedy gravesites are within walking distance of Arlington House. Many who remember the assassination of John F. Kennedy pass by the eternal flame, lit by Jacqueline Kennedy Onassis, who is now buried beside her first husband and the two babies they had who died in infancy. A short distance down the hill is the gravesite of Robert Kennedy, which is composed of a reflecting pool.

The Tomb of the Unknown Soldier

Located near the center of the cemetery, the Tomb of the Unknowns is one of the most visited sites on the grounds. The tomb honors the unknown soldiers of World War I, World War II, and the Korean War; the remains of the soldier who was interred in the Vietnam Tomb were identified in 1998 through DNA technology.

The tomb is guarded twenty-four hours a day by the Third Infantry Division (the Old Guard). The sentinels who guard the tomb perform a changing of the guard every half hour in the warm months and every hour during the winter. There are also many wreath laying ceremonies at the Tomb of the Unknowns.

Iwo Jima Memorial

Iwo Jima, the memorial to the United States Marine Corps, is a powerful tribute to the marines and World War II. If you can manage to drive around the monument, it will appear that the marines are raising the flag (an optical illusion). An Air Force Memorial and Museum are also being planned for the future on this site. Nearby is the Netherlands Carillon, a gift of chimes from the people of the Netherlands that has fifty bells.

Other Sites

At the Arlington National Cemetery, you'll also find the Confederate War Veterans' Memorial, which was erected in 1912 and designed by a Confederate war veteran who is buried beneath it, as well as the Civil War Memorial on the grounds of the Lee home. Also on the grounds of the Lee home is a former village for freed slaves, called the Freedman's Village, which thrived after the Civil War and even had its own hospital and a school with 900 students.

▌ TRAVEL TIP

D.C. is home to other historic cemeteries you can visit, like the Congressional Cemetery on 18th and E Streets (☎202-543-0539). It contains the remains of John Philip Sousa, J. Edgar Hoover, and Civil War photographer Matthew Brady. Rock Creek Cemetery, on Rock Creek Church Road and Webster Avenue NE (☎202-829-0585), is the oldest cemetery in Washington, D.C., established in the early eighteenth century on the grounds of St. Paul's Episcopal Church. People visit this graveyard to see the famous sculpture *Grief* by Augustus Saint-Gaudens.

Other important memorial sites include a memorial to the crew of the space shuttle *Challenger,* two of whom are buried at the memorial site; Lockerbee Memorial Cairn for the 259 people killed on Pan Am Flight 103; an Iran Rescue Mission Memorial for servicemen killed in the hostage rescue attempt; a monument to Teddy Roosevelt's Rough Riders of the Spanish-American War; a memorial to the Hmong, who helped the United States in the secret war in Laos; and the USS *Maine* Monument, which includes the actual mast and anchor of the ship.

Arlington National Cemetery is also the final resting place of some of America's most famous military leaders, as well as people who made an impact on the nation. Famous gravesites are the final resting places of the following luminaries:

- Thurgood Marshall, U.S. Supreme Court justice
- Audie Murphy, most decorated World War II soldier and actor
- Joe Louis (Barrow), World War II veteran and heavyweight boxing champion
- Oliver Wendell Holmes, Jr., Civil War veteran and U.S. Supreme Court justice

- Daniel "Chappie" James, Jr., the first African-American four-star general
- Richard Byrd, polar explorer and admiral
- William Howard Taft, president and chief justice of the U.S. Supreme Court
- Virgil "Gus" Grissom, astronaut
- Medgar Evers, World War II veteran and civil rights leader
- Samuel Dashiell Hammett, army sergeant and Sam Spade author
- Lee Marvin, U.S. Marine Corps private and movie actor
- George Westinghouse, Civil War veteran and inventor

There are an average of twenty funerals at Arlington National Cemetery a day, and approximately a quarter of a million gravesites. In 1980, a columbarium was erected to house cremated remains. Otherwise, it was estimated that at this present burial rate, the cemetery would have been full by 2002.

Location and Hours

The cemetery is located across from the Lincoln Memorial just over the Memorial Bridge in Arlington, Virginia. It's open to visitors from 8:00 A.M. to 5:00 P.M., and from April through September, the evening hours extend to 7:00 P.M.

There is public parking ($1.25 per hour for the first three hours, $2 per hour after that), but the Tourmobile is the best way to get there. (To make reservations, call ☎ 202-554-5100.) You can also go via the Metro to Arlington National Cemetery Metro station.

👫 JUST FOR PARENTS

If your children have ever asked questions about the Kennedy assassination, this is a good place to start your own tale of where you were at the time and what it meant to you. You might also want to remind them that this is the president after whom the Kennedy Center is named and take them by to see the giant bust of Kennedy later on in your trip.

U.S. Holocaust Memorial Museum

✉100 Raoul Wallenberg Pl.
(formerly 15th St. SW)
✆202-488-0400
✍*www.ushmm.org*

This museum and memorial is not for young children. A thoughtful permanent exhibit on the life of a young Jewish boy in Germany ("Daniel's Story: Remember the Children") is, however, suitable for slightly older children (8 to 12 years old). The museum has a sign posted recommending that children under 12 not view the material, but even teenagers need to be prepared for this museum.

Daniel's Story

This walk-through exhibit attempts to explain the events leading up to the Holocaust to children over 8 years old. This exhibit is a Jewish child's personal account of life in Germany during the Holocaust. Daniel takes viewers through his town, his home, the streets of his town in the aftermath of Kristallnacht, the ghetto he was sent to, the cattle-car ride to a concentration camp, and what happened to his family after the war.

Each room of the exhibit has sample diary entries in Daniel's own words. Daniel's diary entries chronicle the confiscation of his parents' store, the burning of their synagogue, being able to buy food and other merchandise only from Jewish merchants, being taunted in school, and being forced to wear the yellow star of David. When his family is forced from their middle-class home and herded into a ghetto, both Daniel and his sister are forced to start working. His family is sent by cattle car to a concentration camp, and a film ends the exhibit explaining what happened to the family after the cattle-car journey, where Daniel was separated from his mother and sister, who were killed in the camps.

For the young and those who have never read *The Diary of Anne Frank,* this is as close to an interactive experience of what happened to those who were children during the Holocaust as one can come.

Other Exhibits

There are a handful of changing and permanent exhibits that you can view, including the Wall of Remembrance, tiles painted by schoolchildren to remember the 1.5 million children killed during the Holocaust, as well as a brief orientation film on the history of the Holocaust and the museum itself that is played every fifteen minutes.

When you get in line to enter the elevator to the fourth floor, where the chronological history of the persecution and elimination of European Jews under Hitler begins, you are given a reproduction of an identity card from one of the Holocaust's victims, two-thirds of whom were killed during this time. An estimated 12 million people were murdered by the Nazis during the Holocaust, a number that includes 6 million Jews as well as gypsies, homosexuals, Jehovah's Witnesses, Soviet prisoners of war, the handicapped, and political dissidents.

The fourth floor tells the story of the Nazi rise to power, with examples of their propaganda against the Jews. The third floor continues the story of the increasing ghettoization of Europe's Jews and includes an authentic cattle car that was once used to transport victims to the camps. This will make the hair on your neck stand as you pass through it. There is also a replica of the wrought-iron sign that hung over the entrance to Auschwitz, "Arbeit Macht Frei" ("Work Will Make You Free"). Here you will also see a disturbing documentation of the Nazi scientific experiments on the camp prisoners.

On the second floor, the story of the liberation of the camps and the end of the war is told. There are relics and a graphic display of the cost of human lives as evidenced by a room full of the shoes of victims and pictures of piles and piles of removed wedding rings and human hair that was used to stuff upholstery. Here, too, are actual pieces of the crematoriums and camps.

The final exhibit is a thirty-minute film called *Testimony*, in which survivors tell their own stories. This leads to the solemn Hall of Remembrance, where an eternal flame burns to remember the victims of the Holocaust.

The museum is also a research center and Holocaust registry. There is a museum store that has a unique collection of books about the Holocaust and its survivors, as well as a museum café that serves both kosher and non-kosher meals.

Location and Hours

The museum is located off the Mall, and it is accessible from the Smithsonian Metro station. You can visit the museum from 10:00 A.M. to 5:30 P.M., but it's closed on the Jewish holiday of Yom Kippur and on Christmas Day.

You need tickets to see the main exhibits—not because it costs money to view them but because there's a need to control the number of people walking through the exhibits at one time. (The memorial receives 2 million visitors a year, and the gallery spaces of the museum itself are small.) You can pick up the tickets at the museum's information desk, or you can order them ahead of time from Protix, at ☎1-800-400-9373.

📖 TRAVEL TIP

The African-American Civil War Memorial is another recent war memorial. The stone-and-bronze tribute to the more than 200,000 African-American soldiers and their white officers who fought for the Union in the Civil War was unveiled off U Street NW in September of 1996. The visitors' center offers a database for researching regiments and battle action.

National World War II Memorial

✑www.wwiimemorial.com
☎1-800-639-4WW2

This memorial opened to the public in May 2004, made possible by private fundraising and ardent support from World War II veterans. Today, it is the only war memorial on the Mall's central axis.

The World War II Memorial is built on a 7.4-acre site between the Washington Monument and the Lincoln Memorial. The white-granite and bronze memorial has two forty-three-foot arches, symbolizing the Atlantic and Pacific theaters of the war, as well as fifty-six granite pillars that form an oval around a plaza with a pool. The pillars represent the states and territories that sent soldiers from the United States to war. Along the ceremonial entrance to the plaza, twenty-four bronze panels show various scenes from the war, both at home and overseas. Across from the pool is the Freedom Wall, where 4,000 gold stars symbolize the 400,000 Americans killed in combat.

As with all things in Washington, there was controversy over the construction of this memorial, from how the funds were raised (pitches from actor Tom Hanks and Senator Bob Dole) to its size and scale and even its location, claiming that it would obstruct the peaceful view of the Reflecting Pool.

Location and Hours

The memorial can be found at the Rainbow Pool site, at the east end of the Reflecting Pool between the Lincoln Memorial and the Washington Monument on the Mall.

CHAPTER 8

Government Buildings

THE THREE BRANCHES of Federal government—executive, legislative, and judicial—are all headquartered in Washington, D.C. Being able to tour the facilities and actually see your government in action will give you a real perspective on those social studies and civics lessons you got back in grade school. In addition to the three major branches, you can see many other government agencies and service organizations to see how the principles worked out by our founding fathers have evolved over the last 200 years.

Everyone who comes to the capital wants to see some of these sites, but access to them may be limited. Some places require visitors to purchase tickets in advance, and many of the sites are closed on weekends.

🧳 TRAVEL TIP

Since the terrorist attacks of September 11, you must get White House tour tickets in advance through your local representative's or senator's office, and there are no tours on Sunday or Monday. Also, the U.S. Mint and the U.S. Supreme Court are closed on the weekends, so head there first on a Friday or save them for Monday (unless it's a federal holiday, when some government agencies are closed—call to make sure).

The White House

✉ 1600 Pennsylvania Ave. NW
✆ 202-456-2121
✑ *www.whitehouse.gov*

The White House is the oldest public building in D.C. and has been the home of all presidents except Washington. It was designed by Irishman James Hoban, who won a competition in 1790, beating out fifty-one designers including Thomas Jefferson, who used a pseudonym when submitting his entry. Originally called the "presidential palace," it acquired the nickname "the White House" after continuous applications of whitewash had been painted on the exterior to fix it up after it was set on fire during the War of 1812.

James Hoban guided the subsequent restoration of the White House, adding space for the presidential staff. In 1902, a West Wing with the Oval Office and the Rose Garden were added under Teddy Roosevelt's administration. The third floor was added in 1927 to provide more living space for the first family. The entire White House was rehabbed in 1948 after the leg of a piano Margaret Truman was playing crashed through the dining room ceiling. The Trumans lived at Blair House, the presidential guest house, for four years, during which time the East Wing, an air-raid shelter, an interior movie theater, and a balcony on the south portico were added.

White House Ghosts

It is said that the White House is haunted by quite a few ghosts. By far the most famous is the ghost of President Lincoln, but ghost hunters and former White House personnel claim he's not the only one. According to various tales and legends, the presidential mansion is haunted by the ghosts of Abigail Adams, Dolley Madison, Lincoln's son Willie (who died at age twelve in the White House), Presidents Jackson and Harrison, and a British soldier who was killed during the burning of the White House in 1814.

The ghost of Abigail Adams is forever attempting to hang her laundry in the grand East Room, and her ghost has been seen approaching the room with her arms out as if carrying a laundry basket. Some have said that they can smell a whiff of soap and damp cotton when her ghost is near.

Dolley Madison cared a great deal about the White House and planted her own garden where the Rose Garden is today. It is reported that when Edith Wilson attempted to tear up this plot of land, the ghost of Dolley Madison terrified the gardeners. Instead, the roses were planted to appease her, and she has not reappeared since then.

The ghost of Lincoln's son is said to appear in the room where he died, and his mother reported that she felt him with her in the White House. A great believer in the spirit world, she also said she could hear Thomas Jefferson playing the violin. The presence of Abraham Lincoln has been recorded throughout the White House ever since his assassination. He is said to walk through the halls and knock on the door of guests staying in the Lincoln Bedroom.

📖 TRAVEL TIP

When you tour the White House, remember that this is not just any museum. Videotaping and photography are not allowed. And the bathrooms inside the White House aren't open to the public, so it's a good idea to stop at the visitor center before you start the tour.

Even before Lincoln's ghost was said to roam the halls, White House servants had said that they could hear laughter coming from the bed where Andrew Jackson slept in the Rose Room, and Mrs. Lincoln reported that she often heard his ghost stomping and swearing. President Harrison is said to haunt the White House attic.

The White House Tour

When you tour the White House, you won't be able to have access to all of it. Only seven rooms and various hallways and corridors of the White House are open to the public. The second and third floors of the White House are the private domain of the first family. The Oval Office and the Lincoln Bedroom are not open to the public.

The Library

First stop on the tour is the Library, where you'll see 2,700 books on display and a chandelier that once belonged to James Fennimore Cooper (author of *The Last of the Mohicans*). The Library is where the president holds private interviews.

The China Room

The next room on the tour is where examples of the table settings from each presidential administration are on display. It is interesting to note that Nancy Reagan wasn't the only first lady to cause an uproar over her china pattern choice. Mary Todd Lincoln's pattern uses a bright purple, which many thought was too royal, and caused quite a stir at the time.

The East Room

The gold-and-white East Room on the second floor has been the site of many of the mansion's biggest events, including the wedding receptions of Nellie Grant, Alice Roosevelt, and Lynda Bird Johnson. It has also been the viewing room for seven presidents' funerals, the site of Susan Ford's senior prom, and the site of Nixon's resignation speech. During the Civil War, Union troops were housed in this room.

═══FAST FACT

The East Room is the largest room in the White House and, according to the secret service tour guide, in the nineteenth century it was the room where Abigail Adams hung the presidential laundry to dry because she didn't want people to see it hanging on the lawn (and this is now the room supposedly haunted by her ghost).

The famous life-sized painting of George Washington by Gilbert Stuart that was saved by Dolley Madison as the White House burned in 1814 is also on display here. Even though Stuart made many Washington portraits, the best will be traveling when the National Portrait Gallery is closed for renovation, so this is the only one you can catch in Washington, D.C. during this time.

The four walls of the East Room are the oldest parts of the White House left after the fire.

The Green Room

This room once served as Jefferson's dining room; today it serves as a parlor. The room gets its name from the green silk that has adorned its walls since the Monroe administration.

The Green Room is furnished in the Federal style of the early 1800s. There's a marvelous painting of Bear Lake, New Mexico, by Georgia O'Keeffe as well as a street scene of Philadelphia that was purchased by an antiques dealer for $10 and turned out to be one of the original White House paintings.

The Blue Room

The most formal room in the White House, this is where presidents often receive guests and where the largest Christmas tree in the mansion is on display. This was also the site of President Cleveland's marriage to Frances Folsom. Cleveland, incidentally, was the only president to get married while in office.

The Red Room

In this room, the first lady traditionally does her entertaining. The Red Room features red walls and red satin chairs, as well as a painting of the Rocky Mountains by Albert Bierstadt. This was also the room in which Abraham Lincoln rescinded Confederate President Davis's citizenship during the Civil War.

The State Dining Room

The dining room, which seats 140 people, is also the site of the G.P.A. Healy portrait of Lincoln, which was given to the White

House by Lincoln's heirs. Carved above the fireplace mantel are the words of President John Adams from his second evening in the White House: "I Pray Heaven to Bestow the Best of Blessings on THIS HOUSE and All that shall hereafter inhabit it."

The Vermeil Room

Also known as the Gold Room, this room was refurbished in 1991. It serves as a display room and has also been the room where first ladies have received visitors. Portraits of seven first ladies are on display here, as well as furniture from the nineteenth century.

═FAST FACT

In 1961, First Lady Jacqueline Kennedy decided to make the White House the showplace it once was. She sent out a worldwide request for original furnishings from the house, and she restored many of the rooms to their earlier splendor. Later, she led the nation on the first-ever televised tour of the White House. To preserve the historical décor, Congress passed an act declaring all furnishings and decorations used by the first family during their stay to be the property of the White House.

White House Visitor Center

The White House Visitor Center has a number of displays itself, including exhibits on the history of the mansion, its architecture, furnishings, and first families; there is also a thirty-minute film available for viewing. Other facilities include a small gift shop and bathrooms. (The public is not allowed to use the bathrooms in the White House.)

When you go through the visitor entrance, there are displays along a hallway looking out onto the Jacqueline Kennedy Gardens that explain the architectural and interior changes within the mansion over the past 150 years.

Location and Hours

The White House is not far from the McPherson Square Metro station; the visitor center is accessible from the Federal Triangle station. The White House Visitor Center is located at ✉1450 Pennsylvania Avenue NW, in the Department of Commerce Building, between 14th and 15th Streets. The White House is a little further down, at ✉1600 Pennsylvania Avenue NW.

The visitor center is open from 7:30 A.M. until 4:00 P.M. White House self-guided tours of up to ten people at a time are allowed between 7:30 A.M. and 11:30 A.M., Tuesday through Saturday only. Don't forget that you'll need to obtain tickets in advance through your congressional representative's office. The White House is occasionally closed for official functions, so call ahead for scheduling.

Before the tour, you'll need to go through a security check, which includes going through a metal detector and having your belongings x-rayed.

🐞 JUST FOR PARENTS

If your tour is early, you might consider having a leisurely breakfast at Old Ebbitt Grill (see Chapter 14), which is almost across the street, or an exquisite breakfast in the Willard Room of the Willard Hotel. Nothing else nearby is open that early.

The United States Capitol

✉E and 1st Streets
☎202-225-6827
🖰 *www.aoc.gov*

The Capitol is home to the U.S. House of Representatives and the U.S. Senate, which together make up the legislative branch of the federal government. House and Senate galleries are open to all visitors, but you must obtain passes when Congress is in session (call ☎202-224-3121). The *Washington Post* also lists the schedule in its "Today in Congress" section.

If you haven't received passes from your representative or sen-ator ahead of time, you can get these by presenting a passport at your senator's office on the Constitution Avenue side of the building or your representative's office on the Independence Avenue side of the building. When either the House or the Senate is in session, a flag flies over the respective side of the building. The Capitol's east front is where most of the recent presidents have taken their oath of office.

Aside from being the seat of our government, where the daily business of legislation is enacted, the Capitol building is itself a work of art, and there's much to see there. The building was designed by William Thornton and amended by Benjamin Latrobe; the cor-nerstone was laid by Washington in 1793. Seven years later, the Capitol was ready for Congress to open its first session in 1800. The Capitol was burned down by the British in 1814, and the famous dome wasn't actually added until the Lincoln administration.

The Rotunda

The Capitol's round structure, the rotunda, is covered by a dome that's 180 feet high and 96 feet wide, and it is jam-packed with more than 800 works of art, as well as artifacts as important as the Magna Carta, which is currently on loan from England and on display in a case in the rotunda.

═FAST FACT

The rotunda also has a number of statues, including the controversial group sculpture of the three leaders of the women's suffrage movement—Elizabeth Cady Stanton, Susan B. Anthony, and Lucretia Mott—which had been kept in the crypt until women's groups campaigned successfully to have it moved to a more prominent position in the building.

The rotunda's bronze doors are a bas relief that depict the life of Christopher Columbus. On the walls are eight giant oil paintings by John Trumbull depicting events in American history, such as the signing of the Declaration of Independence and the presentation of Pocahontas to British royalty. On the dome's ceiling is a fresco by Constantino Brumidi, who has been called the "Michelangelo of the Capitol" for this painting, *Apotheosis of Washington.* It's an allegorical portrait of the first president surrounded by Roman deities who are watching the development of the nation.

The Rest of the Capitol

Beyond the rotunda is the National Statuary Hall, which was the original chamber for the House of Representatives. Each state was invited to send two statues of important regional leaders, and the hall is now so full that statues spill out into adjoining halls and corridors and even show up haphazardly throughout the building. Some of the more prominent figures whose statues are on display include Ethan Allen, Daniel Webster, and Henry Clay; some of the more unusual works of art and personages that can be found elsewhere are Utah's sculpture of Philo Farnsworth, the father of television, and Colorado's painted bronze statue of Jack Swigert, Jr., an Apollo 13 astronaut.

The vaulted ceilings of the first floor of the Senate wing have paintings and panels celebrating American democracy, progress, and technology painted by Brumidi. Known as the Brumidi Corridors, they are based on the loggia of the Vatican. This tradition continues throughout the halls and galleries in the House wing by other artists (after Brumidi's death) and depicts such events in American history as the Boston Tea Party, the Women's Suffrage Movement, the signing of the Declaration of Independence, and the burning of the Capitol in 1814. These scenes continue to the present and include a panel on the space shuttle *Challenger* disaster.

The south and north wings of the Capitol are the House and Senate chambers. The House of Representatives chamber is the largest legislative body in the world and the site of the president's annual state of the union address.

Location and Hours

The Capitol is located at the east end of the Mall, where E and First Street intersect. The closest Metro stations are Capitol South and Union Station.

You can visit the Capitol from 9:00 A.M. until 4:30 P.M., except on Thanksgiving Day, Christmas Day, and New Year's Day. Guided tours of up to forty people are given throughout the day. To take the tour, you'll need timed tickets, which you can pick up on the southwest corner of the building (near the intersection of First Street SW and Independence Avenue). Tickets are available after 9:00 A.M. on a first-come, first-served basis.

RAINY DAY FUN

If you've got time, you can visit the two museums on site: the original U.S. Supreme Court chambers, which have been restored to their original appearance with red velvet upholstery (the Supreme Court moved out of the Capitol to its own building in 1935), and the old Senate chamber, also restored to its original nineteenth-century appearance.

Supreme Court

✉ 1st St. NE
✆ 202-479-3000
🖉 www.supremecourtus.gov

The building that now houses the U.S. Supreme Court was built in 1935 and features a classical Corinthian design of sixteen marble columns topped by a sculpted pediment. (The building was once nicknamed the Marble Palace.) Previously, the Court met in the Merchants Exchange building in New York City and moved a number of times; it was housed in the Capitol prior to 1935.

The U.S. Supreme Court is the highest court of the judicial branch of our government. It is besieged by close to 7,000 requests a year for retrial of controversial cases that bear on issues affecting the nation, but it hears only about 100 cases annually. The Court is in session Monday through Wednesday from 10:00 A.M. until noon, beginning the first Monday in October and ending in late April; brief sessions are held in May and June. The *Washington Post* regularly publishes the Supreme Court's calendar, or you can call ☎202-479-3211 for case information. There are only 150 public seats, so arrive early if you want to get in. No cameras or videotaping are allowed.

Educational programs, a theater, and changing exhibits are located on the ground floor. The Court's Great Hall features a twenty-minute film on how the Supreme Court works, as well as its history and some of its more famous cases. There's a gift shop on the premises, as well as two restaurants.

≡FAST FACT

The first bill introduced in the U.S. Senate was the Judiciary Act of 1789, which established the U.S. Supreme Court, originally composed of five associate justices and a chief justice. Today, there are eight associate justices and one chief justice. Members of the U.S. Supreme Court are appointed by the president, subject to approval by the Senate.

Location and Hours

The U.S. Supreme Court building is located to the side of the Capitol, on First Street NE, between East Capitol Street and Maryland Avenue. Take the Metro to Capitol South or Union Station. Visitor hours are Monday through Friday, from 9:00 A.M. to 4:30 P.M. (The Court is closed on weekends and all federal holidays.) Lectures in the courtroom are given every half hour.

Library of Congress

✉1st St. SE
☎202-707-8000
✐*www.loc.gov*
✐*www.americaslibrary.gov*

This is the world's largest library, with more than 17 million books as well as manuscripts, letters, prints, photographs, recordings, movies, personal papers from scholars and celebrities (from Jefferson to Groucho Marx), and musical instruments. The total collection has more than 131 million items. Of course, only a fraction of this material is on display at any given time, so the exhibits change constantly.

History of the Library

The Library of Congress was created by John Adams in 1800, "for the purchase of such books as may be necessary for the use of Congress." It was originally housed in a boarding house and later moved to the Capitol, where the entire collection was torched by the British in 1814. Thomas Jefferson sold his personal collection of close to 7,000 books to the government to restart the library.

The first permanent home of the library—the Thomas Jefferson Building—was erected in 1897 and was expected to house the growing collection for decades, but it filled up in a mere thirteen years. Two additions have been built: the John Adams Building in 1939 and the James Madison Memorial Building in 1980. The Jefferson building underwent a major twelve-year renovation and reopened to the public in 1997.

There is a twelve-minute orientation film shown in the visitors' center in the Jefferson building, which gives you an overview and history of the library.

Halls and Galleries

The exterior of the Jefferson building was designed to look like the Paris Opera House and has a very European fountain with a bronze statue of Neptune outside its front doors. The Great Hall of the Jefferson building features a domed interior and a stained-glass ceiling plus paintings, sculpture, and mosaics by fifty artists.

In the southwest gallery and pavilion of the Great Hall, you'll find the permanent "Treasures of the Library of Congress" exhibit, which includes historic and rare pieces from the collection, such as a Gutenberg Bible and the Giant Bible of Mainz. Other items that have been on temporary display in the "Treasures of the Library of Congress" exhibit include Jefferson's handwritten draft of the Declaration of Independence, with notations from other signatories; Jelly Roll Morton's early compositions; Maya Lin's original drawing for the Vietnam Veterans Memorial; Alexander Graham Bell's notebooks; and George Gershwin's orchestral score for *Porgy and Bess*.

The gift shop is also located in this building. The Library of Congress celebrated its bicentennial in 2000, and bicentennial posters, stamps, and coins are still available for purchase. Calendars are also popular gift items.

The John Adams Building has murals illustrating scenes from *The Canterbury Tales* painted on its interior walls, and the Madison building is the home of the library's restaurants and a theater that shows rare films.

👫 JUST FOR PARENTS

Anyone over eighteen may use the Library of Congress, but its holdings do not leave the premises. You have to obtain a user card, which is available by showing a valid driver's license or passport or by filling out an information sheet.

Location and Hours

The Library of Congress is located on the Mall, near the Capitol (between East Capitol Street and Independence Avenue). If you plan to take the Metro, you can get off at the Capitol South Metro station.

The Jefferson building is open Monday through Saturday, from 10:00 A.M. to 5:30 P.M. The Madison building is open from 8:30 A.M. to 9:30 P.M. on weekdays and until 6:00 P.M. on Saturdays. All buildings are closed on Sundays and on federal holidays. One-hour guided tours are available every half hour by reservation, but these are not recommended for children under 10. There is a security check when you enter.

National Archives

✉700 Pennsylvania Ave. NW
✆1-86-NARA-NARA
✆202-501-5000
✍*www.archives.gov*

The National Archives and Records Administration is home to the National Archive Exhibition Hall, which displays the originals of our nation's most precious documents—the Declaration of Independence, the Constitution, and the Bill of Rights. Collectively known as the Charters of Freedom, they are all on permanent display here in glass cases in which the air has been replaced by helium. Surrounding these cases are documents, photos, and artifacts that tell the story of our nation's history from the colonies to the present, from the Emancipation Proclamation to the Japanese surrender in World War II.

Although it was constructed relatively recently, in 1932, the building matches the Greek revival style of many other federal buildings with its colonnade façade topped by a pediment and a dome. The design was created by John Russell Pope, who also worked on the National Gallery of Art and the Jefferson Memorial.

The National Archive collection includes more than 3 billion items. On the walls of the Exhibition Hall are two murals by New Yorker Barry Faulkner. The mural on the left shows Jefferson passing the Declaration of Independence to Hancock for his signature, and the mural on the right shows Madison submitting the Constitution to Washington at the Constitutional Convention. The bronze design on the floor represents the four winged figures of Legislation, Justice, History, and War and Defense.

A rotating collection of items from the permanent collection is on view in the rotunda in the "American Originals" panels. These have included the Louisiana Purchase, signed by Napoleon, and Greta Garbo's driver's license. A gallery on the lower level features themed exhibits from the collection. Copies of the documents, as well as books, can be purchased in the museum shop.

Location and Hours

The National Archives are located on the Mall. Although its address places it on Pennsylvania Avenue, the entrance is actually on Constitution Avenue, between 7th and 9th Streets. You can reach the archives from the National Archives Metro station.

During warm weather, the archives are open from 10:00 A.M. until 9:00 P.M. After Labor Day, they close earlier, at 5:30 P.M., and they are closed on Christmas Day. Public tours of the National Archives are available, but you must call to make a reservation at least a month in advance.

The Mint

✉ 14th and C St. SW
☎ 202-874-3188
🖱 *www.moneyfactory.com*

The Bureau of Engraving and Printing, an arm of the U.S. Department of the Treasury (and also known as the U.S. Mint), is a real kid-pleaser, and makes for a fun family tour. Timed tickets are required during the busy season and can be obtained at the visitors' center in front of the building or by writing to your representative or senator ahead of time. Once you have a ticket, you may have to wait awhile for your thirty-minute tour, but it is fascinating to see the bills, stamps, and White House invitations being printed. (Coins are minted in Texas and Philadelphia.)

To enter, you must pass through a security checkpoint. While you wait in line for your tour to begin, you will see a brick of $20 bills that totals a million dollars and television displays of interesting facts about our currency. Did you know, for instance, that dollar bills aren't made out of paper? They're actually 75 percent cotton and 25 percent linen. And did you know that the average lifespan for a dollar bill is a year and a half?

The tour begins with a brief film about the history of the Bureau of Engraving and Printing. (In 1862, it consisted of six employees who separated $1 and $2 bills printed by a private company; the staff is currently about 3,000 people.) The presentation also includes an introduction to the printing of money, with a description of how the U.S. currency was recently redesigned to include a watermark portrait that you can see by holding the bill up to the light. These changes were implemented to make counterfeiting more difficult.

≡FAST FACT

Everyone knows that a dollar bill travels extensively in its lifetime, but now there's a Web site that tracks its journey. If you log on to *www.wheresgeorge.com* you will be able to enter the serial number of a bill currently in your possession, and they will e-mail you back its travel history. One sample dollar bill was tracked at traveling 193 miles in six months.

The "money factory" prints 38 million notes a day, totaling approximately $541 million. The tour leads you through the actual printing process. You witness the giant presses roll behind a Plexiglas wall and smell the paintlike odor of the green and black inks. The production process of U.S. currency involves sixty-five steps, including examining the bill sheets, overprinting, slicing the sheets, and shrink-wrapping the bills.

After the tour, you are let out into the gift shop, which sells such novelties as bags of shredded money and imperfect sheets of currency. It has a number of interactive displays for kids, as well as a photo booth where kids can have their picture imprinted on a $20 bill.

Location and Hours

The U.S. Mint is located on 14th and C Streets, not far from the Smithsonian Metro station. During the winter, tours are given from 9:00 A.M. to 2:00 P.M., Monday through Friday. In the summer, afternoon hours are added from 4:00 to 7:30 P.M. The Mint is closed on weekends, federal holidays, and the week between Christmas Day and New Year's Day.

U.S. Department of Treasury

✉15th St. and Pennsylvania Ave. NW
✆202-662-0896
✐*www.ustreas.gov*

Once money is printed and bundled, it is sent off to the U.S. Treasury, and from there it is dispersed to banks. The white granite building of the U.S. Treasury Department should be familiar to all Americans, because it appears on the back of the $10 bill. It is the third-oldest federal building in the city, after the White House and the Capitol. The building itself is a prime example of the Greek revival architectural style that swept the nation in 1800s, with a façade full of Ionic columns and topped by a pediment.

At the U.S. Department of the Treasury, you can take a tour that will take you through the restored interior of both the east and west wings, featuring vaulted ceilings, chandeliers, and period furniture that includes some chairs with dollar signs on their backs.

The burglarproof vault room is now an office, but you can see its metal walls and federal symbols on its exterior. Another treasury room was the office of Andrew Johnson for six weeks while Mary Todd Lincoln prepared to move from the White House.

═FAST FACT

The best reason for visiting the Treasury Department and going through the annoying tour-request bureaucracy is the Cash Room. A U.S. Treasury–operated bank until the mid-1970s, this small marble room (thirty-two by seventy-two feet) with chandeliers was the site of President Grant's inaugural reception. Six thousand invitations were sold, and the crowd was so tight that people passed out.

Location and Hours

You can reach the Treasury from the Metro Center or Federal Triangle Metro station. At the time of this writing, public tours have been suspended, but call to see if they have resumed.

Federal Bureau of Investigation (FBI)

✉J. Edgar Hoover Building
935 Pennsylvania Ave.
✆202-324-3447
✍*www.fbi.gov*

The Bureau of Investigation was established in 1908 during the Teddy Roosevelt administration by U.S. Attorney General Charles Bonaparte as a force of special agents to investigate a corrupt public land scheme in Idaho.

The first public enemies list was released in April of 1930 and was composed mainly of Chicago gangsters. (Surprisingly, the notorious Al Capone was only number four.)

In 1933, the Bureau of Investigation merged with the Prohibition Bureau and the Bureau of Identification, establishing the FBI as we know it today. At the head of the FBI was J. Edgar Hoover, who had 266 agents and 66 accountants under his direction.

Location and Hours

The FBI building is located on E Street between 9th and 10th Streets in the J. Edgar Hoover Building. Take the Metro to the Metro Center or Federal Triangle Metro station.

The FBI building has been undergoing renovations and is closed to tours, but it should reopen soon, so check with the tour office at ✆202-324-3447. Once it does reopen, you should be able to obtain tickets from your representative's or senator's office.

CHAPTER 9

Other Museums

WASHINGTON, D.C., has the largest number of museums per capita of any city in the world—it has twenty art museums alone. In addition to the national monuments and the Smithsonian museums and galleries, the capital also has a number of fabulous private museums. This means you do have to pay for entrance, but it's well worth it. The one exception to this rule is the National Gallery of Art, which is free, even though it's not part of the Smithsonian Institution.

📰 TRAVEL TIP

Because of so many recent destructive acts aimed at artworks, none of the city's art museums will allow backpacks into the museums. You must check them in the coat-check areas.

The International Spy Museum, which opened in 2003, has caused quite a stir in the city as one of the more offbeat educational experiences in the city. The new City Museum of Washington, D.C., is also a surprisingly entertaining way to learn about the people and culture of the nation's capital.

National Gallery of Art and Sculpture Garden

✉Constitution Ave. NW

☎202-737-4215

✐*www.nga.gov*

This monumental museum of art takes up two city blocks and continues across the street with a new outdoor sculpture garden. Half a day is hardly long enough to see everything.

The original neoclassical West Building was designed by John Russell Pope (who also designed the Jefferson Memorial and the nearby National Archives building). The newer East Building is connected via an underground passageway that includes a gift shop and restaurant. Its H-shaped façade and signature skylights were designed by Chinese-American architect I.M. Pei, who also designed the controversial glass pyramid addition at the Louvre museum in Paris.

The West Building

The gallery was created by Congress after financier Andrew Mellon donated his world-renowned art collection to the nation; the collection included two of the Raphaels on display. Today, the National Gallery has one of the finest collections of Renaissance art outside of Italy, and it may house the only bona fide painting by Leonardo da Vinci in the United States. *Ginevra de Benci,* a noblewoman's portrait, is a double-sided wooden panel, and is believed to be a da Vinci. The museum also displays *Madonna and Child with a Pomegranate,* a painting that some believe was also completed by da Vinci while apprenticing in Verrocchio's studio. Other highlights of the Renaissance collection, which takes up fifteen rooms of the West Building, include five Botticellis, Raphael's *St. George and the Dragon,* a number of Fra Angelicos and Filippo Lippis, as well as a room of Italian frescoes that is the only representatives of their kind in the United States.

The Flemish and Dutch collections are equally stupendous, with some of the finest Rembrandts, Vermeers, Halses, Rubenses and Van Eycks in America. The eighteenth- and nineteenth-century galleries displaying French works include some marvelous rococo Watteaus and Bouchers, as well as David's *Napoleon*, Georges de La Tour's *Repentant Magdalen*, fourteen paintings by El Greco, and Jean Baptiste Siméon Chardin's *(Boy with) Soap Bubbles*, a classic work.

In the galleries that display nineteenth-century English paintings, there are marvelous landscape paintings by Turner and Constable, as well as portraits by Thomas Gainsborough.

≡FAST FACT

One of the most popular Colonial American paintings on display in the American collection—John Singleton Copley's *Watson and the Shark*—tells the story of fourteen-year-old Watson's fall into Havana Harbor, where a shark ate his right foot. Watson survived to become a successful British merchant and politician. This is sure to be a shocker (and pleaser) for bored boys who are tired of all the portraits and landscapes.

You can also view American classics, including a terrific selection of early American paintings by unknown artists, such as *Strawberry Girl*; Augustus Saint-Gaudens' life-sized sculpture of the Shaw Memorial; a tribute to the Buffalo soldiers of the Civil War; and Thomas Coles's four paintings of the stages of man's life. The nineteenth-century American collection also includes a number of Homers, Sargents, Eakinses, Bellowses, and Hassams.

The indoor sculpture collection downstairs spans the fifteenth to nineteenth centuries and includes a fabulous Rodin collection, including studies for *The Kiss* and *The Thinker*, as well as some ballerinas by Degas. This floor also features furniture, tapestries, and ceramics.

Break for lunch after you've seen the West Building, and eat in the full-service Terrace Cafe, which offers a good selection of sandwiches, pastas, and hot meals. You can even enjoy a glass of wine and use your credit card to pay. Then head through the ground-floor gift shop, which features mainly prints, scarves, and posters, and look at the twentieth-century art housed in the East Building.

The East Building

The East Building features an impressive number of large-canvas moderns from the abstract expressionist movement, including Robert Motherwell's gigantic black-and-white painting *Reconciliation Elegy,* Pollock's *Number 1,* and Mark Rothko's *Orange and Tan.* Alexander Calder's orange-and-black finned mobile hangs above you. Barnett Newman's *Stations of the Cross,* as well as works by pop artists Roy Lichtenstein, Claes Oldenburg, and Andy Warhol are also on display. Early twentieth-century works include thirteen Picassos and paintings by Braque, Kandinsky, Mondrian, Rene Magritte, and Edward Hopper.

The Sculpture Garden

The outdoor sculpture garden on 8th Street features about thirty works from the late twentieth century and is a wonderful marriage of large-scale art and public space. A large circular fountain shoots jets of water in the center of the garden—during the winter it's an ice-skating rink—and there is an outdoor cafe. People flock to the giant typewriter eraser by Claes Oldenburg and Lichtenstein's *House I,* a two-dimensional primary-color sculpture that plays with the spatial illusion of the house, as well as the metaphorical. Other artists represented include David Smith, Alexander Calder, Sol Lewitt, and Lucas Samaras.

Location and Hours

The museum is located on Constitution Avenue, between 3rd and 7th Streets on the north side of the Mall. Take the Metro to National Archives, Judiciary Square, or Smithsonian Metro station.

You can visit Monday through Saturday from 10:00 A.M. to 5:00 P.M. or on Sunday between 11:00 A.M. and 6:00 P.M. Inquire about free tours, special exhibits, concerts, and films.

═FAST FACT

Augustus Saint-Gaudens created the Shaw Memorial, a bronze relief in tribute to Robert Gould Shaw and the Buffalo Soldiers of the Massachusetts Fifty-fourth Regiment. The original is on display at the top of Boston Common, but a full-scale plaster cast can be seen at the National Gallery of Art. The memorial is considered one of the most powerful pieces of art dealing with the American Civil War.

Corcoran Gallery of Art

✉500 17th St. NW
✆202-639-1700
⌨www.corcoran.org

An incredible private collection in a beautiful *beaux arts* museum building, the Corcoran was D.C.'s first art museum. Originally housed in what is now the Renwick Gallery, the collection outgrew its space and moved to its current location in 1897. It will be expanding again in the near future, with a new wing designed by Frank Gehry, having once again outgrown its space with 3,000 new objects added in 2003 alone.

Collection Highlights

The collection was amassed by William Corcoran, a Washington banker who realized how important it was to begin collecting American art, not just the European masters that everyone else with money was buying. Highlights of his personal collection include Bierstadt's *Last of the Buffalo* and Frederick Church's

Niagara, as well as Healy's portrait of Abraham Lincoln (a second one is in the White House) and the controversial sculpture of the naked female *Greek Slave* by Hiram Powers.

There are a number of important works by European artists here as well, such as Rubens, Delacroix, Renoir, Monet, Corot, Degas, and Turner. You can also see a working clock that once belonged to Marie Antoinette.

Contemporary Works

Newer works by American artists include canvases by almost all the members of the Hudson River school, as well as paintings by Mary Cassatt, Thomas Eakins, Mark Rothko, and Helen Frankenthaler. In the lower level of the gallery, near the cafe, is a changing exhibit of works by African-American artists—the Corcoran has the largest collection of works by African-American artists in any American art museum and includes 350 works dating back to 1806—that has featured Kara Walker's powerful silhouette works, photos by Gordon Parks, and paintings by Jacob Lawrence, Romare Bearden, and Sam Gilliam. Other special exhibits recently featured at the Corcoran include the sculpture of Roy Lichtenstein and photos by Annie Leibovitz.

Restaurant and Gift Shop

The museum restaurant, Café des Artistes, offers a wonderful lunch that is often tied to the show. On the walls above the restaurant is a copy of a frieze from the Parthenon.

The museum shop offers an eclectic mix of clever art-related items, from Warhol glasses to traditional posters and mouse pads. Because the Corcoran has an art school, it often supports the work of local artists.

Location and Hours

The Corcoran Gallery is located on 17th Street NW, between E Street and New York Avenue. Take the Metro to the Farragut North station.

The Corcoran is open between 10:00 A.M. and 5:00 P.M. on Mondays, Wednesdays, and Thursdays, between 10:00 A.M. and 9:00 P.M. on Thursdays, and between 10:30 A.M. and 12:30 P.M. on Saturdays and Sundays. The gallery is closed on Tuesdays, as well as on Thanksgiving, Christmas Day, and New Year's Day.

Suggested donation for adults is $5, $4 for senior citizens, and $3 for students with valid I.D. You can pay $8 for a family, with children under 12 free. There are fees for special exhibits. Every Sunday afternoon there is an art-making workshop for kids ages 5 to 10. Reservations are required, and there are free family days four times a year with performances and art demonstrations. There's also a Sunday gospel brunch; expect to pay $23.95 for adults, and $10.50 for children.

≡FAST FACT

One of the most influential architects of Washington in the nineteenth century was James Renwick, who brought an American sensibility to the neoclassic style that was prevalent at the time. He designed the Smithsonian Castle, the original Corcoran Gallery (now the Renwick Gallery), and the gatehouse in Georgetown's Oak Hill Cemetery, as well as St. Patrick's Cathedral and Grace Church in New York City, and Vassar College.

The Phillips Collection

✉ 1600 21st St. NW
☎ 202-387-2151
🖉 www.phillipscollection.org

The Phillips Collection is a private collection of a married couple, the steel-fortune heir Duncan Phillips and his wife, Marjorie Phillips. The collection spans the twentieth century, rivaling any modern art museum in the world. In fact, it is considered to be the first modern art museum in the country. Today, the collection is still housed where it was originally shown to the public—in the Phillips's Georgian mansion.

Collection Highlights

Highlights of this incredible personal collection include Renoir's *Luncheon of the Boating Party* and the Rothko room, which features four works in a small room. Marjorie was an artist herself, and her American impressionist work is also on display here. Sometimes when a museum benefactor is also an artist, the work is included to appease the family, but Marjorie Phillips's *Night Baseball* is an American classic. Using post-Impressionistic techniques for its very middle-American subject, it deserves the treatment it receives as one of the icons of this museum.

The collection has grown immensely from the time it was started by the Phillips family. Today, it includes 2,500 works and is known throughout the world for its breadth of European impressionist and postimpressionist works, which the Phillips felt started with El Greco because he was "the first impassioned expressionist" and Chardin because he was "the first modern painter." There are also works by Van Gogh, Monet, Degas, Gauguin, and Cezanne, as well as Pisarro, Bonnard, Vuillard, and Braques (thirteen of these). American painters in the collection include O'Keeffe, Marin, Dove, Hartley, many of the Ashcan School artists, and four striking works by Jacob Lawrence from his *Migration of the Negro* series.

Gift Shop and Café

The museum gift shop is small but clever, featuring many reproductions from the collection as well as unusual modern art items such as a Man Ray teapot. The cafe, located on the lower level, serves a good selection of sandwiches and homemade soup.

Location and Hours

The Phillips is located on 21st Street NW at Q Street. If you take the Metro to the Dupont Circle station (and the Q Street exit), it's a short walk to the museum.

Permanent collection admission is free on weekdays; on week-ends and for special exhibits, the admission price is $8 for adults and $6 for seniors and students. Price of admission includes an audio tour. Children under 18 can enter free, but they have to pur-chase the audio tour for $3.

The museum is closed Monday. It is open Tuesday through Saturday from 10:00 A.M. to 5:00 P.M. (late on Thursday, open until 8:30 P.M.), and on Sunday from noon to 7:00 P.M. The Phillips is also closed for some national holidays, such as Fourth of July, Thanksgiving Day, Christmas Day, and New Year's Day, so call ahead.

👥 JUST FOR PARENTS

On Thursday nights the Phillips hosts "artful evenings" with music, gallery talks, and a cash bar. On Sunday nights during the fall and winter, the museum hosts free concerts in the music room at 5:00 P.M., although you do have to pay the price of museum admission.

The Phillips is undergoing an expansion with construction of a new annex that is set to open in the summer of 2005. Some of the pieces from the permanent collection will tour during that time.

Kreeger Museum

✉2401 Foxhall Rd. NW
☎202-337-3050
✍www.kreegermuseum.com

The Kreeger Museum is one of those incredible places that you can't believe everyone in the world doesn't know about—it is one of the best-kept secrets in the whole city of Washington, D.C. Off the beaten track in the city's exclusive suburbs, the Kreeger houses a breathtaking collection of nineteenth- and twentieth-century modern art.

The Kreeger is located in a private mansion built by noted architect Philip Johnson in the late 1960s when he was at the beginning of his postmodern style. The architecture and the art complement each other so well that it's hard to decide which is the more impressive.

Museum Layout

The Kreeger Museum, a private home until 1994, was designed according to a module system. Every room and public space (including the stupendous pool) is constructed on some variation of a box measuring twenty-two feet on all sides. Areas sometimes consist of two modules, sometimes just half of one, and they are often topped by a dome. The entire structure is composed of beige limestone, and the museum's acoustics (both indoors and outside in the sculpture garden) are wonderful.

Although there are more than 180 works in this collection, the most memorable are in the dining room, where nine paintings by Monet catch the sunlight through glass door panels that overlook the sculpture terrace.

Collection Highlights

David Kreeger, founder of GEICO insurance, and his wife, Carmen, were responsible for amassing the collection and it is said that they agreed on every piece they purchased, though Carmen was more partial to nineteenth-century works and David liked those of the twentieth century. The collection begins with French masters of the nineteenth century, such as Corot, Courbet, and Renoir and continues through every modern art movement from the Cubists to the Symbolists to Pop. The Kreegers also collected African art, from masks to sculpture, and the presence of it here certainly helps reveal the connections among the influences this art had on the art of the twentieth century.

Artists in the collection read like a Who's Who in modern art, from thirteen Picassos that span his entire career to Braque, Cezanne, Man Ray, Kandinsky, Degas, Bonnard, Van Gogh, Léger,

Mondrian, Munch, Stella, Rodin, and Chagall, to name only a fraction. It is truly amazing that all these wonderful works once hung on the walls of a private home, which itself is a work of art, and that the owners had the generosity and vision to leave it all to the public.

Location and Hours

The Kreeger is located in a residential neighborhood and isn't accessible by public transportation. If you have a car, parking is available. A taxi-cab ride from downtown will run about $8.

You may choose to take a docent-led tour, available at 10:30 A.M. and 1:30 P.M. on Tuesdays through Saturdays. The tour takes about an hour and a half and is limited to fifteen people. Call to make a reservation, or send an e-mail to ✍*visitorservices@kreegermuseum.com*. The museum is also open for visitors to browse the collection on Saturdays from 10 A.M. to 4 P.M. Tickets are free, but there's a suggested donation of $8 for adults and $5 for seniors. Children under 12 are discouraged, but if your children are used to touring museums and they are well-behaved, this is a not-to-be-missed experience. Also note that the museum is closed the entire month of August.

National Museum of Women in the Arts

✉1250 New York Ave. NW
✆202-783-5000
✍*www.nmwa.org*

Do you have a daughter or granddaughter who is interested in art? This is a must-see museum that is sure to inspire her. Another gem in D.C.'s museum crown, the National Museum of Women in the Arts features more than 250 works by female artists housed in a restored Masonic temple.

Collection Highlights

In this museum, you will find the work of two of the Peale sisters, who were as talented as their father and his brother (nineteenth-century portrait painters James and Charles Peale) but whose work is virtually unknown. The permanent collection also features early Italian Renaissance and Flemish works by female artists, as well as seventeenth-century female silversmiths. Rosa Bonheur, considered the best painter of animals in the nineteenth century, had to dress as a man to paint in public.

≡FAST FACT

The niece of one of the first successful artists in America, Sarah Miriam Peale is considered one of the first American women to have a successful career as an artist. Her uncle was Charles Wilson Peale, whose portraits of pals George Washington and Thomas Jefferson are famous. Her father, James Peale, had sixteen nieces and nephews, ten of whom were named after famous artists, such as Rembrandt and Rubens. Her sister's work can also be found at the National Museum of Women in the Arts.

Also on display are works by Elizabeth Lebrun, who was the court painter to Marie Antoinette and one of the few known female portrait painters of her time. Mary Cassatt's Japanese-inspired prints are all on view here, as are two Frida Kahlos, including her *Self-Portrait Dedicated to Leon Trotsky*, which some art historians believe was a visual love letter between the painter and the Communist philosopher.

Other Highlights

Other works on display include those by Georgia O'Keeffe, Lee Krasner, and Helen Frankenthaler, as well as Alice Neel's powerful *T.B. Harlem*. There's a quirky sculpture on the landing outside the second-floor elevator near the restaurant that caught my eye and stayed with me: Petah Coyne's dripped pink-and-white wax ballerina costume suspended from the ceiling.

The museum's small restaurant has a surprisingly good and clever selection of sandwiches, such as the Frida Kahlo, a toasted cheese, havarti, and spinach sandwich; or the Mary Cassatt, tuna with Swiss. The gift shop features a terrific collection of books and posters about female artists, as well as a creative jewelry display. There are special exhibits year-round, so call for information.

Location and Hours

The National Museum of Women in the Arts is located on New York Avenue and is accessible from the Metro Center Metro station. Hours are Monday through Saturday 10:00 A.M. to 5:00 P.M., and Sunday noon to 5:00 P.M. Admission is $8 for adults, $6 seniors and students, children 18 and under free. Additionally, admission on the first Wednesday and Sunday of the month is free. The museum is closed on Thanksgiving Day, Christmas Day, and New Year's Day.

National Museum of Health and Medicine

✉6825 16th St. NW, Bldg. 54
✆202-782-2200
⌨www.nlm.nih.gov

Does your child want to be a doctor? This is the museum for kids interested in biology and slightly gross stuff (which means it's not for kids under five). If this sounds like something your kids may enjoy, they'll be talking about what they saw here for the next year!

An Unusual Collection

A little off the beaten track, but certainly one of the most interesting and unusual museums in existence, the National Museum of Health and Medicine is one of the nation's oldest medical museums, with 12,000 medical and anatomical items in its collection. Where else could you find the bullet that killed Lincoln or see Civil War–era surgical tools? You can also see centuries-old Inca skulls that show the results of head surgery, and Paul Revere's dental tools.

The National Museum of Health and Medicine, which was founded after the Civil War, was primarily focused on military medicine and pathology until World War II. It has a wonderful collection of old medical instruments and machines, as well as an extensive collection of skeletons and body parts, the first heart-lung machine, and prosthetic limbs.

It will take about two hours to fully explore this unusual museum. Its four permanent exhibits include "To Bind Up the Nation's Wounds," which focuses on medicine during and after the Civil War; "Living in a World with AIDS"; "Human Body Human Being," which offers a look at a smoker's lung and the opportunity to touch a human brain; and the Billings Microscope Collection, which features the world's most comprehensive collection of microscopes from the earliest in the 1600s to the first electron microscopes of the 1930s.

The museum also has a number of special exhibits, so call for more information.

RAINY DAY FUN

U.S. Navy and Marine Corps museums share a space at 9th and M Street SE (202-433-3534), near the Navy Yard Metro station. The Navy Museum is open Monday through Friday from 9:00 A.M. to 4:00 P.M., and on Saturday and Sunday from 10:00 A.M. to 5:00 P.M. The Marine Corps Museum is open from 10:00 A.M. to 5:00 P.M. every day except Tuesday. It's open on Sunday from noon to 5:00 P.M. The Navy Museum features a rigged fighting top from the frigate *Constitution* and a Gulf War Tomahawk missile. The Marine Corps Museum features memorabilia from the Marines' history, going back to 1775. Outside, a decommissioned Navy destroyer from 1955 allows visitors a peek into life at sea.

Location and Hours

The museum is housed in the Walter Reed Army Medical Center, accessible via the Elder Street NW gate off of Georgia Avenue NW. To get there, you'll have to take the Metro to the Silver Springs or Tacoma Metro station and take a short bus ride. Hours of operation are from 10:00 A.M. until 5:30 P.M. Guided tours are available. The museum is closed on Christmas Day.

The International Spy Museum

✉800 F St. NW
✆202-393-7798
⌨*www.spymuseum.org*

This is a really fun and quirky museum with something for everyone in the family, which is why there are lines for the International Spy Museum on most weekends. This is a private (for profit) museum dedicated to the history and craft of spying.

An Intriguing Collection

Although there are some examples from ancient and European history, the bulk of the museum covers twentieth-century espionage involving Americans, and the exhibits are fascinating and fun.

Kids can crawl though an air-duct tunnel, watch a film on how to pick a lock, place a bug, spot a bug, listen to conversations with the KGB, and learn how to disguise themselves. James Bond's famous Aston Martin is on display, with all its wonderful gadgets, and there's a media room of pop culture spying, with *I Spy* games and *Get Smart* gadgets that never fail to entertain.

What's Covered in the Exhibits

It will take about two hours to see the museum from start to finish. You can pick an alias when you enter, which you are quizzed on when you leave to see if you have successfully completed your mission. The next section is the School for Spies, where the tricks of the trade (use of cameras, bugs, disguises) are explained. Then it's on to the Secret History of History, with displays on spying in the Soviet Union, female spies throughout history, and use of birds and balloons in early spying. There's even a section on spying during the American Revolution.

The next section is on celebrity spies of World War II, where you are reminded that Josephine Baker and Marlene Dietrich did some espionage work for the Allies, with an overview of spying during World War II. Then it's on to the Cold War and spying in Berlin during the 1950s and 1960s, and Eastern Europe until the present. When you exit, you are asked a number of questions about your cover to see if you have been successful at your own spying missions.

The International Spy Museum store is wonderful, and there's something for everyone, from Spy Museum T-shirts for teens to espionage kits to a pen shaped like a lipstick holder (only $4). The Spy City Café is large and offers a good selection of "Killer Sandwiches," salads and soup.

Location and Hours

The museum is located on F Street, accessible from the Gallery Place/Chinatown Metro station in the heart of the city. It is open daily from 10:00 A.M. to 8:00 P.M., but expect lines on weekends and during school holidays. Admission is $13 for adults, $12 for seniors, and $10 for children. Advance tickets can be purchased at the museum or through TicketMaster.

≡FAST FACT

The Martin Luther King Jr. Memorial Library is the main city library of Washington, D.C., and an architectural landmark. It is the only building in this city designed by the founder of the International style of architecture, Ludwig Mies van der Rohe. It is a stark black and glass-paneled rectangle on the street facing the Museum of American Art and the American Portrait Gallery.

The City Museum of Washington, D.C.

✉801 K St.
☎202-383-1870
✎*www.citymuseum.org*

Finally, here's a museum that tells the history of the city of Washington, D.C., from its roots in the Civil War as a mecca for freed slaves to its cultural icons such as the rise and fall and rise and fall again of the Washington Senators, the old D.C. professional baseball team.

There's a great twenty-three-minute film on the history of the city and its neighborhoods that sets the tone for the main exhibit. The exhibit was originally designed as a Web site, so that as you grow more and more interested in a subject, you can open drawers and examine more artifacts from that time. There's a giant illuminated map of the city on the floor, and you can find your hotel on it. A visit to this museum is a great way to start a trip to the city, so kids can really get an overview of where things are.

There is a terrific gift shop on the ground floor that offers such offbeat gifts as White House Christmas ornaments and local cornmeal. There is also a café on the premises.

Location and Hours

Located on K Street in the heart of the city, the City Museum is accessible from the Gallery Place/Chinatown Metro station. Hours of operation are from 10:00 A.M. to 5:00 P.M. Tuesday through Sunday. The museum is closed on Mondays, but it does open on Mondays that fall on holidays. It's also closed on the Fourth of July, Thanksgiving Day, Christmas Day, and New Year's Eve. Admission with multimedia show is $7 for adults and $5 for children, students, and seniors. The price for just touring the exhibits is $3 for adults and $2 for children, seniors, and students.

More Museums

Washington, D.C., has no shortage of museums. Most tourists gravitate toward the National Gallery or the Corcoran, but there are a multitude of smaller museums that have something for everyone. Here are your many options to choose from.

American Red Cross Headquarters and Museum

✉ 1730 E St. NW

✆ 202-639-3300

🖳 *www.redcross.org*

The museum is located at the Board of Governors building, which was turned into a memorial building to honor the heroic women of World War I and can be recognized by the giant white banner with the red cross that hangs on the outside of the beaux arts building.

In 1996, three Tiffany windows dating from 1917 were relit after having been dark since the blackouts of World War II. Funds for the windows were raised by the Women's Relief Corps of the North and the United Daughters of the Confederacy, two organizations of Civil War women. The museum features regular exhibits on Red Cross efforts worldwide, as well as a history of this organization, which was started by Clara Barton after the Civil War.

There is a gift shop on the premises that features such unusual items as a Faberge-style Red Cross egg pendant and earrings modeled after a Faberge Red Cross egg presented by Czar Nicholas to his wife, Alexandra, and his mother on Easter 1915; a plate with a replica of the Tiffany windows; Red Cross Christmas ornaments; and mugs, scarves, and ties. Needless to say, these items make wonderful gifts for nurses.

Location and Hours

The museum is located on E Street near 17th Street and can be reached from either the Farragut West or Farragut North Metro station. You can visit on Monday through Friday between 8:30 A.M.

and 4:00 P.M. Tours of the visitors' center and headquarters building are offered on Tuesdays and Fridays at 9:00 A.M.

Art Museum of the Americas

✉201 18th St. NW

☎202-458-6016

🖉*www.museum.oas.org*

Free admission is just one reason to check out this museum, which you'll find located a stone's throw from the White House and just behind the House of the Americas in a Spanish Colonial structure that was once the home of the Organization of American States. In keeping with the international theme set down by that history, the museum is dedicated to Latin American and Caribbean art. See contemporary works on all kinds of themes by artists and sculptors from Mexico, Venezuela, the Galapagos Islands, and more. The permanent collection includes works by Botero, Roberto Matta, and others, and there is a sculpture garden.

Location and Hours

The Art Museum of the Americas is located on 18th Street and is accessible from the Farragut West Metro station. Visitors are welcomed on Tuesday through Saturday, from 10:00 A.M. to 5:00 P.M.

💼 TRAVEL TIP

Another interesting destination is the Black Fashion Museum, 207 Vermont Avenue, ☎202-667-0744. This is a private museum started by Lois K. Alexander-Lane, a former president of the National Association of Fashion and Accessory Designers. The museum features the designs of Anne Lowe, Elizabeth Beckley, Patrick Kelly, Thony Anyiam, Edward Burke, Bill Washington, and others. It also displays a collection of bridal gowns from the slave era to the present. You can visit the museum by appointment only.

Capital Children's Museum

✉800 3rd St. NW

✆202-675-4120

✍*www.ccm.org*

A hands-on education complex right next to Union Station, the Capital Children's Museum has a number of intriguing permanent as well as changing exhibits. The Chemical Science Center features interactive experiments with "scientists" in lab coats for children over 6. The "Cityscapes" exhibit gives children a chance to slide down a fire pole, drive a Metrobus, navigate a maze, and stand inside a bubble. Kids can also put on their own puppet show and have their faces painted. There's also the opportunity to explore an Ice Age cave.

Another popular exhibit is on animation, in which an interactive demonstration teaches children how cartoons are made from start to finish. There are old-fashioned animation machines, as well as sound-effects machines, and kids can create their own cartoons and view their work.

There are two exhibit areas on the cultures of Japan and Mexico. In the Mexican exhibit area, kids can make and taste chocolate and tortillas, and they can make arts and crafts to take home. There is also a replica of a Mayan pyramid and a Yucatan beach. The Japanese exhibit features a Japanese home, including a Tatami Room where kids can sit at the traditional low table (*kotatsu*) and learn to use chopsticks. They can also try on Japanese school-children's uniforms, examine kimonos, and learn the Japanese language and alphabet. The exhibit also features a simulated ride on a bullet train and a Japanese shopping street, where children can put together their own bento box lunch with plastic items.

Location and Hours

Located on 3rd Street, the museum may be reached from the Union Station Metro stop. Visit the Capital Children's Museum from 10:00 A.M. to 5:00 P.M. Admission prices are $7 for adults, $6 for seniors, and $5 for children, and please note that children must be accompanied by an adult. The museum also offers craft activities every Saturday and Sunday, from noon until 3:00 P.M.

☂ RAINY DAY FUN

Step out of the rain and into the National Building Museum, which is located at ✉401 F Street NW ☎202-272-2448. The museum is open Monday through Saturday from 10:00 A.M. to 5:00 P.M. and on Sunday from noon to 5:00 P.M. Reach it from the Judiciary Square Metro station. Housed in the giant U.S. Pension building, the National Building Museum is dedicated to the architecture and technology of American building. The first major exhibit here was on air conditioning.

College Park Aviation Museum
✉1909 Corporal Frank Scott Dr., College Park, Maryland
☎301-864-6029
🖥*www.collegeparkaviationmuseum.com*

The world's oldest operating airport was established here in 1909, when two guys by the names of Orville and Wilbur brought their "aeroplane" to a field in Maryland. It led to the creation of the first Army Aviation School, one of many firsts to occur at this site. The airport continues to operate today.

Much newer is the museum, filled with displays and artifacts on these and other important contributions to aviation. Each fall, the museum hosts the Air Fair, featuring stunt shows and historical aircraft. (Call the museum to request a copy of its newsletter, *The Wright Flyer,* for more information.)

Location and Hours
College Park Aviation Museum is located in College Park, Maryland, near the University of Maryland, between Route 1 and

Kenilworth Avenue (Route 201). You can reach it via the Metro—it's accessible from the College Park/University of Maryland Metro station.

Hours of operation are from 11:00 A.M. to 3:00 P.M. on Wednesday through Friday, and the museum is open until 5:00 P.M. on weekends. (The museum is closed Monday and Tuesday.) Admission is $4 for adults and $3 for seniors and children.

Daughters of the American Revolution Museum

✉ 1776 D St. NW
✆ 202-879-3241
⌨ http://dar.org/museum

This is the museum of the National Society of the Daughters of the American Revolution. It houses a collection of American decorative arts from the seventeenth to the nineteenth century in thirty-three period rooms organized around thirty-three states. There is also an extensive genealogy library. Members donated all objects in the museum's extensive collection.

Location and Hours

The museum is located on D Street and is a ten- to fifteen-minute walk from either of the nearest two Metro stations, Farragut West or Farragut North. Docent-led tours are available from 10:00 A.M. to 2:30 P.M. on weekdays and from 9:30 A.M. to 4:30 P.M. on Saturday. The museum is closed on Sunday.

Textile Museum

✉ 2330 S St. NW
✆ 202-667-0441
⌨ www.textilemuseum.org

This museum features samples of textiles and fabrics from all over the world. Exhibits also display looms and hand tools. On the fourth floor, there is an interactive exhibit on textile-making for children.

Location and Hours

Located near the Woodrow Wilson House on S Street, the museum can be reached from the Dupont Circle Metro station. Hours of operation are Monday through Saturday, 10:00 A.M. to 5:00 P.M., and on Sunday from 1:00 to 5:00 P.M. A donation of $5 per visitor is requested.

CHAPTER 10

Sites of Historical Interest

WASHINGTON, D.C., IS ONE OF the oldest cities in the nation, and because the city was planned as the nation's capital, it is full of historic places that tell its story. What makes D.C. different is that many of these historic moments were preplanned. Their importance was known from the onset, and preservation was in mind at the time of their occurrence.

Washington, D.C., is also a city that has expanded outward, around the Potomac, so that the older, original parts of the city never had to be torn down and rebuilt for the next generation. This is only one of the reasons that a neighborhood like Georgetown, which was established before the city itself, can remain so full of the restored historic homes and sites we see today.

≡FAST FACT

Though only one Civil War battle took place in Washington, D.C., it is amazing how much of the city's history, from the Arlington House and Arlington National Cemetery to Ford's Theatre and the Petersen House, was shaped by the Civil War years.

Ford's Theatre

✉517 10th St. NW
☎202-426-6924
🖱*www.nps.gov*

In 1865, less than a week after General Lee had surrendered, the actor and Confederate sympathizer John Wilkes Booth shot President Lincoln at close range in the back of the head while the president was watching the play *Our American Cousin*. Ford's Theatre has remained occupied in one way or another to this day, and the second-story balcony booth where Lincoln was shot is now draped in presidential bunting.

From the time of Lincoln's death until the 1930s, Ford's Theatre was used as an office building and storage space, but when the Lincoln Museum was opened there in 1932, funds were raised for its restoration, and it has been managed by the National Park Service since then. The theatre was beautifully restored and now hosts a full season of theatrical performances, including an annual production of Dickens's *A Christmas Carol*.

☂RAINY DAY FUN

Although the Lincoln Museum at Ford's Theatre has a wealth of items from Lincoln's assassination, other artifacts from that night can be seen at different locations throughout the city. The National Museum of Health and Medicine has the bullet that killed Lincoln. The Library of Congress has the contents of Lincoln's pockets from the night he was killed. A blood-soaked pillow can be seen at the Petersen House.

Downstairs you will find an extensive Lincoln Museum that exhibits artifacts from the night Lincoln was shot, such as the gun Booth used, the clothes Lincoln was wearing when he was shot, bloodstained pillowcases and towels, mourning memorabilia collected from throughout the nation, a cast of Lincoln's face and hand, and photos of the other conspirators in the assassination.

There is an extensive bookstore that includes videos, biographies, and even puzzles featuring Abraham Lincoln.

Location and Hours

Ford's Theatre is located on 10th Street NW and is accessible from the Metro Center Metro station. You can tour the theater each day of the week from 9:00 A.M. to 5:00 P.M., and hour-long tours are offered by National Park Service Rangers every fifteen minutes, except during rehearsals and performances. The theater is closed on Christmas Day.

Martin Luther King Jr. Memorial Library

✉901 G St. NW
☎202-727-1126
🖊*www.dclibrary.org*

The great architect of the International style, Ludwig Mies van der Rohe, designed the main branch of the Washington, D.C., library and an architectural landmark, the Martin Luther King Jr. Memorial Library. The library serves as a memorial to the slain civil rights leader and contains a large mural by Don Miller on the life of Martin Luther King Jr. that rivals any of the WPA murals of the 1930s. The library often hosts events related to the life of Martin Luther King Jr. as well as special events during Black History Month.

Location and Hours

The library is located on G Street, diagonally across from the National Museum of American Art. It is accessible from Gallery Place/Chinatown and Metro Center Metro stations. You can visit the library on Mondays through Thursdays from 9:30 A.M. to 9 P.M., on

Fridays and Saturdays from 9:30 A.M. to 5:30 P.M., and on Sundays from 1 P.M. to 5 P.M.

The Charles Sumner School

✉ 1201 17th St. NW
✆ 202-442-6060

Local legend has it that U.S. Senator Charles Sumner petitioned for this school for freed slaves to be taxed so that it could be accredited. It opened in 1872 and became the city's first public school for African-Americans. Today it is also the archive center for the D.C. public-school system, as well as a museum on Martin Luther King Jr., Frederick Douglass, and Washington, D.C., history. In the permanent collection, there is an 1877 diploma from one of the first graduates.

Location and Hours
The Charles Sumner School, where the museum and archive are housed, is located on 17th Street NW. It is accessible from the Farragut North Metro station. You can visit the museum on Monday through Saturday from 10:00 A.M. to 5:00 P.M.; the archives are open by appointment only, Monday through Friday, from 8:00 A.M. to 4:00 P.M.

African-American Civil War Memorial

✉ 10th and U Sts. NW
✆ 202-667-2667
✎ *www.afroamcivilwar.org*

The memorial is a stone-and-bronze commemorative statue grouping created by sculptor Ed Hamilton in honor of over 200,000 African-American Union soldiers and their white officers who fought during the Civil War. The relatively new memorial stands on the former grounds of Union barracks for black soldiers. There is a visitors' center with a database where you can look up the history of those honored by the memorial.

Location and Hours

The memorial is located between 10th and U Streets NW, near the U Street/Cardozo Metro station. The visitors' center is open Monday through Friday from 10:00 A.M. to 5:00 P.M., and Saturday and Sunday from 2:00 to 5:00 P.M.

💼 TRAVEL TIP

L'Enfant Plaza, near Maine and Water Streets SW, is a commemorative tribute to the African-American mathematician and astronomer Benjamin Banneker, who worked with Pierre L'Enfant to create the original design for the city of Washington, D.C., in 1791.

Howard University

✉ 2400 6th St. NW
☎ 202-806-6100
✍ *www.howard.edu*

Howard University was founded in 1866 as a liberal-arts college and university to educate the nearly 4 million emancipated African-Americans of the time. Famous alumnae include U.S. Supreme Court Justice Thurgood Marshall and novelist Toni Morrison.

Howard University was named after white Civil War General Oliver O. Howard, who was Commissioner of the Freedman's Bureau, one of the university's founders, and its third president. His home on Georgia Avenue is a historic landmark.

The Gallery of Art in the College of Fine Arts features the permanent Alain Locke African collection and changing exhibitions.

The Moorland-Springarn Research center houses the country's largest collection of information on the history and culture of African-Americans.

Location and Hours

Howard University is accessible from the Shaw/Howard U Metro station. Tours are available, but call ahead for scheduling.

Georgetown University

Georgetown, founded in 1751, is the oldest part of Washington, D.C. It was a town before there was even a nation to build a capital city for. It was named after King George II and featured cobblestone streets, some of which still exist around Georgetown University, where Bill Clinton went to school. (Clinton is the only president to have gone to college in D.C.). Many of the houses are very narrow—a pink one-bedroom on M Street that is only 9.5 feet wide recently sold for $375,000—because houses in the colonies were taxed by width.

A Tour of Georgetown

Start your walking tour at the Old Stone House (⌂3051 N Street), considered to be the oldest building in the city. It was built in 1765 by carpenter Christopher Layman, who had his workshop on the first floor. This four-room museum is now furnished in eighteenth-century décor, and it is open free to the public Wednesday through Sunday from 9:00 A.M. to 5:00 P.M.

Walk down Jefferson Street to the Chesapeake & Ohio Canal Lock (between M and K Streets), where you can see this important link to the shipping history of Georgetown. The C&O Canal was supposed to link with the Ohio River so that products could be shipped a total of 185 miles, but the quick development of the railroad made this method of transportation a thing of the past. Visitors can still travel on barges (mule-drawn ones, at that) and canoes along the canal.

≡FAST FACT

According to Georgetown University records from 1967, as a junior at the school of Foreign Service, William Jefferson Clinton ran for president of the East Campus Student Council. However, he lost to a classmate. G.U. legend has it that Clinton lost to a much less widely known candidate on the basis of Clinton's desire to unite all five of G.U.'s undergraduate schools. Many felt he had collaborated with the university's administration, which wanted the unification.

Walk down K Street until it intersects with Wisconsin Avenue, and you should find a fence, inside of which is a worn plaque identifying this site as Suter's Tavern, where George Washington and Pierre L'Enfant are said to have planned the city of Washington in 1790. No one knows for sure exactly where the tavern was situated.

Up Wisconsin Avenue and on the corner of Grace Street, you will find the C&O Canal Commemorative Marker. This granite stone is the only record of the canal in existence today, and it commemorates the completion of the canal in 1850. It lies right outside The Shops at Georgetown, a four-story mall that features a food court, Benihana, and Clyde's restaurants, and everything from bead stores to barber shops.

At 1066 Wisconsin Avenue is the Vigilant Firehouse, the oldest volunteer firefighter brigade in Washington, which was founded in 1817. The firehouse was built in 1844 and is now a restaurant that still bears the large "V" for Vigilant near its roof.

Further along M Street is the City Tavern (⊠3206 M Street). Built in 1796, this tavern was the main terminal for the stagecoach line in Georgetown. It once hosted President John Adams for dinner on his inspection of the new city.

It's hard to believe that a city that has preserved so much of its history allowed Francis Scott Key's house to be torn down to make way for a freeway exit ramp. All that is left is the Francis

Scott Key Memorial Site (✉3518 M St.), which is a public park and a marker for the former home of the author of "The Star-Spangled Banner."

═══FAST FACT

Georgetown has always been the home to the city's influential and well-known, and houses here have belonged to Alexander Graham Bell, Louisa May Alcott, Sylvester Stallone, Arnold Schwarzenegger, and countless politicians such as Kennedy and Kissinger. A number of movies have been filmed in Georgetown as well. The most famous are *The Exorcist, St. Elmo's Fire, The Pelican Brief,* and *No Way Out.*

Further along M Street, turn at 35th Street and you will reach Prospect Street. Here you will find the site of *The Exorcist* stairs, which were built on the site of Southworth Cottage (✉3600 Prospect St.), the former home of a Victorian novelist. There are now two townhouses and the long stairs to Canal Street where the movie was shot. This is a favorite haunt of the university crowd around Halloween.

Walk up 35th Street to N Street, and on the corner of 33rd Street you will find The Marbury House (✉3307 N St.) where U.S. Senator and Mrs. John F. Kennedy lived before they moved into the White House in 1961. It had been built for William Marbury in 1812.

Walk up 33rd Street, and turn right at Q Street, and you will come to Tudor Place (✉1644 31st Street, ☎202-965-0400). William Thornton, who designed the Octagon and had a hand in the design of the U.S. Capitol, designed this home for Martha Washington's granddaughter, who married the mayor of Georgetown. The house is now a museum of Washington memorabilia. Tudor Place is open Tuesday through Saturday for guided tours only with admission.

Walk along Q Street until you get to 29th Street, and then head to R Street, where you will come to the large, fenced Victorian Oak

Hill Cemetery. The cemetery was established by William Corcoran, who is also buried here, in 1850.

🧳 TRAVEL TIP

The chapel of Oak Hill Cemetery was designed by James Renwick, and even the gatehouse (3001 R Street) is quite beautiful. If you stroll the grounds, you will see Southern-style Victorian mourning sculptures, like winged angels. You can get a map of the gravesites at the gatehouse, and the cemetery is open from 10:00 A.M. to 4:00 P.M. on weekdays.

Just around the corner from the Oak Hill Cemetery is Evermay (✉1623 28th Street NW), a huge, quirky, red-brick mansion that looks like something out of an Edgar Allan Poe story. You can't enter, but you can walk along its brick wall and peer in at this home of Scottish bachelor Samuel Davidson, who once took out an ad about his property that warned his neighbors to avoid "Evermay as they would a den of evils, or rattlesnakes, and thereby save themselves and me much vexation and trouble." When he died, his will forced his nephew to change his name to Davidson in exchange for the estate.

On Q and 28th Streets is the Gun Barrel Fence, which stretches about a half a block and looks wholly unspectacular—until you realize that it was made from the guns and metal that were recovered from the Old Navy Yard after it was burned by the British in 1814.

Walk back down 28th Street to N Street until you get to 30th Street, and you will be standing in front of The French House (✉3017 N Street), which is where Jacqueline Kennedy lived for a year after her husband's assassination in 1963.

Historic Houses

Washington, D.C., is a terrific city for visiting historic homes that have been wonderfully preserved. Because so many of them were the sites of historic events, such as the Petersen House, they have been left almost unchanged since the event that made them a piece of living history.

Petersen House

✉516 10th St. NW
✆202-426-6924

Lincoln died in a first-floor back bedroom of the home of William Petersen, a tailor. Doctors knew immediately after he was shot that the head wound was mortal, and they did not dare move him to the Civil War hospital less than two blocks away (now the National Portrait Gallery on 10th Street).

The bed Lincoln was laid in was too short for him, and he lay sideways for part of the night until the end piece was sawed off so his feet could hang out. Blood from his head injury is said to have soaked through seven pillows. It's said that a psychic who visited the room said she could see a mist rising from one of the blood-soaked pillows.

You can pay a visit to the Petersen House, which is now maintained by the National Park Service. It's accessible from the Metro Center Metro station.

═══FAST FACT

According to White House legend and John Alexander's *Ghosts: Washington Revisited*, one evening Lincoln dreamed that he heard crying throughout the White House. He left his bedroom to see what was going on and discovered a crowd of people around a coffin. When he asked who had died, he was told, "The assassinated president." It is reported that when he looked in the open casket, he saw himself.

Dumbarton Oaks Estate and Gardens

✉ 1703 32nd St. NW

✆ 202-339-6401

✎ *www.doaks.org*

Dumbarton Oaks was the site of an international conference that led to the creation of the United Nations in 1944. Today, the original Georgian mansion is the site of a museum of Byzantine art, and a newer addition designed by Philip Johnson houses a pre-Columbian art collection.

This Georgetown mansion sits on a sixteen-acre plot that features some of the most beautiful gardens in Washington, D.C., which are open to the public in warm weather as part of the house tour. The historic music room, where the Dumbarton Oaks conversations took place, has a sixteenth-century stone fireplace as its focal point. It also features French tapestries on the walls, and El Greco's *Visitation.*

Location and Hours

The mansion is located on 32nd Street NW, and is not accessible by public transportation. Hours of operation are on Tuesdays through Sundays from 2:00 to 5:00 P.M. It's closed on Mondays, federal holidays, and Christmas Eve. Admission for entrance to the mansion is a recommended donation of $1. For admission to the garden, the fee is $5.

Hillwood Museum

✉ 4155 Linnean Ave. NW

✆ 202-686-5807

✎ *www.hillwoodmuseum.org*

This is the restored mansion of Post cereal heiress Marjorie Merriweather Post, who, with her ambassador-to-Russia husband, managed to buy up many of the Russian aristocracy's confiscated trinkets and jewels as the Communists were selling them for cash in the 1930s. She had a splendid collection of Faberge eggs and rare Russian books, as well as icons. There is also a lovely Japanese-style garden on the grounds. You will find a museum shop and a café on the premises.

💼 TRAVEL TIP

If you're interested in feminist history, visit the Sewall-Belmont House, ✉144 Constitution Ave. NE, ✆202-546-1210. The house is open on Tuesdays through Fridays, from 11:00 A.M. to 3:00 P.M., and on Saturdays from noon to 4:00 P.M. Instead of a fixed admission, donations are requested from visitors. This feminist museum and library—in the home of suffrage leader Alice Paul, founder of the National Women's Party and drafter of the Equal Rights Amendment—is the oldest house on Capitol Hill, with some parts dating back to 1680.

Location and Hours

Located on Linnean Avenue NW, between Upton and Tilden Streets, the Hillwood Museum is accessible from the Van Ness Metro station. Parking on the premises is also available.

The museum is open Tuesday through Saturday, from 9:30 A.M. to 5:00 P.M. Reservations are required for house tours. A refundable reservation deposit is required: $10 for adults, $8 for seniors, and $5 for students. Children under 12 are not permitted.

Woodrow Wilson House
✉2340 S St. NW
✆202-387-4062
🖱www.woodrowwilsonhouse.org

The Wilson House is the only museum in Washington, D.C., of a former president. After Wilson left the presidency, private groups of friends and benefactors bought him this house and a car to make sure that he lived the remainder of his years in comfort.

Wilson and his second wife, Edith, lived here from 1921 until his death in 1924. The house offers a wonderfully preserved glimpse into the 1920s, with an antique phone, Victrola, radio consoles, and even an early GE refrigerator. The parlor still holds wedding presents the couple received, such as a tapestry from the ambassador to France. Long after Wilson left the presidency, rules were passed to prevent presidents from taking official gifts and memorabilia from the White House, but the Wilson House is peppered with bits and pieces from his days in the White House, such as his White House desk chair and even presidential china.

≡FAST FACT

Rumor has it that Wilson's ghost haunts the house, shuffling up and down stairs with the aid of his cane (which he used after a stroke), still disgruntled that his plans for the League of Nations did not come to fruition in his lifetime.

Special events at the Wilson House include a preservation garden party in May and a spot on the annual Kalorama and Embassy tour in September. There is a small gift shop on the premises that sells Wilson memorabilia, including replicas of the Wilson china pattern.

Location and Hours

The Woodrow Wilson House is located on S Street NW and is accessible from the Dupont Circle Metro station. Hours of operation are Tuesdays through Sundays from 10:00 A.M. to 4:00 P.M. You cannot wander the house on your own, but docents offer tours beginning every half-hour. Admission is $5 for adults and $4 for children. The house is closed on federal holidays, Thanksgiving Day, Christmas Day, and New Year's Day.

Decatur House

✉748 Jackson Place NW

✆202-842-0920

✍*www.decaturhouse.org*

This red-brick Federal-style home was considered one of the first "decent" homes in the city when it was built in 1817. A War of 1812 naval hero and commodore, Stephen Decatur hired Benjamin Latrobe, who also contributed to the design of the U.S. Capitol, to design his home. It quickly became a gathering place for the city's upper crust until Commodore Decatur was killed in a duel only fourteen months after moving in.

His widow moved to Georgetown and quickly sold the house, which over the years has been home to Henry Clay, Martin Van Buren, and George Dallas. In the 1870s it was bought by a California family, who furnished it according to the Victorian tastes of the time.

There is a large gift shop with an excellent selection of Americana and Victorian gifts. Special events include a showing of quilts with architectural themes in January and February; Mother's Day Open House in May; participation in the Federal City walking tour and Lafayette Square Open House in September, and a three-week-long nineteenth-century Christmas display in December.

Location and Hours

Located on the corner of Jackson Place and H Street in Lafayette Square, the Decatur House is accessible from the Farragut West and Farragut North Metro stations. Hours of operation are Tuesdays through Fridays from 10:00 A.M. to 3:00 P.M. and Saturdays and Sundays from noon to 4:00 P.M. Docents lead tours every half-hour that last about forty minutes. Tours are $4 for adults and $2.50 for students and seniors.

The Octagon Museum

✉ 1799 New York Ave. NW
✆ 202-638-3105
✐ *www.archfoundation.org*

One of the oldest houses in the city (from 1789 to 1801), this was the temporary home of Dolley Madison and President

Madison—they lived here while the White House was rebuilt after it burned down. The Madisons could watch the White House being constructed from the windows of this six-sided house; the children of its first occupants gave it its current name. Madison signed the Treaty of Ghent that ended the War of 1812 in the circular room at the circular desk on the second floor.

🧳 TRAVEL TIP

The Freedom Plaza is a national park that lies between the Ronald Reagan Building, the National Theatre, the Warner Theatre, and the J.W. Marriott Hotel near the Federal Triangle Metro station. The park is named after the freedom rally in which Martin Luther King Jr. delivered his "I Have a Dream" speech. In the summer, there are concerts and performances. It is also a favorite hangout for the city's skateboarders.

The townhouse was designed by Dr. William Thornton, one of the many architects of the U.S. Capitol building. It was built for the wealthy Tayloe family, who lived here with their fifteen children and slaves. The house has a number of unique design features, such as a three-story oval staircase and hidden doors. The English basement features a working kitchen and the servants' quarters, which offer a glimpse of what life was like for servants during this time.

After the Tayloes moved out, the house became a girls' school and eventually became a boarding house. The museum is now run by the American Architectural Foundation, which puts up changing exhibits about American architecture.

Location and Hours

The Octagon Museum is located on New York Avenue NW and is accessible from the Farragut West Metro station. Hours of operation are Tuesday through Sunday from 10:00 A.M. to 4:00 P.M.; the museum is closed Monday. Guided tours are offered every half hour at a fee of $5 for adults and $3 for students and seniors.

Heurich House

✉ 1307 New Hampshire Ave. NW

☎ 202-429-1894

Even if you do not like meandering around old houses, the Heurich House is a one-of-a-kind experience and should not be missed. Eccentric beer magnate Christian Heurich, whose grandson has revived the family business and now offers a Foggy Bottom Ale on sale throughout the city, built it at the turn of the century.

The house is a unique combination of German beer garden and ornate Victorian flourishes. From the outside it looks like a castle, with a tower and arched portico doorway and a handful of gargoyles and carved human heads and animals thrown in as design elements.

Inside, the Heurich House is crammed full of the carved wooden panels, wainscoting, and matching furniture that was popular with the nouveau riche of the time but that rarely survives today. The front parlor's ceiling is a painting of blue sky with angels of the seasons. The dining room is wall-to-ceiling carved oak and mahogany with matching fireplaces; carved wooden tables and chairs feature berries, fruit, and animals. The hallway is mauve with a stenciled gold fleur-de-lis-pattern. On the lower level, where the kitchen is, there is a tavern room where Heurich had eight German drinking mottoes painted as frescos on the walls, offering such wisdom as "There is room in the smallest chamber for the biggest hangover."

Heurich had suffered two fires in his beer factories, so he ordered that his home be fireproof. As a result, this house on Dupont Circle is one of the first private residences in the country that used poured concrete as a foundation and is the first fireproof building in the city. Heurich was ahead of his time in many building innovations. His was one of the first homes to use electricity throughout the house (because of his fear of fire) as well as a "speaking tube" to communicate from one floor to the other and an electric bell system. He also used a coal-burning steam boiler to heat the house.

There's a small shop on the premises that sells old postcards of Washington, D.C., and Victorian tea items and that also features a section for children. You will also find a Victorian garden that is open to the public. During the holiday season, the house is done up with Victorian Christmas decorations.

Location and Hours

The Heurich House is located on the corner of Twentieth Street and New Hampshire Avenue. You can get there from the Dupont Circle Metro station. The museum has recently reopened under new management, so call for hours. Admission is $3 for adults and $2 for students and seniors. Docent-guided tours are $5.

🚶 JUST FOR PARENTS

If you want to take a break from museums, take a stroll around Lincoln Park (East Capitol Street between 11th and 13th Streets NE). Although the park honors Abraham Lincoln and features a statue of him that was commissioned in 1876, the real draw here is the Emancipation Statue. This statue, which was built from funds raised by freed slaves, depicts Archer Alexander, the last slave captured under the Fugitive Slave Law, breaking the chains of slavery while President Lincoln reads the Emancipation Proclamation.

Cedar Hill

✉ 1411 W St. SE
☎ 202-426-5961

This last home of Frederick Douglass—freed slave, author, civil and women's rights orator, and U.S. Marshall of the District of Columbia in 1877—is far off the beaten track, but the tour is well worth it.

Frederick Douglass was the first African-American who was nationally renowned as a civil rights leader. After he escaped from slavery and purchased his freedom, he wrote and published his autobiography, *Life of Frederick Douglass*, which became an international bestseller. He traveled extensively throughout the north and the world, telling firsthand of the injustices and horrors of slavery in the South.

When he returned to the United States, he printed an abolitionist newspaper out of Rochester, New York, and oversaw the Rochester activities of the Underground Railroad. When he attended the first women's-rights convention in 1848, he also became an ardent supporter of rights for women.

Douglass became a confidant to Presidents Abraham Lincoln and Andrew Johnson regarding black suffrage, but he turned down Johnson's offer to be the head of the Freedman's Bureau. Instead, he became the first president of the Freedman's Bank, where he thought he could do more good.

He served the country as U.S. Marshall, recorder of deeds in Washington, D.C., and the American consul-general to Haiti. When he died in 1895, thousands attended his funeral.

═FAST FACT

Starting with its role as the mecca for freed slaves during and after the Civil War, and continuing through this century as the site of many major civil rights demonstrations, Washington, D.C., has one of the nation's most extensive groupings of sites of historic significance to African-Americans. However, most of them are not close together.

Douglass bought Cedar Hill, a twenty-one-room mansion on a hill overlooking the Capitol, for $6,700 as a bankruptcy foreclosure and broke the neighborhood's "whites only" barrier. He moved into the house at the age of sixty, and walked the two miles to the Capitol every morning. He lived here with his first wife and five children for years. When she died, he married his white secretary, an act that many considered scandalous; in response, he said that his first wife had been the color of his mother and his second was the color of his father.

The house is furnished with the memories of a long career in public service. He was a close friend of Harriet Beecher Stowe and Abraham Lincoln, and Mrs. Lincoln had given him one of the president's canes. He had served as the U.S. Ambassador to Haiti, and a prized possession in the house is a leather rocking chair bestowed on him from the people of Haiti. He also had an extensive library and built himself a small brick house in the back of the property where he liked to work alone. Family members dubbed it "the Growlery" because he growled at anyone who bothered him there.

There is a half-hour movie of Douglass's life, which is extremely well done, that plays in the visitors' center. There is also a gift shop that sells copies of his famous autobiography.

Location and Hours

You can reach Cedar Hill by taking the Metro to Anacostia station and transferring to the B2 bus, which stops in front of the house. The house is open daily from 9:00 A.M. to 4:00 P.M., except Thanksgiving Day, Christmas Day, and New Year's Day. A National Park Service Ranger tour is $3 for adults and $1.40 for seniors.

Mary McLeod Bethune House

✉ 1318 Vermont Ave. NW

☎ 202-673-2402

✐ www.nps.gov

Every July 10, there is a birthday celebration at the Victorian residence of Mary McLeod Bethune. Bethune, one of seventeen children of freed slaves, advised Franklin Delano Roosevelt and three other presidents and created the National Council of Negro Women. She was also the founder of Bethune-Cookman College in Daytona, Florida. The visitors' center shows a twenty-five-minute film on Bethune's life. This is also the site of the National Archives for Black Women's History, which is open by appointment. There is a treasure hunt through the Council house for children.

Location and Hours
You can reach the Mary McLeod Bethune House from McPherson Square Metro station. Tours are available Mondays through Saturdays from 10:00 A.M. to 4:00 P.M.

Churches and Cathedrals

Washington, D.C., also has several historic churches and cathedrals that are open to visitors. You don't have to be religious to appreciate their art and architecture.

Franciscan Monastery
✉1400 Quincy St. NE
✆202-526-6800

Located on forty-four acres of land, the monastery is dotted with replicas of Holy Land shrines surrounding a turn-of-the-twentieth-century Byzantine-style church. Tours of Roman-style catacombs are given on the hour. Visit the monastery Monday through Saturday from 9:00 A.M. to 4:00 P.M. and on Sunday from 1:00 to 4:00 P.M. The monastery is about three-quarters of a mile away from the Brookland/CUA Metro station.

St. John's Episcopal Church
✉16th & H Sts. NW
✆202-347-7866

Called the Church of Presidents, this nineteenth-century Episcopalian church has seen every president from James Madison to Bill Clinton worship here. The church is located in Lafayette Square and is accessible from the Farragut West and Farragut North Metro stations.

St. Matthew's Cathedral
✉1725 Rhode Island Ave. NW
✆202-347-3215
🖱*www.stmatthewscathedral.org*

St. Matthew's is open Sundays through Fridays from 6:30 A.M. to 6:30 P.M. and on Saturdays from 7:30 A.M. to 6:30 P.M. You can take a guided tour on Sunday at 2:30 P.M. Most Washingtonians pass this red-brick church without realizing it was the site of John F. Kennedy's funeral in 1963. You can reach St. Matthew's Cathedral from the Farragut North or Dupont Circle Metro stations.

Calvary Baptist Church
✉755 8th St. NW
✆202-347-8355
🖱*www.calvarydc.com*

One of the oldest black churches in D.C. and one of the stops on the Underground Railroad, this church was attended by General Oliver Howard, one of the founders of Howard University. The church is accessible from Gallery Place/Chinatown Metro station.

Ebenezer Methodist Church
✉420 D St. SE
✆202-544-1415

This church was the site of the first public school for African-Americans. In 1975, the Ebenezer Methodist Church was designated as a landmark by the D.C. government. The church is open to visitors Mondays through Fridays from 8:30 A.M. to 3:00 P.M. You can get there by taking the Metro to the Capitol South station.

CHAPTER 11

Other Attractions

NOT ONLY IS WASHINGTON, D.C., a great city for museums and historical and government sites, but it has some truly fabulous buildings and arts centers that compete with those of other major cities, some that are truly unique.

Much of D.C. was built in the 1950s and 1960s. It is an American city that features significant architectural accomplishments of the International architectural style of glass and steel, such as the Martin Luther King Jr. Memorial Library and the Kennedy Center.

John F. Kennedy Center for the Performing Arts

✉2700 F St.

✆1-800-444-1324

⌨*www.kennedy-center.org*

The John F. Kennedy Center for the Performing Arts (known as the Kennedy Center) is a living memorial tribute to President Kennedy and is our nation's premier performing arts center. It houses four theaters and is home to the National Symphony Orchestra, the Washington Opera, and the American Film Institute.

The Kennedy Center is built on seventeen acres of land over-looking the Potomac. It was designed by Edward Stone (who designed the General Motors building in New York) in the International architectural style of the 70s, with lots of marble and glass.

The John F. Kennedy Center Tour

The free fifty-minute guided tour starts at the Hall of Nations, where the flags of the countries that the United States has diplo-matic relations with are on display, in alphabetical order. Throughout the Kennedy Center are gifts sent by various nations, such as the Swedish modern chandeliers and the Belgian mirrors. Even the marble was a gift, contributed by Italy.

The next stop on the tour is the Grand Foyer, where free con-certs are given and the signature giant bronze bust of President Kennedy (sculpted by Robert Berks) is on view. It is also the recep-tion area for all three theaters on the main floor.

TRAVEL TIP

The Millennium Stage at the John F. Kennedy Center for the Performing Arts features free concerts for 400 people every evening at 6:00 P.M. (The concerts are also broadcast on the Internet). The series was started in 1997 as part of the Performing Arts for Everyone Initiative, and it has been so successful that a mirror project was started in 1998 on the grounds of the U.S. Capitol during the summer months.

The tour will take you through the Israeli Room, where panels depicting scenes from the Old Testament adorn the walls, and the African Room, which displays beautiful tapestries donated by var-ious African nations. You'll then continue through the Concert Hall, which is the largest auditorium in the building with 2,700 seats, where the National Symphony Orchestra performs.

Next, you'll tour the Opera House, which has 2,200 seats and an interior décor of red and gold. There is also a smaller Eisenhower Theatre, which seats 1,100 and is wood paneled, and the newer Terrace Theatre, which was donated by Japan as a bicentennial gift. The Terrace Theater is used for chamber concerts.

There are also two smaller theaters: the Theatre Lab, which seats 380 people, and the American Film Institute's theater, which seats 200. You will end your tour in the Hall of States, where the flags of the fifty states and four territories are displayed in the order they joined the nation.

The view from the Roof Terrace Restaurant is stupendous. If there are no performances, you will be allowed to visit. If a performance is in progress in the restaurant, they don't want to disturb the diners who are watching. You can just go up to the Roof Terrace and take a look as part of the tour or on your own, if it's not closed. In addition to the Roof Terrace Restaurant, the center boasts another restaurant, and there's also a gift shop.

Location and Hours

The Kennedy Center is located on F Street, near New Hampshire Ave. and 25th Street NW (at Rock Creek Parkway at the tip of F Street). Take the Metro to the Foggy Bottom station and transfer to a free shuttle. Parking is also available on site.

The Kennedy Center is open daily for tours from 10:00 A.M. until midnight. Free guided tours are given Mondays through Fridays from 10:00 A.M. to 5:00 P.M. On Saturdays and Sundays the hours are 10:00 A.M. to 1:00 P.M.

You can obtain free tickets for Millennium performances (at 6:00 P.M. daily) by writing to your representative or senator before your arrival. Tickets to other performances run between $10 and $75, depending on the event, but tickets are half-price for seniors and students. The box office is open Monday through Friday from 10:00 A.M. to 5:30 P.M.

Folger Shakespeare Library

✉201 E. Capitol St. SE
☎202-544-7077
✎*www.folger.edu*

This incredible collection of Shakespearean plays, memorabilia, and artifacts was amassed by an Amherst student after hearing Ralph Waldo Emerson lecture on his love of the Bard. Henry Clay Folger began the collection by buying a cheap set of Shakespeare's plays and from there went on to put together the world's largest collection of Shakespeare's printed works, now housed in the Folger Shakespeare Library.

On the exterior of the marble building are nine raised art deco reliefs depicting scenes from Shakespeare's plays. A statue of Puck, from *A Midsummer's Night Dream,* stands in the west garden, and there are quotes from Shakespeare and his contemporaries etched onto the façade.

On the east side of the building is an Elizabethan garden, with flowers and herbs from Shakespeare's time. In warm weather the garden is included in the library tour.

☂RAINY DAY FUN

The Folger Library has a great interactive Web site for kids, featuring games and fun facts from the collection. In addition, every Saturday morning there is a performance workshop for families with children ages 8 to 14 on such things as Elizabethan swordplay. Tickets are $10. There's usually a matinee performance, so it might be fun to perform in a Shakespeare play in the morning and then see one that afternoon!

The Library

The Folger Library is an active research center for both Shakespearean scholars and those who wish to research English and Renaissance history and literature. There are more than a quarter of a million books on hand, many of which are very rare, such as early editions of Shakespeare's plays. The collection also features a number of rare Renaissance manuscripts, musical instruments, costumes, and paintings. The Reading Room, which is only open to the public in April during the library's annual celebration of Shakespeare's birth, houses a replica of the bust of Shakespeare on view at Stratford's Trinity Church. At the other end is a stained-glass window showing the seven ages of man from *As You Like It*.

TRAVEL TIP

Washington, D.C., has one of the best Shakespearean theater companies in the country, dedicated to classical theater. The Shakespeare Theatre in the Nation's Capital performs five Shakespeare plays a year at its home—downtown at 516 8th Street SE—and two weeks of free Shakespeare every summer at the "Shakespeare Free for All" in Rock Creek Park. Call ☎202-547-3230 for information.

The interior Great Hall is chock-full of Shakespeare-related decor, from the wood-paneled walls with a carved relief of the Bard, to the painted plaster ceiling depicting Shakespeare's coat of arms, to the tiled floor inlaid with the masks of Comedy and Tragedy.

Other Facilities

Special exhibits on the works of Shakespeare, as well as other Renaissance interests, are on view throughout the year. The Library also hosts PEN-Faulkner readings, poetry readings, and a concert series. There is a performance space designed to resemble an Elizabethan theater with a three-tiered gallery, carved oak columns, and a sky balcony at the end of the Great Hall. Performances are given here throughout the year.

There is also an extensive gift shop on the premises.

Location and Hours

The Folger Shakespeare Library is located on Capitol Street, near the Capitol South Metro station. Visitor hours are Monday through Saturday from 10:00 A.M. to 4:00 P.M.; the library is closed on federal holidays. Free guided tours are offered at 11:00 A.M. Matinee performances are held every Saturday.

Union Station

✉50 Massachusetts Ave. NE
✆202-289-1908
🖰*www.unionstationdc.com*

Built at the turn of the century during the great railroad age, Union Station was once the largest railway station in the world. It was an important center of Washington, D.C., life for many years. (Roosevelt's funeral train left here amidst thousands of mourners.) The station later fell into disrepair and became a place that people avoided. In 1981 it was renovated to the tune of $160 million and has once again become an important part of Washington's bustling life. It is now the site of a number of charity events and gala evenings, hosted in the station's Main Hall beneath its ninety-six-foot-high gilded vaulted ceiling. The Main Hall is visited by 25 million people annually, making it the most visited site in the capital.

Daniel Burnham incorporated a number of neoclassical design elements and American motifs in his designs of the station. The design was based on the ancient Baths of Diocletian and the Arch of Constantine in Rome, featuring arches, Ionic columns, and 100 eagles on the white-granite façade. In front of the building is a replica of the Liberty Bell, and a huge statue of Columbus greets visitors as they disembark and grab a cab. Above the arched entryway are six carved figures representing Fire, Electricity, Freedom, Imagination, Agriculture, and Mechanics.

Inside the Main Hall are a total of forty-eight statues of Roman soldiers designed by Augustus Saint-Gaudens (one each for the states that were in existence at the time of the station's construction). The

East Hall, with its marble walls, a hand-stenciled skylight, and bright murals, is now a shopping arcade that features more than 135 stores from Ann Taylor to The Gap.

A number of very good restaurants are featured in the Main Hall of the Station (America, B. Smith, Thunder Grill), as well as a food court on the lower level that supplies more than forty varieties of faster food, from burgers to sushi. The lower level also features a nine-theater movie complex, where films are shown in the carved-out underground passageways of the former train station.

≡ FAST FACT

The larger-than-life bronze statue that welcomes visitors to Union Station when they arrive by train at Gate C depicts Philip Randolph, the founder of the Sleeping Car Porters Union and the civil rights activist who organized the famous 1963 March on Washington.

Location and Hours

Union Station is located on Massachusetts Avenue. Both Amtrak trains and Greyhound buses come and go from the station, as well as the D.C. Ducks and Old Town Trolley tours. The station is open twenty-four hours a day, but most restaurants and the movie theaters close by 11:00 P.M.

If you go to the Union Station Web site, ✐www.unionstation dc.com, you can print out a coupon for 15 percent off at many of the 135 shops and cateries in the station.

Washington National Cathedral

✉Massachusetts and Wisconsin Avenues NW
✆202-537-6200
✐www.cathedral.org

Designed to be "Your Church in the Nation's Capital" (it is an Episcopal church with a nondenominational congregation), the

Washington National Cathedral stands higher than the Washington Monument and crowns a fifty-seven-acre plot of land at the capital's highest point. It is the sixth largest cathedral in the world and took a total of eighty-three years to complete (in 1990).

This church is designed in the fourteenth-century English Gothic style, complete with flying buttresses. It has many beautiful stained-glass windows, but the one that draws the most attention is the "space" window commemorating Apollo 11, which contains a chunk of moon rock.

Its exterior and interior feature an incredible collection of gargoyles from the traditional to one that looks like Darth Vader, which was designed by a twelve-year-old boy in an annual competition. New gargoyles are added every year.

═FAST FACT

The Darth Vader gargoyle at the National Cathedral is one of the most famous offbeat sights in the capital. It was designed by twelve-year-old Christopher Rader, who read of the national competition for children in *National Geographic* magazine. The Darth Vader gargoyle is located on the northwest corner of the nave, and you really need binoculars to see it well.

In the crypts on the lower level lie the sarcophagi of President and Mrs. Wilson, as well as Helen Keller and her companion, Anne Sullivan.

There is an observation gallery that you get to by elevator where you can see a panoramic view of Washington, D.C., from a very different perspective. There is also a lovely garden and an extensive gift shop that offers many gargoyle-related items, tea services, and cookbooks. The selection of jewelry for sale is quite comprehensive.

There are wonderful programs for children offered throughout the week, and an occasional medieval arts-and-craft workshop for children on some Saturdays from noon to 4:00 P.M. You can find afternoon tea being served on Tuesday and Wednesday afternoons. (See Chapter 15 for more information.)

Location and Hours

The cathedral is located at the intersection of Massachusetts and Wisconsin Avenues NW and is accessible from the Tenleytown Metro station, though you should expect a fairly long walk along Wisconsin Avenue or to catch the bus.

Visiting hours are from 10:00 A.M. to 4:30 P.M. daily; the nave level is open weeknights until 9:00 P.M. Daily evensong service is held at 4:00 P.M., with a noon service held Monday through Saturday. Sunday services are held at 11:00 A.M.

Guided tours are given all day and highlight many of the different and offbeat aspects of the cathedral, from a gargoyle tour to a behind-the-scenes tour that takes you up slender staircases. Tours suggest a donation of $2 per adult, $1 per child.

The Pentagon

☎ 703-695-1776

✐ www.defenselink.mil

Since the Pentagon was attacked on September 11, 2001, public touring has been greatly curtailed, but tours are available for groups, and you may be able to schedule a tour or join an existing tour by calling ahead. The side of the building that was hit by the airplane has been completely restored, and the Pentagon has been operating at full capacity.

World's Largest Office Building

The five-sided headquarters of the U.S. military is the world's largest office building and houses more than 24,000 employees. It is huge in every sense of the word, from the 583 acres of land it occupies on to the 17.5 miles of interior corridors, about a mile of which you will have to walk through on the hour-and-a-half tour, so wear very comfortable shoes. Here are some other facts about the Pentagon:

- It is twice the size of the Mercantile Mart in Chicago and has three times the office space as the Empire State Building in New York.
- The 24,000 people who work in the Pentagon park approximately 8,770 cars in sixteen parking lots. There are 4,200 clocks, 691 water fountains, and 284 bathrooms. Two hundred telephone calls are made daily through 100,000 miles of telephone cables.
- The building was designed in such a way that even though there are 17.5 miles of corridors, it takes only seven minutes to walk between any two points in the building!

The Tour

You have to pass through airport-quality security before you begin the tour, which starts at the Concourse area of the Metro station. There is a short film about the development of the Pentagon, which was built just after World War II in sixteen months on former swampland. The new structure consolidated seventeen buildings of the War Department. Tours were offered to the public in 1976 and were expected to be discontinued after the Fourth of July, but they turned out to be very popular so the Pentagon has continued the service.

Part of the tour is a visit to the Air Force Art Collection, which includes some of Walt Disney's early cartoons, which he did while he was an ambulance driver in World War I, as well as more traditional art depicting historic events in air force history. You then pass the executive offices of the U.S. Air Force and the POW Alcove, where paintings of prisoner-of-war camps are displayed. Next you will pass the Marine Corps Corridor and then the Navy Corridor, where models of ships and submarines are on display in glass cases. Then you'll tour the Army Corridor, which displays the army command and divisional flags and 172 army campaign streamers from just after the Revolutionary War to the present.

Next up is the Time-Life Corridor, where civilian artists' paintings of war commissioned by Time-Life during World War I hang. The MacArthur Corridor honors General MacArthur's fifty-two-year military career. The hall of heroes commemorates the 3,409 Medal of Honor recipients. The Military Women's Corridor tells the story of women in the military. The Navajo Code Talkers Corridor honors the 400 Navajo marines who created an indecipherable-to-enemies communication code based on the Navajo language to use during World War II. The two newest additions to the Pentagon tour are the African-Americans Corridor and the Hispanic Heroes Corridor. The Flag Corridor displays state and territorial flags throughout the nation's history.

The Pentagon cafeterias are not open to the public, but there is a mall inside the Pentagon with two banks, an Amtrak station, and a post office.

Location and Hours

The Pentagon is located off I-309; you can get there on the Metro (the Pentagon station); if you choose to drive, be aware that limited parking is available. Guided tours are offered Mondays through Fridays from 9:00 A.M. to 3:00 P.M. for parties of ten to forty-five visitors, but you must call ahead for reservations. The Pentagon is closed on weekends and federal holidays.

National Geographic Society's Explorers Hall

✉ 17th & M St. NW
☎ 202-857-7588
✍ www.nationalgeographic.com

Kids love this place almost as much as the huge National Museum of Natural History, and as it's much smaller, it's also easier to visit in a short period of time. There are many interactive exhibits, such as giant slides in a microscope and a display in which kids can touch a tornado. Everyone comes here to see the *Aepyornis maximus* egg from the extinct elephant bird. Other objects on display include a replica of a giant Olmec stone from 32 B.C., the dogsled from Admiral Perry's trek to the North Pole, and a full-scale model of Jacques Cousteau's diving craft.

There's a geology exhibit where you can see inside the Earth and another where you can explore Martian terrain. A theater-in-the-round exhibit explains Earth's weather and ecology.

The Explorer's Hall also has exhibits that change monthly. The museum store has an extensive display of books, science-related toys, and ecological items for kids.

Location and Hours

Located at the intersection of 17th and M Streets NW, the museum is accessible from the Farragut North and Farragut West Metro stations. Visiting hours are Monday through Saturday 9:00 A.M. to 5:00 P.M. and Sunday from 10:00 A.M. to 5:00 P.M. The museum is closed on Christmas Day.

National Aquarium

✉14th and Constitution Ave.
✆202-482-2825
✐*www.nationalaquarium.com*

This is a 125-year-old aquarium, and certainly one of the quirkiest—where else would you find piranhas in a government building? It's small by big-city standards, but that's one of its charms. It's also old and much less high-tech than many other aquariums around the country, which again makes it very child-friendly. There's a tidal pool where kids can touch horseshoe crabs and rather large snails, and there's a fairly large and ominous-looking electric eel.

The big kid-pleasers are the shark and piranha feedings, which take place every day at 2:00 P.M. You can visit the aquarium in the morning (on your way to the Mall) and have your hand stamped to return for the feeding in the afternoon. The alligator exhibit has recently been expanded, and new touch-tanks have been added.

≡FAST FACT

According to the guides at the aquarium, piranhas aren't as vicious as we've been led to believe. When President Roosevelt visited South America and saw a school of piranhas eat a cow that had been lowered into the water, the fish hadn't been fed in a month, and as guides will point out, they are usually not that vicious. To prove the point, a fillet of flounder is lowered into the piranha tank, and it takes a good ten minutes for the rather small fish to eat the whole thing.

Location and Hours

The aquarium is located on the corner of 14th Street and Constitution Avenue, in the basement of the Department of Commerce Building. It is accessible from the Federal Triangle Metro station.

Hours of operation are from 9:00 A.M. to 5:00 P.M. daily; the last admission is at 4:30 P.M. Shark feedings take place on Mondays, Wednesdays, and Saturdays at 2:00 P.M.; the piranhas are fed on Tuesdays, Thursdays, and Sundays at 2:00 P.M.; finally, the alligators are fed on Fridays at 2:00 P.M. Admission is $3.50 for adults and $1 for children ages 2 to 10. The aquarium is closed on weekends.

National Academy of Sciences

✉2100 C St. NW
☎202-334-2436
✎www.nas.edu

Have a young scientist in the family? Take him or her to pose in front of the twenty-one-foot statue of Albert Einstein (by Robert Berks, the same sculptor who did the bust of Kennedy at the Kennedy Center) that adorns the front of the National Academy of Sciences building, and have a picture taken. There's an example of Foucault's pendulum, as well as science-related panels on the walls, depicting some of the greatest scientists in history. The Academy also has changing exhibits on art and science.

Location and Hours

The National Academy of Sciences is located on the corner of C Street and 22nd Street; it's accessible from the Farragut West Metro station. The hours of operation are Monday through Friday, 7:30 A.M. to 5:30 P.M.

Pope John Paul II Cultural Center

✉3900 Harewood Rd. NE
✆202-635-5400
✍*www.jp2cc.org*

The cultural center is a relatively new museum, opened in 2001 in a postmodernist building. The center is devoted to faith and culture; for instance, there's a Polish Heritage Room. Another room features Pope John Paul II's personal memorabilia. The basement level offers interactive activities such as bell ringing. There are special exhibits, as well as a museum store, a café, and a chapel.

Location and Hours

The Pope John Paul II Cultural Center is located on Harewood Road NE. If you don't mind a walk, you can get there from the Brookland/CUA Metro station. The center is open Tuesdays through Saturdays from 10:00 A.M. to 5:00 P.M. and Sundays from noon to 5:00 P.M. Admission is free, but a donation is suggested.

Freedom Park

✉1101 Wilson Blvd., Arlington, Virginia
✆703-284-3710

Until recently, Freedom Park was the site of Newseum, a popular interactive museum dedicated to journalism, its history, and changing technology. Newseum is moving to a new site near the Mall in downtown D.C. in 2006. However, Freedom Park is still worth visiting.

The park is dedicated to the spirit of freedom throughout the world. On display in the park are articles that represent freedom all over the world, including the following:

- A chunk of the Berlin Wall
- A former watchtower
- A toppled, headless statue of Lenin
- A bronze casting of Martin Luther King Jr.'s Birmingham, Alabama, jail-cell door
- Stones from the Warsaw ghetto
- A casting of a South African ballot box

📑 TRAVEL TIP

The New Newseum will encompass six levels and will contain three times the exhibition space of the former Newseum in Arlington. It will be located on Pennsylvania Avenue and 6th Street and is set to open in 2006.

At the center of Freedom Park is the glass and steel Freedom Forum Journalists Memorial, which honors journalists who have died while trying to report the news. The monument bears 1,000 names of journalists, whose deaths date back to 1812.

Location and Hours

Freedom Park is located on Wilson Boulevard in Arlington, Virginia. It is accessible from the Rosslyn Metro station. The park is open from dawn until dusk. Free tours are given every thirty minutes on a first-come, first-served basis from 11:00 A.M. until 2:00 P.M. The tours are limited to twenty people.

Reagan Trade Building

✉ 1300 Pennsylvania Ave. NW
✆ 202-312-1300
🖳 *www.itcdc.com*

One of the newest federal buildings in the city, the Ronald Reagan Building and International Trade Center was designed by James Ingo Freed, the architect for the U.S. Holocaust Museum and Memorial. You'll see a giant slab of the Berlin Wall covered with graffiti when you enter from the Federal Triangle side, and an underground food court that caters to office workers. The walls are lined with contemporary artworks, and there is a gift shop selling Reagan memorabilia. With its Federal Triangle entrance, the Trade Center is also a great air-conditioned shortcut to the Mall on an extremely hot day (or a heated one on a cold day).

Location and Hours

The Reagan building is located on Pennsylvania Avenue NW and is accessible from the Federal Triangle Metro station. It's open during business hours and closed Sundays. The food court is open until 8:00 P.M. Guided tours are available on Mondays, Wednesdays, and Fridays at 11:00 A.M.

Old Post Office Pavilion

✉1100 Pennsylvania Ave. NW
☏202-606-8691
🖱*www.oldpostofficedc.com*

Built in 1899, the Old Post Office Pavilion was once the largest government building in Washington, D.C. It was the first public building with a clock tower and electric power. Only eighteen years after it was built, people began referring to it as "old" because a new post office had been constructed at Union Station.

The old post office was slated for demolition in the 1920s, but the Depression saved the building, which many now appreciate for its design. The building now houses a number of shops, a food court, and the office of TICKETplace (☏202-TICKETS) where you can buy half-price tickets for concert and theater events the day of the show. The Clock Tower is open for tours and offers a splendid view of the city from a vantage point which is the second highest in the city (after the Washington Monument). A statue of Benjamin Franklin stands outside the building to remind us that he was our first postmaster general.

Location and Hours

The pavilion is located on Pennsylvania Avenue NW and is accessible from the Federal Triangle Metro station. Free tours are available daily between 8:00 A.M. and 11:00 P.M.

The *Washington Post* Newsroom

✉1150 15th St. NW
☎202-334-7969

This is a great tour for a budding journalist or anyone interested in Watergate lore. The tour is led by a specially trained *Post* guide who will take you through the newsroom, where you can see reporters gathering information and writing their stories. Stops include prepress production and a visit to the presses, which print the day's papers. You will also be taken to the circulation department and the hot type museum, where you'll see how newspapers were once produced.

Location and Hours

The *Washington Post* building is located on 15th Street NW, near the F Street Metro station. Group tours are offered Mondays from 11:00 A.M. until 3:00 P.M. and take about an hour. To tour the newsroom, you must make reservations well in advance. Children under 11 are not allowed.

CHAPTER 12

Gardens, Parks, and Recreation

WASHINGTON, D.C., is a great outdoor city, with terrific parks and public spaces. From spring until late fall, the National Mall is really a giant park, where you will often see people running, walking dogs, playing Frisbee, and flying a kite. But the city also has a terrific array of parks, playgrounds, recreational facilities, and gardens, as well as circles and squares where you can sit and relax.

Because of its moderate weather, Washington, D.C., is actually a gardener's dream. There are many places to have family picnics and enjoy outdoor sporting activities from ice-skating in the winter to sailing, bicycling, and fishing in the warmer months.

The National Mall

The long lawn between the Jefferson Memorial on the south and the Lincoln Memorial to the west, with the Smithsonian museums and the National Gallery to the east is really a giant park, which is why the National Park Service oversees it. The Mall is lined by 2,000 American elms and the famous 3,000 cherry trees.

At the turn of the last century, the area was a railway yard, but construction of the Smithsonian museums turned it into the public space it is today. Sometimes called the nation's backyard, the Mall is a wonderful public space for national expressions of remembrance, observance, and protest. In the summer months, free screenings of classic movies are shown here.

The Mall is accessible from the Smithsonian, L'Enfant Plaza, and Archives/Navy Memorial Metro stations.

≡FAST FACT

The Smithsonian Carousel is a nineteenth-century carousel that features beautiful horses for kids to ride when the weather is nice. It may remind you of the many merry-go-rounds in Paris that are near all the major sights. The carousel is located across the street from the Arts and Industries Building on the Mall. Kids can take a ride for $2 on weekdays from 11:00 A.M. to 5:00 P.M. or on weekends between 10:00 A.M. and 6:00 P.M.

U.S. Botanic Garden

✉100 Maryland Ave.
✆202-225-8333
www.usbg.gov

The U.S. Botanic Garden is a surprisingly fun place for kids and parents alike. The concept for the creation of a national garden was conceived by our founding fathers, and many of the plants on view here have their roots (literally) in our nation's past.

The newly renovated garden reopened in December 2001, with a new conservatory and lots of exhibits for kids, such as a Jurassic plant re-creation, a tropical rain forest, and many exhibits on endangered plant species, as well as a children's garden. Among its many highlights are the orchid collection, which features 10,000 varieties.

Visitors to the reopened botanical gardens will find new exhibits, upgraded interiors, an enlarged gift shop, and an entrance on Independence Avenue. Themes within the newly renovated glass house focus on plant conservation and endangered species, plant discoveries, orchids, and tropical medicinal plants. Case exhibits explore how plants have influenced the development of civilization, their therapeutic value, and how plants are represented in the arts.

Exhibits in the east half of the conservatory focus on the ecology and evolution of plants. There are exhibits on primitive plants in a reconstructed Jurassic landscape (which is sure to be of interest to kids who are serious about dinosaurs), an oasis, plants of the desert, and a Japanese meditation garden.

The former Palm House has been redesigned as a jungle, representing the reclaiming of an abandoned plantation by the surrounding tropical rain forest. The former Subtropical House has turned into an expanded exhibit of economic plants, focusing on crops that are used to make cosmetics, fiber, food, and industrial products.

The national garden features a First Ladies Water Garden and a lawn terrace for outdoor events. The Showcase Garden displays native plants in ecological settings, such as a wet meadow bog, stream pool, and woodland habitats.

Bartholdi Park

Bartholdi Park, located across the street from the U.S. Botanic Gardens at Independence Avenue, features the botanic gardens home-gardening demonstration landscape, which displays plants that are suitable for urban growth. Among the displays are the following:

- The all-seasons garden, where plants that have four seasons are on display
- The heritage garden, which features North American plantings
- The romantic garden, which features beautiful roses and a secluded park bench
- The rock garden, which features unusual plants in raised rock beds

═FAST FACT

At the entrance of Bartholdi Park, you'll find the Bartholdi Fountain. The park and the fountain are named in honor of Frédéric Auguste Bartholdi, the sculptor of the Statue of Liberty.

Location and Hours

The U.S. Botanic Gardens are located at 100 Maryland Avenue and First Street SW, at the east end of the Mall. Bartholdi Park is located across the street, with entrances on Independence Avenue, Washington Avenue, and First Street. Both are accessible from the Capitol South Metro station.

Admission to all public areas of the U.S. Botanic Garden (USBG) is free. The conservatory is open from 10 A.M. to 5 P.M. daily. Visitors are welcome in Bartholdi Park from dawn until dusk.

U.S. National Arboretum

✉3501 New York Ave. NE
✆202-245-2776
✍www.usna.gov

The National Arboretum is a 446-acre preserve dedicated to research, education, and conservation of trees, shrubs, flowers, and other plants. Among the highlights are the National Bonsai and Penjing Museum, which includes fifty-three miniature trees given to the United States by Japan as part of its bicentennial gift.

The arboretum also features a conservatory for tropical bonsai trees that includes a Japanese garden. Across the road from the bonsai collection, the National Herb Garden features an extensive spread of antique roses and ten specialty herb gardens sorted by their functions, from fragrance herbs to herbs used by Native Americans.

The largest planting of azaleas in the nation can be found at the arboretum, as well as a historic rose garden and the Franklin tree, which is a species of tree now extinct in the wild, discovered by a botanist friend of Benjamin Franklin in 1765. There is also a national grove of state trees.

The arboretum also has a lovely gift shop with all sorts of books about plants, as well as planting and gardening-related paraphernalia. If you call ahead, you can find out about any special workshops or lectures that may be offered on the day of your visit.

Hours and Location

The Arboretum is located on New York Avenue NE. To get there, take the Metro to Stadium Armory station, then transfer to the B2 bus to get to the intersection of Bladensburg Road and R Street NE.

Hours of operation are 8:00 A.M. to 5:00 P.M. daily. The arboretum is closed on Christmas Day. The National Bonsai and Penjing Museum is open from 10:00 A.M. to 3:30 P.M. Admission and parking are free.

Tram tours are available on Saturdays and Sundays from April through October. The forty-minute, narrated, open-air tram tour of the entire site is available at 10:30 A.M., 11:30 a.m., 1:00 P.M., 3:00 P.M., and 4:00 P.M. You can buy tickets at the ticket kiosk in the administration building. Tours are $3 for adults, $2 for seniors, and $1 for children ages 4 to 16.

Other Gardens and Botanical Exhibits

Washington, D.C., is a planned city, and its architect, Pierre L'Enfant, made sure that there would be plenty of gardens and parks to decorate its streets. The many flowers—daffodils, tulips, roses, and the famous cherry blossoms—that line the city's streets provide wonderful green natural beauty in an urban setting.

Enid A. Haupt Garden
✉10th St. and Independence Ave. NW
☎202-357-2700

Enid Haupt, the donor after whom this garden was named, was an avid horticulturist who also has a conservatory named after her in New York's Botanical Gardens. These four acres of gardens, enclosed by the National Museum of African Art, Smithsonian Castle, the Arts and Industries Building, the Sackler and Freer galleries, and the Ripley center, provide a wonderful respite for kids after a long day of touring museums. While most children won't appreciate the central floral bed that copies the rose window design of the Smithsonian Castle, they will enjoy the fountain garden outside the African Art Museum and the large signs explaining various botanical experiments throughout the garden.

Location and Hours

Located in the inner courtyard of the Smithsonian museums on the Mall, the garden is accessible from Smithsonian and L'Enfant Plaza Metro stations. You can visit the Enid A. Haupt Garden from 7:00 A.M. to 9:00 P.M. in the summer and 7:00 A.M. to 5:45 P.M. during colder weather. Admission is free.

Kenilworth Park and Aquatic Gardens

✉ 1900 Anacostia Drive SE

✆ 202-426-6905

✍ www.nps.gov

Kenilworth Aquatic Gardens, a twelve-acre garden devoted to water-living plants, is considered one of D.C.'s greatest natural wonders. There are more than 100,000 water plants, and more than forty ponds are filled with water lilies, lotus flowers, and other aquatic flora. Cattails and yellow flag irises edge the ponds. Completing this watery world, the garden naturally attracts an interesting ecosystem of turtles, snakes, frogs, and ducks.

Bordering all this is the Kenilworth Marsh, the last remaining tidal marsh in the District. Walk the garden's River Trail for spectacular views of the marsh, the Anacostia River, and nearby wooded swamps.

Location and Hours

Not far from the U.S. National Arboretum, Kenilworth Aquatic Gardens are open to the public free of charge. Visitors are welcome to picnic in designated areas. The gardens are open daily until late afternoon, but evening walks can be arranged. The best time to visit is June and July to see the hardy water lilies, and July into August for tropical plants and lotuses.

Washington National Cathedral Gardens

✉Massachusetts and Wisconsin Avenues NW

✆202-537-6200

✍www.cathedral.org

The Washington National Cathedral features fifty-seven acres of gardens above the city. There is a small herb garden, where visitors can purchase herbs, and the Bishop's Garden, which features magnolias, orchids, and other exquisite flowers.

══FAST FACT

The Cathedral Gardens are home to the English Tree, which, according to legend, only blooms on Christmas Day—or when British royalty visits. The tree has lived up to its legend. It has bloomed every Christmas and three other times: in 1951 and 1957 when Queen Elizabeth visited, and in 1981 when Prince Charles was in town.

Location and Hours

The cathedral is located at the intersection of Massachusetts and Wisconsin Avenues NW and is accessible from the Tenleytown Metro station, though you should expect a fairly long walk along Wisconsin Avenue or to catch the bus.

You can stroll around the gardens on your own from 10:00 A.M. until 9:00 P.M. For more information about visiting the cathedral, see Chapter 11.

Brookside Gardens

Wheaton Regional Park, MD
✆301-962-1427
✑*www.brooksidegardens.org*

Just north of the city, this is a 50-acre botanical garden with both indoor and outdoor gardens and two conservatories. Kids will love the annual summer butterfly show. There is also an annual chrysanthemum show featuring the city's landmarks, as well as animals, sculpted out of flowers.

Location and Hours

The gardens are accessible from the Glenmont Metro station. You can visit from sunrise to sunset any day of the year except Christmas Day. Admission is free of charge, though fees do apply to some special programs and events.

Constitution Gardens

✉900 Ohio Drive SW
✆202-426-6841
✑*www.nps.gov*

The Constitution Gardens are composed of forty-five acres of landscaped grounds, which include a lake and an island, and are considered to be one of the prime picnic spots in the capital. Located near the Vietnam Veterans Memorial on the Mall, the gardens are home to 5,000 oak, maple, dogwood, elm, and crabapple trees spread over fourteen acres. The gardens also include a memorial to the signers of the Declaration of Independence. You can reach the Constitution Gardens from the Farragut West Metro station.

Franciscan Monastery Garden

✉1400 Quincy St. NE
✆202-526-6800
✑*www.gardenvisit.com.ge/francis.htm*

The Franciscan Monastery features forty acres of land planted with daffodils, flowering dogwood, cherry, and tulip trees. The garden pathways are lined with authentic replicas of Holy Land shrines. The monastery's greenhouse features hibiscus, lantanas, tiger lilies, giant caladiums and palms, and banana trees.

Location and Hours

Visit the monastery Mondays through Saturdays from 9:00 A.M. to 4:00 P.M. and Sundays from 1:00 to 4:00 P.M. The monastery is about three-quarters of a mile away from the Brookland/CUA Metro station.

▐ TRAVEL TIP

Here's another off-the-beaten-track option. Visit Guston Hall Gardens, located just south of D.C., overlooking the Potomac. The 550 acres of gardens and wooded countryside are home to plants and shrubs that were found there during Colonial times! For more Information, call ✆ 703-550-9220 or visit ✉ www.gustonhall.org.

Lady Bird Johnson Park and Lyndon Baines Johnson Memorial Grove

✆ 703-285-2600

✉ www.nps.gov

The Lady Bird Johnson Park is an island in the Potomac that was built from material dredged from the river in 1916. The resulting park was named after the former first lady in 1968 in honor of her efforts to revamp Washington, D.C.

The island sits at the Virginia end of the Memorial Bridge. In the spring, more than a million daffodils bloom throughout the park and along the highway. At the south end of the park, a fifteen-acre grove of trees was planted in honor of President Johnson and marked by a large block of pink Texas granite.

Location and Hours

To get to the island, you'll need to take the George Washington Memorial Parkway. You can also take the Metro to the Arlington National Cemetery Metro station (the Lyndon Baines Johnson grove is located adjacent to the Arlington National Cemetery). The park is open from sunrise to sunset. Restroom facilities are available from 7 A.M. to 10 P.M.

D.C.'s Parks

In addition to the many beautiful gardens, D.C. offers quite a few options to visitors who are interested in visiting a park—whether to see the memorials, to have a picnic, or to play Frisbee with the kids.

Fort Dupont Park
✉Minnesota and Massachusetts Avenues
✆202-426-7745
✑*www.nps.gov*

One of Washington's largest parks, Fort Dupont offers 376 acres of wooded land, which serve as a friendly haven for picnics, nature walks, and various outdoor sports. Although the Civil War fort itself is no more, earthworks and an explanatory plaque mark the former site. Runaway slaves found safety within its walls; Dupont was one of sixty-eight forts encircling Washington in the 1860s.

Today, the grounds feature a sizable garden, a skating rink, and a sports complex, among other amenities. A hiking-biking trail surrounds the park, while an activity center includes workshops and walks led by park rangers; nature studies; and Civil War exhibits. Most presentations are free, though there is a small charge for the ice rink and sports complex activities. Summers feature weekend jazz concerts at an outdoor stage, free to all.

Location and Hours

The park is located between Minnesota and Massachusetts Avenues at Randle Circle. Take the Metro to the Potomac Avenue station and transfer to a V4 or V6 bus. The activity center's hours vary by season. The center is open Tuesdays through Saturdays in the summer and weekdays only the rest of the year.

TRAVEL TIP

The ruins of some of the other sixty-seven forts may be seen while walking the marked trails that make up the Fort Circle Parks. Maps are available showing the approximate location of the various forts in the ring; call the National Park Service at ✆202-343-4747 for more information.

Potomac Park

✆202-619-7222 (NPS)

✉www.nps.gov

Potomac Park consists of the 722 acres of land around the Tidal Basin surrounding most of the presidential memorials, and it's here that you will find all the lovely Japanese cherry trees. Potomac Park is divided into East Potomac and West Potomac Park.

West Potomac Park includes Constitution Gardens as well as the Vietnam Veterans, Korean War, Lincoln, and Jefferson Memorials and the reflecting pool. East Potomac Park has picnic grounds, three golf courses, a swimming pool, and biking and hiking trails overlooking the Potomac. At the southern tip of the park is Hains Point, which features ball fields, a golf course, picnic grounds, and *The Awakening,* the famous sculpture of a giant emerging from underground.

Rock Creek Park

✉Glover Road

✆202-282-1063 (headquarters)

✆202-426-6829 (Nature Center and Planetarium)

✆202-426-6908 (Peirce Mill)

✆202-426-6851 (Old Stone House)

✉www.nps.gov

Rock Creek Park, established in 1890, is one of the oldest national parks in the country and one of the largest forested urban parks in the United States. The park offers an undisturbed 1,754-acre expanse of urban forest, open fields, and creeks with running water. According to some locals, parts of it are still so wild that you can occasionally see deer in the fall and winter.

The main visitor center is the nature center and planetarium (⊠5200 Glover Road NW) where much of the information on the history of the park is located. You can view exhibits about the park's wildlife, visit a hands-on discovery center for children, view an observation beehive, and get your kids to participate in many child-oriented workshops and activities. The planetarium offers a daily showing of "Tonight's Sky" at 4:00 P.M., and a weekend showing of "The Night Sky" at 1:00 P.M. Programs last between forty and sixty minutes. From April through November there are meetings of the National Capital Astronomers, who hold a once-a-month evening stargazing session.

The park's grounds contain a wealth of hiking and biking trails, picnic facilities, tennis courts, a skating rink, horseback riding, and a golf course. Call ahead for fees and reservations.

≡FAST FACT

Rock Creek Park contains the Old Stone House, the oldest house in Washington, D.C., and Peirce Mill (currently closed for renovations), which was once an active gristmill where corn and wheat were ground into flour using water power from Rock Creek. The park grounds also contain remains of Civil War fortifications, including Fort Stevens, the site of the only battle within the District of Columbia during the Civil War.

Location and Hours

You can reach Rock Creek Park via public transportation. Take the Metro to Friendship Heights, then transfer to E2 bus, which should take you to the intersection of Glover and Military Roads.

The park is open seven days a week during daylight hours. The nature center and planetarium are open Wednesdays through Sundays from 9:00 A.M. to 5:00 P.M. The Old Stone House is open Wednesdays through Sundays from 9:00 A.M. to 4:00 P.M. These features are all closed New Year's Day, Fourth of July, Thanksgiving, and Christmas Days.

Admission to the planetarium is free, but you must pick up tickets at the nature center in advance.

Discovery Creek Children's Museum
✉4954 MacArthur Blvd.
✆202-337-5111
✍www.discoverycreek.org

Located in the only remaining one-room schoolhouse in Washington, D.C., this children's museum's focus is on interacting with nature, since it lies in the beautiful Glen Echo Park. The museum's events change seasonally, especially since so much of the program is based on interacting with nature.

Location and Hours
The children's museum is located on MacArthur Boulevard. Take the D6 Metrobus to Silbey Hospital, and get off at the intersection of MacArthur and Ashby Avenues. You can tour the schoolhouse on Saturdays from 10:00 A.M. to 3:00 P.M. and on Sundays from noon to 3:00 P.M. Admission is $4 for children; free for adults.

Theodore Roosevelt Island
✆703-285-2598
✍www.nps.org

Roosevelt Island is a memorial to the conservation efforts of President Teddy Roosevelt. Soon after his death in 1919, a memorial association was put together to purchase the ninety-one-acre island for this purpose.

Roosevelt Island is one of the locals' favorite places to picnic and just enjoy the wooded outdoors. There are a number of trails through the marsh, swamp, and forest where visitors can see birds and small mammals. There is also an outdoor memorial with a statue of Roosevelt, with quotes about his conservation beliefs. You can also rent canoes at Thompson Boat Center.

Location and Hours

The park is open seven days a week during daylight hours. The nearest Metro station is Rosslyn. Get off there, then walk across the pedestrian bridge at Rosslyn Circle. By car, take the George Washington Memorial Parkway exit north from the Theodore Roosevelt Bridge.

Sports and Recreation

If you are interested in staying active while you're visiting D.C., this city has a lot to offer. There are hiking and biking trails, boating opportunities, tennis courts, golf courses, and more.

Hiking Paths

There are many hiking paths throughout the urban area and, therefore, many local hiking clubs. The *Washington Post* weekend section always lists hiking activities of the local clubs, which you can usually join. In addition, the C&O Canal in Georgetown has an eighteen-mile hiking path, which is fairly easy, so you can take slightly older children.

Both Rock Creek and Theodore Roosevelt Island have extensive hiking trails, but they are slightly more rugged. The hiking paths along East Potomac Park are fairly easy to navigate. There are also hiking trails in Mount Vernon.

Bike Paths

Again, check the *Washington Post* weekend section for bicycling tours, or call one of the many organized bicycling tours. (Bike the Sites ☎202-966-8662 is the best known.) If you want to rent bikes and ride through a park, you can do so at Fletcher's Boat House at the C&O Canal ☎202-244-0461 or at Thompson Boat Center ☎202-333-9543 in Rock Creek Park. You can also rent bikes at Big Wheel Bikes, ✉1034 33rd Street NW in Georgetown, which is right near the C&O Canal and its extensive bike path.

There is also a new seven-mile bike path that takes you from Georgetown to Bethesda, Maryland, along an abandoned railroad track on the Potomac known as the Capital Crescent Trail.

💼 TRAVEL TIP

You can rent a two-seater or four-seater paddleboat at the Tidal Basin. Kids also love the mule barge rides at the C&O Canal, where boat guides, dressed in costumes from the 1870s, often have a box of old-fashioned toys for kids to play with.

Canoes and Paddle Boats

Thompson Boat Center (☎202-333-9543) in Rock Creek Park rents canoes, kayaks, rowing boats, and paddle boats, as long as you leave a photo I.D. and a credit card with your rental fee. Fletcher's Boat House (☎202-244-0461) on the C&O Canal also rents canoes and rowboats and sells fishing licenses, with bait and tackle.

Tennis

There are public tennis courts at Rock Creek Park (☎202-722-5949) and East Potomac Park (☎202-554-5962), but you should call ahead for availability and fees. The D.C. Department of Parks and Recreation (☎202-673-7660) will also give you a list of other outdoor tennis courts in the district.

Ice Skating

The newly opened National Gallery of Art Sculpture Garden (☎202-737-4215) offers ice-skating on the fountain pool in the winter. You can also skate on the C&O Canal in the winter (☎301-299-3613), but you must bring your own skates. Pershing Park at 14th Street and Pennsylvania Avenue (☎202-737-6938) also features outdoor skating.

Horseback Riding

The stables at Rock Creek (☎202-362-0117), near the nature center, offer a one-hour guided trail tour on Tuesdays, Wednesdays, and Thursdays.

Fishing

The Potomac River is a great place for freshwater fishing with a good catch of smallmouth bass, rainbow trout, and perch. There are several fly-fishing shops and guides in Georgetown, Arlington, and Alexandria.

Sailing

The Potomac is a great river for sailing. There are several marinas on the southwest waterfront, as well as in Old Town Alexandria and Arlington. Lessons and rentals are available at the Washington Sailing Marina, just south of Reagan National Airport on US 1.

🚶 JUST FOR PARENTS

If you would like to play golf, you've got two options. The two public golf courses in D.C. are in Rock Creek Park (☎202-882-7332) and East Potomac Park (☎202-554-7600). Call for fees and other information.

Professional Sports

Washington has a full array of professional sports teams—the only sport it fails to host a team for is baseball, although there are always rumors that a team will be fielded again someday.

Washington Redskins

www.redskins.com

The Redskins play football at the FedEx field in nearby Landover, Maryland. Tickets are hard to come by for regular season games, but preseason games are generally available.

Washington Capitals

202-661-5050
www.washingtoncaps.com

Hockey fans can watch the Washington Capitals at the MCI Center. It is possible to get tickets at the box office or over the phone.

Washington Wizards

202-661-5050
www.nba.com

If you're lucky, you might be able to catch a game with Michael Jordan's former home team at the MCI Center.

Washington Mystics

202-661-5050
www.wnba.com

The newest member of the Washington professional teams, the Mystics are a female basketball team in the WNBA league. They play at the MCI Center.

D.C. United and Washington Freedom

703-397-5450 (D.C. United)
202-547-3137 (Washington Freedom)

The three-time MLS Cup champions, D.C. United play their games at the RFK Stadium. The Washington Freedom, the women's soccer team, has a growing fan base.

CHAPTER 13

Shopping in D.C.

SHOPPING IN THE NATION'S CAPITAL is surprisingly diverse and exciting. Of course, there's a wealth of souvenirs available from street vendors, museum shops, and tourist attractions, but D.C. itself has a number of terrific outdoor flea markets that offer everything from handmade jewelry to ceramics, and fabulous consignment shops where you can buy slightly worn designer clothing. Georgetown also features a wealth of trendy shops.

D.C. and the surrounding areas also have a number of malls and shopping centers and three great outlet centers that bring shoppers from Maryland and Virginia. And Dupont Circle features an incredible collection of first-rate art galleries, offering works by local artists and internationally famous ones, as well as a terrific selection of new- and used-book stores.

💼 TRAVEL TIP

T-shirt wagons and souvenir stands line the side streets of the Mall and the streets along 10th and F Streets surrounding Ford's Theatre and the Petersen House. If you are planning on taking T-shirts or hats to the folks back home, these street vendors offer a good selection of FBI and Washington, D.C., tie-dyes at a fraction of the cost of more expensive locations. Some offer miniature D.C. monument paperweights and large Lincoln penny souvenirs as well.

Markets and Fairs

Washingtonians are lucky urban dwellers. They have some of the best year-round markets and craft and food fairs in the country because of the mostly mild weather and the many farms that surround the city in neighboring Virginia and Maryland.

Eastern Market

✉225 7th St. SE
✆202-546-2698
✎*www.easternmarket.net*

This is an all-week indoor market with a weekend crafts fair. Outside there are arts-and-crafts vendors (many of whom take MasterCard and/or Visa) where you can buy homemade jewelry, soaps, ceramics, and clothing and even get a tarot card reading. Indoors there's a fantastic sit-down counter with the best blueberry buckwheat pancakes, and specialty meat-and-cheese shops that rival the best that New York and Paris have to offer. The market is open on Tuesdays through Fridays from 10:00 A.M. to 6:00 P.M., on Saturdays from 8:00 A.M. to 6:00 P.M., and on Sundays from 8:00 A.M. to 4:00 P.M. Accessible by the Metro Eastern Market station.

Dupont Market

This is a wonderful seasonal farmer's market with grand floral displays and terrific homemade organic fare (sausages and cheeses) and homemade specialties (jams and even chocolates), and there are usually free samples.

Dupont Market is located on Twentieth Street between Q Street and Massachusetts Avenue NW. It's open every Sunday from April through December from 9:00 A.M. to 1:00 P.M.

Georgetown Flea Market

Another Sunday market, this is one where you can browse through antiques, from home furnishings to old records and vintage clothing, as well as food, candy, and dessert vendors. Open year-round, weather permitting, the Georgetown Flea Market is located on Wisconsin Avenue, between S and T Streets, NW.

Shopping for Souvenirs

Washington souvenirs are fun to shop for. You can bring home anything from an FBI baseball cap purchased from a street vendor to a Planet Hollywood T-shirt. But it's also a lot of fun to visit the souvenir shops and see what they have to offer in terms of miniature Washington monument paperweights or commemorative plates.

Capital Coin and Stamp
⊠ 1701 L St. NW
✆ 202-296-0400

This is a shop that specializes in political paraphernalia, so it's perfect for the nation's capital. The merchandise here is mainly post–World War II objects, although there are items going as far back as Lincoln's time. The offerings include buttons, bumper stickers, and T-shirts, as well as video- and audiotapes of famous speeches. To visit the Capital Coin and Stamp shop, take the Metro to the Metro Center station.

Destination D.C.
⊠ 50 Massachusetts Ave.
✆ 202-371-6688
✍ *www.destinationclothing.com*

Destination D.C. offers everything your heart could desire in T-shirts and D.C.-related souvenirs such as postcards, buttons, and sports bottles. Most items are under $10.

Destination D.C. is located at Union Station; another branch can be found at the Fashion Center, Pentagon City, in Arlington, Virginia.

Museum Shops

This is almost one of the reasons to go to Washington. You can find great items, at fairly low prices, for just about everyone on your Christmas list, no matter what time of the year you're shopping.

National Building Museum
✉401 F St. NW
✆202-272-2448

This gift shop offers a great selection of antiques and current photographs and witty office-related supplies. The museum is accessible from the Judiciary Square Metro station.

ｉ JUST FOR PARENTS

Adams Morgan and Capitol Hill are the two neighborhoods known for their antiques, even if they're less than fifty years old. You can't possibly go home empty-handed.

International Spy Museum
✉501 Pennsylvania Ave.
✆202-393-7798
✐*www.spymuseum.org*

The International Spy Museum gift shop has a wonderful array of spying gadgets for kids and grownups, as well as clever spy-related jewelry, items from classic television shows, scarves, and note cards. The museum is located on F Street, and it is accessible from the Gallery Place/Chinatown Metro station in the heart of the city.

National Gallery of Art
✉Constitution Ave. NW
✆202-737-4215
✐*www.nga.gov*

The National Gallery of Art's gift shops feature calendars, note cards, journals, wall plaques, scarves, and jewelry based on the permanent collection. There are always some items on sale. The museum is located on Constitution Avenue, between 3rd and 7th Streets on the north side of the Mall. Take the Metro to the National Archives, Judiciary Square, or Smithsonian station.

Corcoran Gallery of Art
✉500 17th St. NW
✆202-639-1700
✐*www.corcoran.org*

The Corcoran gift shop offers a wonderful, somewhat wacky collection of art-related jewelry (often connected to a show), as well as a great selection of Pop Art dishes and glassware, and fun children's art projects. The Corcoran Gallery is located on 17th Street NW, between E Street and New York Avenue. Take the Metro to the Farragut North station.

Phillips Collection
✉1600 21st St.
✆202-387-2151
✐*www.phillipscollection.org*

If you're interested in Man Ray teacups and a great bag with Marjorie Phillips's impressionist painting of American baseball, be sure to stop at the Phillips gift shop when you visit the museum. The Phillips is located on 21st Street NW at Q Street. If you take the Metro to the Dupont Circle station (the Q Street exit), it's a short walk to the museum.

National Museum of Women in the Arts
✉1250 New York Ave. NW
✆202-783-5000
✐*www.mnwa.org*

The gift shop of the National Museum of Women in the Arts features an interesting selection of jewelry, women-empowering note cards and journals, glassware, handbags, and lots of hard-to-find books about female artists. The museum is located on New York Avenue and is accessible from the Metro Center Metro station.

Smithsonian Institution Museums

☎ 202-357-2700 (general)

✍ *www.si.edu*

And then, of course, there are the fabulous Smithsonian Institution museums, including the National Air and Space Museum, the National Museum of Natural History, and the National Museum of American History. Each of them is a shopper's delight, and you could easily spend an hour browsing in each one. Air and Space (on 6th Street and Independence Ave.) is a three-floor museum, and has the astronaut ice cream and every Star Trek–related model you could ever want. The Museum of American History (between 12th and 14th Streets on Constitution Avenue) sells a replica of the Hope diamond, as well as all sorts of presidential memorabilia, and incredible Christmas ornaments, such as Dorothy's ruby slippers. You can buy dinosaur-fossil-making kits at the National Museum of Natural History (on 10th Street and Constitution Avenue), as well as those fantastic Smithsonian science-project kits.

═FAST FACT

The Smithsonian Institution publishes an extensive four-color catalog of gifts and souvenirs that features everything from furniture reproductions and jewelry (the Hope diamond copy is here) to prints, scarves, and clothing. You can order the catalog by calling ☎ 1-800-322-0344.

Washington Dolls' House and Toy Museum
✉5236 44th St. NW
✆202-244-0024
⊘www.dollshousemuseum.com

Washington Dolls' House and Toy Museum sells replicas of old toys, as well as wonderful miniature-sized home furnishings for doll houses or collectors. The museum is accessible from the Friendship Heights Metro station.

Malls and Department Stores

Most D.C. department stores are located in malls throughout the city and suburbs; the one exception is Hecht's (⊘www.hechts.com), the only local D.C. department store that stands on its own. Its flagship store, located at 12th and G Streets, has been at that location for more than fifty years, and from there its Christmas display windows have delighted city residents for decades.

Cady's Alley
✉3318 M St. NW, Georgetown
⊘www.cadyalley.com

Cady's Alley is a group of converted nineteenth-century buildings that are home to ten home furnishing and décor shops.

Chevy Chase Pavilion and the Mazza Gallerie
✉5355 Wisconsin Ave.
✆202-686-5335

This upscale mall is located in Friendship Heights and includes more than forty-five specialty shops. There is a Georgette Klinger spa and Filene's Basement, a wonderful discount store. The anchor store in this mall is the Neiman Marcus department store. There's also a movie theater.

Fashion Center at Pentagon City
✉ 1100 Hayes St., Arlington

This is a mega-mall, located near the Pentagon. There are 163 shops here, with Macy's and Nordstrom as the anchors. There is a food court here as well.

Shops at Georgetown Park
✉ 3222 M St. NW
✆ 202-298-5577

This is a lovely mall inside a rehabbed former Colonial-era tobacco warehouse. There are snack spots where you can get pretzels and coffee, and terrific original stores as well as chain store offerings, such as Polo/Ralph Lauren and J. Crew.

Union Station
✉ 50 Massachusetts Ave.
✆ 202-371-9441
✍ *www.unionstationdc.com*

There are at least 150 stores here, from 9 West and B. Dalton to Bath & Body Works and a Discovery Channel store. If you go to the Web site, there is a printable coupon for 15 percent off at many of the stores. There is a forty-kiosk food court on the lower level, along with a nine-screen cinema.

Outlet Shopping

One of the best things about outlet shopping is that if you are a truly savvy shopper, you'll come prepared with coupons to save money on already marked-down merchandise. If you can't find your own coupons, locate the customer service desk and ask if they have any. Sometimes all you have to do is show your AAA membership card.

Leesburg Corner Premium Outlets

✉241 Fort Evans Rd., Leesburg, Virginia

✆703-737-3071

🖝www.outletsonline.com

This sixty-store outlet shop just past Dulles Airport offers popular designer shops at up to 70 percent off, such as DKNY and Tommy Hilfiger, a Gap outlet, as well as an Off Saks Fifth Avenue store. There are also a number of specialty shops selling children's clothes, shoes, and housewares.

Take Route 267 (Dulles Toll Rd./Greenway) or Route 7 to Route 15 N. Follow the signs, and turn right at the top of Ft. Evans Road. Stores are open Mondays through Saturdays from 10:00 A.M. to 9:00 P.M. and on Sundays from 11:00 A.M. to 6:00 P.M.

🧳 TRAVEL TIP

Most outlet centers have a Web site where you can download a certificate for a coupon book, or there might be a coupon for additional discounts in a local travel magazine or guide.

Prime Outlets, Hagerstown

✉495 Prime Outlets Blvd., Hagerstown, Maryland

✆1-888-883-6288

🖝www.primeoutlets.com

Seventy-five minutes outside D.C., this sixty-store outlet and discount center offers many of the same stores as Leesburg, as well as a KB Toys. Go to the Web site or find a customer service booth for discount coupons.

Take I-495 to I-270, which leads to I-70, and exit 29 will lead you to Hagerstown Outlet Center. The outlets at Hagerstown are open Mondays through Saturdays from 10:00 to 9:00 P.M. and on Sundays from 11:00 A.M. to 6:00 P.M. Closed Easter Sunday, Thanksgiving Day, and Christmas Day.

Tyson's Corner Center and Tyson's Galleria

✉1961 Chain Bridge Rd., McLean, Virginia

✆1-888-2TYSONS

✎*www.shoptysons.com*

With more than 400 stores within seven miles of the city, Tyson's is where D.C. goes to shop. There are eight major department stores—among them, Bloomingdale's, Macy's, Hecht's, Nordstrom's and Lord & Taylor as well as The Gap, L.L. Bean, Coach, and a Disney Store. A Rainforest Cafe is here for the kids.

If you e-mail or call Tyson's, you can get a coupon book to use at various stores. Take the Capital Beltway (I-495) to the intersection of Route 7 and 123. The mall is open Mondays through Saturdays from 10 A.M. to 9:30 P.M. and Sundays from 11 A.M. to 6 P.M.

Bookstores

If you're a bookworm, you're in luck. Washington, D.C., has some terrific bookstores, from the serious to the quirky.

A Likely Story Children's Books

✉1555 King St., Alexandria, Virginia

✆703-836-2498

✎*www.alikelystorybooks.com*

Child Magazine called this the best children's bookstore in the country. It's well stocked and has a regular series of readings and character presentations. You can get to the bookstore via the Metro; get off at King Street and walk two blocks east.

Chapter Literary Bookstore

✉1512 K St. NW

✆202-347-5495

This is a very literary bookstore where authors frequently come to give readings—check with the bookstore about the schedule.

Every July, Chapter Literary Bookstore holds a birthday party for Proust, and on Fridays there are free cookies and tea.

Idle Time Books
✉4219 18th St. NW
☎202-232-4774

This is a used-book store in the Adams Morgan section where you can get former bestsellers for as little as $3, since they specialize in used paperbacks. You'll have to hunt, but it's worth your time.

Kramerbooks and Afterwords Café
✉1517 Connecticut Ave. NW
☎202-387-1400

Some people spend the better part of their day at this cyber café, bookstore, and restaurant in Dupont Circle. It's open twenty-four hours on weekend days.

Lantern Bryn Mawr Bookshop
✉3241 P St. NW
☎202-333-3222

This Georgetown used-book store is a favorite for local university students, because you can purchase slightly worn hardcovers for as little as $3 and paperbacks for $1. Old records (lots of '70s rock) and used CDs are also available.

Politics and Prose Bookstore
✉5015 Connecticut Ave. NW
☎202-364-1919

Another Dupont Circle institution, even D.C. politicians come here to shop for books on history, political theory, and scandal. The store often features heavy-duty political speakers and heated discussions, so call for events and scheduling.

Consignment Shops and Thrift Stores

If you have a teenager who's looking for "retro" clothing, or if you're interested in finding a classic Coach bag for yourself, D.C.'s consignment shops and thrift stores are a gold mine.

Clothes Encounters of a Second Kind
✉202 7th St. SE
✆202-546-4004

This is a great consignment shop where you can find bags and shoes and designer suits for a fraction of their original cost. The shop is located across the street from the Eastern Market and is accessible from the Eastern Market Metro station.

Funk & Junk
✉106½ N. Columbus St., Alexandria, Virginia
✆703-836-0748

Funk & Junk is located in Alexandria, but you can reach it via the Metro (King Street station). This thrift shop is a great place for teens looking for old jeans, Hawaiian shirts, and "classic" T-shirts.

Rage Clothing
✉1069 Wisconsin Ave. NW
✆202-333-1069

A Georgetown staple, Rage Clothing features tons of jeans and vintage clothing from the 1970s. There's a $10 bargain section on the second floor.

Secondi Consignment Clothing
✉1702 Connecticut Ave.
✆202-667-1122

Secondi is a store that specializes in secondhand designer clothing, shoes, and accessories.

Toy Stores

Washington, D.C., has a number of delightful independent toy stores that are thriving because the chain toy stores are located in the malls on the outskirts of the city. Many of the stores have a regular program of readings and milk and cookies, so call before you visit.

🧳 TRAVEL TIP

Although D.C. has so many museums, and so many museum stores, even in airports and locations throughout the city, it's hard to find a regular chain toy store in the city itself. You have to go to the suburbs to find a Toys Я Us or a KB Toys.

Child's Play
✉5536 Connecticut Ave. NW

Located in the Friendship Heights neighborhood, this toy store features building toys, computer software, art supplies, and games.

Sullivan's Toy Store
✉4312 Wisconsin Ave. NW
☎202-362-1343

A terrific little toy store for younger children featuring learning games, costumes, stickers, and a great selection of books and stuffed animals. There is an art-supply store next door that might be of interest to slightly older children.

Tree Tops Toys
✉3301 New Mexico Ave. NW
☎202-244-3500

This store specializes in plush dolls, European toys, books, and even children's clothing.

Other Specialty Shops

From a magic shop your kids are sure to enjoy to a comics store and martial arts center, here are a few other shops worth a visit.

Al's Magic Shop

✉ 1012 Vermont Ave. NW

✆ 202-789-2800

✍ *www.alsmagic.com*

Al's Magic Shop is a classic magic shop, with tricks for sale, as well as pranks that children of all ages never seem to get tired of.

Big Planet Comics

✉ 3145 Dumbarton Ave. NW

✆ 202-342-1961

If you're in Georgetown and interested in comic books, this store is a classic. You can get the latest graphic novels and comics, as well as back issues of the old DC and Marvel comics here.

Dollar Station

✉ 1320 U St. NW

✆ 202-232-4052

Everything in the store is a dollar, which is wonderful when your kids want to go on a buying rampage. Sometimes there are local souvenirs for sale, and there's always candy and snacks.

Martial Arts World

✉ 1105 F St. NW

✆ 202-437-2455

If you have a karate kid in your family, you might want to pop into this store, which has a great selection of martial arts videos and DVDs, and all sorts of Kung Fu gear.

CHAPTER 14

Family Dining

WASHINGTON, D.C., IS A GREAT PLACE TO EAT. With so many tourist attractions, there is a restaurant for every palate, from haute cuisine to Japanese teahouses to cafeterias. The museum restaurants can also be surprisingly good (try the Corcoran Café and the restaurant at the National Gallery of Art, or the tiny restaurant at the National Museum of Women in the Arts). And many of the hotel restaurants are surprisingly family-friendly.

There are familiar chains like TGI Friday's and Planet Hollywood as well as the less familiar ones: New York's Smith & Wollensky, Morton's of Chicago, and Washington's own pub chain, Clyde's. There's also a Hard Rock Cafe, a Planet Hollywood, and a Rainforest Cafe (in Virginia) from which you can bring back souvenir Washington, D.C., T-shirts.

🧳 TRAVEL TIP

Special attire recommendations (such as jacket and tie, or no shorts) are noted in the reviews. Otherwise, you should be able to wear whatever you are sightseeing in.

The list of restaurants in this chapter is for sit-down family dining. Many of these restaurants are for slightly older children, ages 7 and up. For families with younger children, the chain or hotel restaurants are probably your best bet for dinner. The listings are organized into sections by location; within each section they are listed in alphabetical order.

Downtown D.C.

Anadale
✉401 7th St. NW
✆202-783-3133

This trendy new hotspot, painted emerald green and mustard yellow with contemporary art on the walls, is located in one of the art gallery centers of Washington, D.C. Chef Alison Swope serves up American/Southern/Santa Fe food that's original and creative, with a good by-the-glass wine list and fabulous desserts. Dinner entrees run $13 to $20; lunch is about half that. Reservations are suggested. Major credit cards are accepted. Take the Metro to the National Archives station.

Arena Cafe
✉521 G St. NW
✆202-789-2055

While the former Velocity Grill in the MCI Center is remodeled into a steakhouse, this nearby restaurant that looks like a diner from the outside is a real treat. It is known for its excellent salads, great crab cake sandwiches, and a full selection of beers. Entrees run $10 to $18. Major credit cards are accepted. Take the Metro to the Gallery Place station.

Bis
✉15th E St. NW
✆202-661-2700

Located in the trendy Hotel George, and now part of the Kimpton Hotel chain, Bis has been one of the hottest restaurants in town for the past few years, so make reservations. Its food is Parisian bistro with an American flair as evidenced by such entrees as calamari with chorizo or duck breast with olives and citrus fruit. Still, the hotel chain is exceedingly family-friendly, and there should be items on the menu for all age groups. Entrees range from $17.50 to $25. Major credit cards are accepted. Take the Metro to the Union Station stop.

Capitol Grille

✉601 Pennsylvania Ave. NW

✆202-737-6200

This is a popular bar and restaurant where locals eat and hang out. Noted for its steaks and dry-aged cuts of beef, there's an aging room on the premises with sides of beef hanging on display. They also serve lobster, large portions of fish, and generous side dishes. Some seats have a view of the Capitol Building. Entrees run $19 to $27. Jacket and tie are strongly suggested. Major credit cards are accepted. Take the Metro to the National Archives station.

Coeur de Lion

✉926 Massachusetts Ave. NW

✆202-414-0500

Located in the Henley Park Hotel, this restaurant is ideal for romantic couples, which is precisely why older children (especially teenage girls) might like it. Coeur de Lion is a local favorite because of its romantic, elegant décor and cozy atmosphere, and it serves a wonderfully rich continental cuisine with an American flair. The cognac-flavored lobster bisque is a favorite, as are the crab cakes, but the menu changes seasonally, and there are a lot of lighter entrees. Desserts are a specialty, so save room for the cheesecake or crème brulée. Entrees run $15 to $22. For men, a jacket is required. This is an intimate restaurant with candlelight tables, so reservations are recommended. Major credit cards are accepted. Take the Metro to the Metro Center station.

D.C. Coast
✉ 1401 K St. NW
📞 202-216-5988

This is one of the hottest new restaurants, so don't even think about going without making reservations. Set in the Tower Building, the art deco interior with its two-story dining room and glass-enclosed balcony make the place airy, and the bronze mermaid at the door lets you know you're in for some fun too. Seafood is a specialty here—try the crab cakes, tuna tartare, or Chinese smoked lobster—and there are also some hearty entrees like the double-cut pork chop. Entrees run $12 to $30. Major credit cards are accepted. Take the Metro to the McPherson Square station.

Equinox
✉ 818 Connecticut Ave. NW
📞 202-331-8118

Founded by Todd Gray, one of chef Roberto Donna's disciples, this is one of the hottest restaurants in town. The food is American bistro fare with a wide variety of creative appetizers, as well as a good selection of meat, fish, and game. Everyone raves about the lamb with beans. A honey butter and a fruit butter are served with your bread basket, and homemade cookies are served after the meal, so you don't need dessert. Entrees run $12 to $26, but there are a number of more elaborate tasting menus. Major credit cards are accepted. Take the Metro to the Farragut West station.

Georgia Brown's
✉ 950 15th St. NW
📞 202-393-4499

This restaurant offers Southern cooking that everyone loves. Signature dishes include shrimp and grits, Southern fried chicken, and bourbon pecan pie. The Sunday brunch is considered one of the best in the city ($23.95 for adults, and $17.95 for children). Major credit cards are accepted. Take the Metro to the McPherson Square station. Parking is also available.

Hard Rock Cafe

✉999 E St.

✆202-737-7625

This theme restaurant is located right around the corner from Ford's Theatre and the Petersen House, and it might be a good lunch stop for children or teens who are tired of "ancient" history. It serves average American fare in a fun atmosphere jam-packed with rock memorabilia. Clever items on the menu include Tupelo chicken with apricot sauce and honey mustard ($7), the Ringo Combo of rings, rolls, and chicken ($9), Bruce's ribs ($17), and Hunka Hunka Chocolate Banana Love ($5.99), as well as burgers, chili, and pizza. The kids' menu includes macaroni and cheese, pizza, Jimi Tenderstix, or a cheese sandwich for $6.99, with a souvenir cup.

═FAST FACT

Among the rock memorabilia on view at the Washington, D.C., Hard Rock Cafe are a green leisure suit once worn by James Brown, Freddy Mercury's red leather pants from 1982, eight Beatles gold records, the piccolo trumpet used in "Penny Lane," Led Zeppelin's Jimmy Page's guitar, Rolling Stones' Brian Jones's Nehru jacket, and Jimi Hendrix's brown leather shoulder bag, in which he kept his lyrics.

An amusing painting depicts George Washington in a Hard Rock T-shirt. Other items of interest include displays on the Beatles, the Rolling Stones, the Jackson Five, Jimi Hendrix, and The Doors, as well as some of Elvis's gold records and the saxophone President Clinton played at his 1993 inauguration. The souvenir shop on premises sells a very cute D.C. T-shirt featuring the Capitol and the Washington Monument ($24). Major credit cards are accepted. There is a coupon in various hotel handouts for a free souvenir with the purchase of an entree. Take the Metro to the Metro Center station.

Jordan's
✉ 1300 Pennsylvania Ave. NW
✆ 202-589-1223

The success of Michael Jordan's restaurant in New York City launched this sister eatery next door to the Ronald Reagan Trade Building. It features American cuisine with an international flair and is surprisingly good. The dinner menu is a little expensive, offering steak and oysters, but there are wonderful appetizers. The lunch menu is affordable with hamburgers, salads, and crab cakes. Major credit cards are accepted. Take the Metro to the Federal Triangle station.

Legal Seafoods
✉ 716 7th St. NW
✆ 202-347-6181

Located on the outskirts of Chinatown, near the MCI Center, this is a Boston-based seafood chain that has won awards for its kids' menu, which offers macaroni and cheese, hot dogs, hamburgers, and a kids' portion of steamed lobster, popcorn shrimp, or a small fisherman's platter of shrimp, clams, and scallops. The kids' menu runs from $4 to $16 on the upper end for the one-pound lobster.

The clam chowder is highly regarded, and the fresh fish is always good. Boston cream pie is always served. Dinner runs anywhere from $12 to $20. Major credit cards are accepted. Take the Metro to the Metro Center station.

🧳 TRAVEL TIP

Another branch of Legal Seafoods is located at ✉ 2020 K Street NW (✆ 202-496-1111). It was actually the first to open, in 1995, and the eatery proved so successful and popular that two more have followed (the one near the MCI Center and another at Reagan National Airport).

Les Halles
✉1201 Pennsylvania Ave. NW
☎202-347-6848

A slightly expensive French restaurant with an emphasis on beef and desserts, Les Halles is located just opposite the Federal Triangle Metro stop. The décor is authentically French, with lace curtains, a homey wooden interior, and popular French songs playing in the background. The fare is mainly beef, which is well prepared—the filet with béarnaise sauce is divine—but there are also other traditionally French items on the menu, such as cassoulet and a marvelous onion soup, which is a meal in itself. They also feature rich and wonderful desserts, such as peach melba. A meal for one with a glass of wine will run about $40. Major credit cards are accepted.

McCormick & Schmick's Seafood Restaurant
✉1652 K St. at Connecticut Ave. NW
☎202-861-2233

Part of an Oregon chain, this is one of the better restaurants in town. It features linen tablecloths and fancy chandeliers. People come here for the oyster bar and the crab cakes, and the desserts are highly recommended. There is an all-day light-fare menu with entrees under $10; otherwise, entrees are priced from $11 to $24. A daily happy hour offers appetizers for about $2, which makes this a very popular after-work hangout. Major credit cards are accepted. Business attire is suggested. Take the Metro to the Farragut North or West Metro station.

Morrison-Clark Historic Inn Restaurant
✉1015 L St. NW
☎1-800-332-7898

Award-winning creative cuisine served amid Victorian décor in a historic landmark. The goat cheese and phyllo rolls are excellent, as are the many delicious desserts such as the homemade chocolate napoleon. Entrees change from season to season, but the menu offers a full array of fish, duck, rabbit, pork, and lamb on a regular basis. All the ice cream is made on the premises.

Reservations are strongly suggested since the dining area only seats about forty, and this restaurant is popular with the local crowd for business lunches and romantic dinners. Entrees run $15 to $30. Major credit cards are accepted. Take the Metro to the Metro Center station, but be prepared for a bit of a walk.

Morton's of Chicago
✉1050 Connecticut Ave. NW
✆202-955-5997

This is the quintessential Washington, D.C., steakhouse where Washingtonians go for prime rib, which is thick and juicy but runs out early in the evening—if you want to try it, you should get there early. Meals run $20 to $65, slightly less for lunch. Most major credit cards are accepted. Portions are generous; most people, even the swells, leave with doggy bags. Business attire is essential. Reservations are strongly suggested. Take the Metro to the Metro Center station.

═FAST FACT

In addition to Morton's of Chicago in downtown D.C., there's another Morton's branch in Georgetown (✆202-342-6258). The address is ✉3251 Prospect Street NW. This branch offers an impressive collection of paintings by Leroy Neiman.

M & S Grill
✉600 13th St. at F St. NW
✆202-347-0234

This is the surf-and-turf sister restaurant of McCormick & Schmick's, and it's right near the MCI Center. This one is a little more relaxed and much heavier on the meat (ribs and steaks abound). There's a regular happy-hour special of $2 appetizers and plenty of sandwiches under $10. Meals run $7 to $22. Major credit cards are accepted. Take the Metro to the Metro Center or Gallery Place station.

Old Ebbitt Grill

✉675 15th St.

☎202-437-4801

Now part of the Clyde's chain, this very old Washington watering hole is still a popular place for the power lunch and is well known for its Sunday brunches. Famous patrons include most presidents (including Clinton) as well as the Rolling Stones and Clint Eastwood.

Clyde's was opened as a saloon in 1856, and its etched-glass partitions and paneled wooden booths are surrounded by political memorabilia, such as Teddy Roosevelt's animal trophies and Alexander Hamilton's wooden bears. While a restaurant this old has standards that regulars return for—the burgers, the New England clam chowder, and the Maryland crab cakes—the menu does vary seasonally, and it is said that this is the only place in Washington where you can get fresh Alaskan halibut when it's in season.

Entrees run $10 to $20; lunch is a little less expensive. This is one of the few restaurants downtown that serves breakfast ($4 to $8), and Sunday brunch is $6 to $16. Major credit cards are accepted. Take the Metro to the McPherson Square or Metro Center station.

Oval Room

✉800 Connecticut Ave. NW

☎202-463-8700

The Oval Room is located within walking distance of the White House. Inside, you'll find some charming murals of Washington, D.C., past and present (presidents and Hollywood stars). The restaurant's soups are highly recommended, as are the tuna tartare and crab-cake appetizers; there's also a wide selection of meat and seafood entrees. Entrees run $6 to $25. Major credit cards accepted. Jacket and tie required. Complimentary valet parking is available with dinner. Take the Metro to the Farragut West station.

Palette
✉ 15th and M Streets
☎ 202-587-2700

The newly opened Palette, which offers modern American cuisine, also allows diners to view art exhibits on loan from private galleries. Signature dishes include citrus sweetbread appetizer and rabbit with truffles and pistachio cream. The creative menu also features clever combinations, such as foie gras and ahi tuna club with blood-orange mayonnaise. The signature drink, Warhol, is a vodka-based grape-and-berry-juice concoction with a hint of caraway seeds. Meals run $15 to $35, but there is lighter fare in the lounge area. Major credit cards are accepted. Take the Metro to the Metro Center station.

Pier 7
✉ Maine Ave. and 7th St. Waterfront
☎ 202-554-2500

This restaurant offers a wonderful waterfront dining experience with panoramic views of the Potomac and various monuments. Pier 7 is known for its seafood, such as the crab cakes and bouillabaisse, but there is also a wide selection of pastas and meat dishes on the menu, as well as a pre-theater *prix fixe* menu. Entrees run $15 to $30. Major credit cards are accepted. Take the Metro to the L'Enfant Plaza station.

Planet Hollywood
✉ 1101 Pennsylvania Ave. NW
☎ 202-783-7827

The food here is pretty standard (burgers, salads, pizzas) and moderately priced, with a good children's menu. Kids love this popular food attraction when visiting the White House or Mall because there is some unique Hollywood memorabilia to see. Don't miss Darth Vader's helmet, Arnold Schwarzenegger's *Terminator* costume, Freddy Krueger's *Nightmare on Elm Street* glove, Jack Nicholson's ax from *The Shining,* and the props from *Titanic.*

Specific to the Washington, D.C., locale are the computer set from *WarGames*, which is in the back of the restaurant toward the ceiling (it's used as a frame for the second video screen), the desk from *Mr. Smith Goes to Washington*, and the gun Wesley Snipes used in *Murder at 1600*. Two video screens play nonstop Hollywood snippets.

There is a coupon in the Old Town Trolley map and various hotel handouts that gives you a free magnet with your meal of over $15. Major credit cards are accepted. Take the Metro to the Federal Triangle station.

📁 TRAVEL TIP

Lunch is also a good way to experience some of the city's more expensive or trendy restaurants, without having to pay top dollar. For instance, should your child be a Michael Jordan fan and want to eat in his new restaurant, lunch is definitely the more affordable option.

Poste
✉558 8th St. NW
☎202-783-6060

Located in the trendy Hotel Monaco, former home of the Tariff Building, Poste is an American brasserie that features a wonderful selection of seasonal meals from the traditional steak frites to a mixed grill, cinnamon duck, and lobster risotto by Chef Joseph Comfort, founder and co-owner of Bistro 309 in Frederick, Virginia. The crème brulée is perfect, and the Postemint, a parfait of mint and cream and chocolate, is good for an afternoon treat any time of the year. House cocktails are superb, especially the Big Ten (a delicious mix of gin, blue Curacao, and pineapple juice) and Sealed with a Kiss (a champagne and strawberry vodka concoction). There is also a bar menu.

Dinner runs between $18 and $23, but salads and lighter fare are available. This is a nice treat for youngsters who enjoy a fancier meal. Major credit cards are accepted, and valet parking is available. Take the Metro to the Gallery Place/Chinatown station.

Prime Rib
✉2020 K St. NW
☎202-466-8811

This restaurant is considered one of Washington's best places for roast beef, and it has a real men's-club feel with lots of wood and leather. Steaks are thick and juicy, and the prime rib served with fresh horseradish is excellent. There's plenty of fish on the menu too. There's a pianist in the evenings.

Meals run $18 to $30, less for lunch, and for men a jacket and tie are required. Most major credit cards are accepted. Take the Metro to the Farragut West station.

Red Sage
✉605 14th St. NW
☎202-638-4444

Ask anyone who's been here, and they'll refer to this restaurant as "a Wild West fantasy." Think of it as an upscale theme restaurant, with unique Western touches such as buffalo horn chandeliers. The menu offers many creative Southwestern opportunities, such as barbecued ostrich and catfish tacos, but it's best when you stick to traditional Western food like chili, burritos, or the fabulous homemade sausage. Reservations are recommended for the main dining area (a very popular tourist draw in the summer), but the café and chili bar don't accept them. Meals run $12 to $31.50, but the café and chili bar are less expensive, as is lunch. Major credit cards are accepted. Take the Metro to the Metro Center station.

Willard Room
✉1401 Pennsylvania Ave. NW
☎202-637-7440

The Willard Room in the Willard Hotel is the very best that D.C. dining has to offer, so it might not be appropriate for your children. The setting is palatial, restored to its turn-of-the-century grandeur with chandeliers, wood paneling, and columns. It is considered one of the most romantic settings in town, and many marriage proposals have been made in this dining room.

≡FAST FACT

> The Willard Room is known as the "residence of the presidents" because it has served most presidents dinner the night before their inauguration. Lincoln is said to have come here for the corned beef and blueberry pie, and Henry Clay is said to have invented the mint julep at Willard's bar.

For such a spectacular, historical setting, the food is reasonably priced. The menu changes daily, but the seafood is especially wonderful, as are the desserts. Main courses run $15 to $40. Major credit cards are accepted. Jacket and tie are required, and reservations are a must. Take the Metro to the Metro Center station. Complimentary valet parking with dinner is also available.

Zola
✉800 F St. NW
✆202-654-0999

Zola is located right next door to the International Spy Museum and a stone's throw from the National Portrait gallery (and the American Museum of Art, when it opens). This is a surprisingly affordable sit-down restaurant that runs between $7 and $17 for lunch and $7 to $24 for dinner. Major credit cards are accepted. Take the Metro to the Gallery Place/Chinatown station.

Capitol Hill

America
✉50 Massachusetts Ave. NE
✆202-682-9555

This is a great spot for a leisurely meal after getting off the train at Union Station. As you eat, you can watch passersby head to and fro, and the fourth floor offers a view of the Capitol building.

The food offered at America is supposed to be traditional American, and there are dishes from all fifty states, with selections like roast turkey and stuffing, macaroni and cheese, and spaghetti and meatballs. Meals run $12 to $17 for dinner, though lunches are less expensive. Major credit cards are accepted. Take the Metro to the Union Station station.

B. Smith's
✉50 Massachusetts Ave.
✆202-289-6188

This is the most expensive restaurant in Union Station and is a branch of a New York restaurant founded by model Barbara Smith (the Oil of Olay beauty). It is built in a beautiful Beaux Arts building and former presidential waiting area, where presidents once greeted visiting dignitaries.

The food is creative Southern/Creole/soul food with a French flair, which means wonderful Maryland crab cakes, red beans and rice, fried green tomatoes, catfish, jambalaya, and pecan and sweet potato pies. Brunch is outstanding. Meals run $11 to $25. Major credit cards are accepted. Take the Metro to the Union Station station.

Thunder Grill
✉50 Massachusetts Ave.
✆202-898-0051

This high-concept Southwestern restaurant with a beautiful wooden interior and portraits of Native Americans on the walls is also located at Union Station. Entrees include traditional Southwestern fare such as fajitas and quesadillas, as well as hot-and-spicy shrimp, salads, and sandwiches. There's a selection of thirty-one tequilas on the menu, and happy hour features a different frozen margarita every day. Most entrees are under $15. Major credit cards are accepted. Take the Metro to the Union Station station.

Adams Morgan/Woodley Park

Cashion's Eat Place

✉1819 Columbia Rd. NW

✆202-797-1819

This is an all-American-style restaurant decorated with the owner, An Cashion's, family photos. The menu changes daily, but there's a variety of comfort food like roast chicken and steak and wonderful garlic mashed potatoes, as well as some pretty exotic fare such as buffalo steak and roasted duck breast with beets. The goat cheese ice cream is always recommended if it's on the menu, and locals say the desserts are not to be missed, so save room. Also a local choice for Sunday brunch.

Dinner runs between $18 and $30, and Cashion's takes MasterCard and Visa only. No lunch is served Tuesdays through Saturdays. Take the Metro to the Woodley Park station. Valet parking is also available.

New Heights

✉2317 Calvert St. NW at Connecticut Ave.

✆202-234-4110

This two-story restaurant with large windows is popular because you can order any selection in appetizer or meal sizes, and the menu is creative but dependable. People come back for the butter-fried oysters and the crab cakes. Full entrees run from $16 to $25, but appetizer portions are about half that. Major credit cards are accepted. Free valet parking is available. Take the Metro to the Woodley Park station.

Perry's

✉1811 Columbia Rd.

✆202-234-6218

Perry's is a former disco; today it's a hip, fun restaurant with cozy sofas around tables and a funky, bizarre, alienlike chandelier. Perry's serves Asian fusion food in the evenings, and there's a rooftop dining area open in the spring and summer where you can eat sushi or sesame-crusted tuna with mango salad. Most meals run between $10 and $17, but you can make a meal out of sushi and an appetizer. Major credit cards are accepted. Take the Metro to Woodley Park station.

 JUST FOR PARENTS

Perry's hosts a famous and fabulous drag-queen brunch every Sunday that serves up a display of pan-Asian and American breakfast treats with a wicked cocktail. It may not be appropriate for children between the ages of 5 and the late teens, but there are plenty of baby-boomers with strollers and toddlers in attendance every Sunday.

Georgetown

1789
✉ 1226 36th St. NW
✆ 202-965-1789

This upscale restaurant, named for the year that Georgetown was founded, is located in an old townhouse with working fireplaces and old maps of Washington, D.C., on the walls. The food is based on traditional American cooking, with an updated twist by Chef Ris Lacoste, who varies the menu according to what's available seasonally.

The emphasis here is definitely on seafood. The oyster stew is creamy, and the desserts are rich. Entrees run from $18 to $39, but there is a pre-theater *prix fixe* menu that offers three courses for $25. Jacket is required for men, and free valet parking is available. Major credit cards are accepted.

Michel Richard Citronelle
✉ 3000 M St. NW
✆ 202-625-2150

This is the place to dine in Washington, where everyone who is anyone goes for both the food and to be seen. (Reservations are a must!) The award-winning chef and owner, Michel Richard, left his Citrus Restaurant in Los Angeles to set up this signature contemporary French restaurant located at the Latham Hotel, and everyone in D.C. seems to have appreciated his move.

There is a wall in the restaurant that changes colors (sort of a mood wall), and a see-through, glass-enclosed wine "library" of thousands of bottles surrounds the dining area. The menu is exotic and comprehensive; you can get everything from sweetbreads to lamb and duck, and each dish is creatively displayed with wonderful sauces. Meals run $16 to $32. Jacket and tie are required of men at dinner, and business attire is necessary for lunch.

▥ TRAVEL TIP

While Georgetown has some of the best restaurants in the city, you will probably have to take a cab back and forth because the area is not accessible by Metro. Fortunately, the distance from downtown D.C. is fairly short, so a cab ride shouldn't cost too much.

Old Glory Barbeque
✉3139 M St. NW
✆202-337-3406

Ample American barbeque with a Southern flair is served here. Although there's an excellent children's menu, portions are so wonderfully generous that you might want to order family-style and share. There's a terrific appetizer sampler, the Whole Lotta Glory, which features a little bit of everything—pit barbeque shrimp, fried green tomatoes, buffalo wings, oak-grilled chicken wings, and St. Louis–style spareribs. And the entire shebang costs a mere $10! Entrees include ribs, ham, and even barbequed lamb, as well as pulled chicken and pork. Major credit cards are accepted.

Sea Catch
✉1054 31st St. NW
✆202-337-8855

Conveniently located in a courtyard of art galleries in the Georgetown mall, Sea Catch overlooks the C&O Canal and features a fireplace and tables on a deck. The raw bar features oysters and clams, and Sea Catch also serves up great shrimp and lobster. Entrees run the gamut from shellfish to tuna nicoise and sesame-crusted scallops. Most entrees run from $13 to $20. Major credit cards are accepted, and parking is free.

Sequoia
✉3000 K St. NW at 30th St.
✆202-944-4200

Sequoia is located at Washington Harbor, and it's one of the most spectacular view-with-a-meal dining experiences in D.C. Most people come for the view of the Potomac (especially for drinks after work), but the food is decent too—crab cakes, calamari, pizza, catfish, and salads. There's a pre- and post-theater special *prix fixe* menu Monday through Thursday that offers house wine, soup or salad, choice of entree, and dessert for $19.95. Meals run $8 to $29. If you want a table with a view, it's a good idea to make a reservation. Major credit cards are accepted.

Dupont Circle

Dupont Grille
✉1500 New Hampshire Ave. NW
✆202-939-9596

Situated right on Dupont Circle, this a great location for people-watching, which makes it a terrific summer Sunday brunch site. The fish dishes are excellent, from the crab cakes to the cashew-crusted tempeh, and the menu offers a variety of chicken and beef. Dinner runs between $17 and $26, but the appetizer portions are large enough for smaller appetites. Breakfast is served every day, and the

Sunday brunch is $20 for a champagne mimosa or Bloody Mary with a fruit cocktail and a choice of original entrees such as the lump crab and mushroom cheesecake (a sort of quiche) or the Eggs Dupont (with crab cakes). This restaurant also serves wonderful waffles and French toast. Major credit cards are accepted. Take the Metro to the Dupont Circle station.

Firefly
✉ 1310 New Hampshire Ave. NW
☎ 202-861-1310

Located in the Hotel Madera, this is a one-of-a-kind dining experience that should entrance children and adults alike. The interior features a replica of a tree festooned with summer lights, and birch trunks lining the wall give the atmosphere of a summer evening, even in the dead of winter. The fried oysters and onion-and-sausage tart appetizers are delicious, as are the lamb, chicken, and salmon main courses, which vary slightly with the season. Dinner entrées run from $13 to $23. If the pumpkin pudding is on the menu, order it.

The bill is presented in a mason jar with holes in the lid. A Sunday brunch is also offered, and major credit cards are accepted. Firefly is a small restaurant, so make a reservation, especially on the weekend. Take the Metro to the Dupont Circle station.

🚶 JUST FOR PARENTS

Coeur de Lion in the Henley Park Hotel (downtown D.C.) is considered by many to be one of the most romantic hotel restaurants in town, for both its setting of fireplaces and candlesticks as well as its superb food.

The Jockey Club
✉ 2100 Massachusetts Ave. NW
☎ 202-293-2100

The Jockey Club has been a Washington, D.C., standby since the Kennedy days, located in the Westin Fairfax Hotel. Today it remains a popular place for a power lunch. In spite of a number of renovations and changes in hotel management, it remains pretty much the same, with red-leather banquettes, red-and-white tablecloths, and horse-y doodads. The menu changes from chef to chef and food trend to food trend, but the standards are still there— French onion soup, Caesar salad, and crab cakes, as well as the pommes soufflés side dish of puffy French fries. There's a dessert cart for those who care to indulge.

Reservations are a must. Jacket and tie are required of men at dinner and strongly suggested for lunch. Complimentary valet parking is available with dinner. Entrees run $24 to $34 for dinner and less for breakfast and lunch. Most major credit cards are accepted. Take the Metro to the Dupont Circle station.

Nora
✉ 2132 Florida Ave. NW at R St.
✆ 202-462-5143

This is one of the best restaurants in Washington, D.C., in spite of the fact (or because of it, depending upon your culinary tastes) that all the food is organically grown. The setting is lovely, in a private townhouse with a skylight and restored stable as the main dining room with quilts and local art on the walls. This is not your tofu-and-bean-sprout burger restaurant but, rather, haute cuisine for the culinary correct. There's an emphasis on seafood, but there's also free-range chicken and even kidney on the menu. Desserts are wonderful, especially the pies and homemade ice cream, and there's a varied wine list. Of course, a restaurant like this varies the menu depending upon seasonal produce, so there is always something new and different to try. Entrees range from $20 to $25. Reservations are strongly recommended. Nora takes MasterCard, Visa, and Discover only. Take the Metro to the Dupont Circle station.

Smith & Wollensky
✉ 1112 19th St. NW (between L and M Streets)
✆ 202-466-1100

Because Washington, D.C., is a town that loves its red meat, this is just the restaurant that the city needs. This branch of the renowned New York steakhouse, with its famous green-and-white exterior, serves lots of steak (even a double sirloin for close to $60), as well as lamb chops and lobster. There's a smaller, sister restaurant next door, Wollensky's Grill, that is open until 2:00 A.M. Entrees run $15 to $60. Major credit cards are accepted. Business attire is suggested. Take the Metro to the Farragut West station.

Vidalia

✉1990 M St. NW

✆202-659-1990

Considered one of the most creative Southern restaurants in D.C., Vidalia has been a popular favorite for a long time. The dining room is down a flight of stairs and has no windows, but no one seems to mind as they slap apple butter on the delicious corn bread and try the new ways that the chef has come up with to flavor grits (such as goat cheese and mushrooms). There are many interesting seafood entrees on the menu, and desserts are superb too. Try the pecan pie. Entrees run $13 to $27. Most major credit cards are accepted. Take the Metro to the Dupont Circle station.

Foggy Bottom/West End

Aquarelle

✉2650 Virginia Ave. NW

✆202-298-4455

Here's your chance to get inside the infamous Watergate Hotel and see how the other half lives, or eats. If you're going to the Kennedy Center, this is actually a good place to go for an exquisite pre-theater meal (*prix fixe* $38, which is a bargain at this upscale restaurant) and some fabulous views of the Potomac. (Call ahead for a reservation if you want a good table with a view.)

The menu includes such upper-crust entrees as quail, rack of lamb, squab, and sweetbreads, all wonderfully prepared. Entrees run $18.50 to $45. Free valet parking is available. Men are required to wear a jacket at dinner. Major credit cards are accepted. Take the Metro to the Foggy Bottom station.

▮ TRAVEL TIP

Aquarelle, in the Watergate Hotel, offers spectacular views of the Potomac and is a great place to go for drinks, appetizers (often with a theme, such as Japanese sushi or Spanish tapas), or dinner when you are taking in a show at the Kennedy Center for the Performing Arts.

Dish
✉924 25th St. NW
☎202-338-8707

Dish is located near the Kennedy Center and Georgetown. At this casual and friendly restaurant, the attention to detail—whether it's the playful sizes and shapes of the Crate & Barrel dishes, servers clad in Brooks Brothers suits, or the eight-foot diptych of a weimaraner dog photograph by William Wegman—sets the tone. During the winter months, a gas-lit fireplace warms the guests.

Menu favorites include crispy fried chicken, blackened pork chops, and a New England clambake. At lunch, hearty sandwiches such as meatloaf and Colorado turkey melt are big enough to share. The brown cow ice-cream float is a perfect ending. Dinner entrees run between $16 and $22. Breakfast is served daily. Major credit cards are accepted. Take the Metro to the Foggy Bottom station.

Galileo
✉1110 21st St. NW
☎202-293-7191

This was one of the most talked-about restaurants of the late 1980s, as it was the first restaurant in chef Roberto Donna's Italian eatery empire (others include the Il Radicchio chain and Pesce). It's so popular you cannot get in for dinner without a reservation, and some book weeks in advance. The food is rich (Italian with French and Swiss influences), and hazelnuts and porcini mushrooms seem to be a chef's favorite as they appear on everything from fish to game. Entrees are on the expensive side, with pasta dishes starting at $22, but it's worth it. Major credit cards are accepted. Take the Metro to the Foggy Bottom station.

Goldoni
✉1120 20th St. NW
✆202-293-1511

This highly praised restaurant with Venetian Italian cuisine has just moved to a new location. The food is a little more complicated than southern Italian—lots of light sauces and intricate food layering. The rack of lamb is a favorite, as is the salmon wrapped in prosciutto. The desserts are supreme. Entrees run from $12 to $18. Major credit cards accepted. Parking is available in a validated lot. Take the Metro to the Foggy Bottom station.

🚶 JUST FOR PARENTS

The Willard Room is said to be one of the places where Washingtonians propose to one another, with cozy, yet elegant table settings (lots of chandeliers) and consistently fabulous food.

Kinkead's
✉2000 Pennsylvania Ave. NW
✆202-296-7700

This is a popular American brasserie just a few blocks west of the White House. It is known for its seafood entrees, such as the grilled squid and polenta appetizer, and the signature dish of a pepita-crusted salmon with shellfish and chili ragout, but there is always at least one meat and poultry entree on the menu. During evenings and Sunday brunch, the restaurant features a jazz group or a pianist. Dinner entrees run $18 to $25; lunch is less expensive. Major credit cards are accepted. Take the Metro to the Foggy Bottom station.

Melrose
✉ 1201 24th St. NW at M St.
✆ 202-955-3899

Melrose is a very popular seafood restaurant in the upscale Park Hyatt Hotel; reservations are strongly recommended for the weekends, when there's dancing, and for lunch, when the business crowd comes here. The glass-enclosed dining area overlooks a sunken terrace with a garden and fountain for warm-weather dining. Everyone loves the shrimp-filled ravioli and the house crab cakes. Meals run $14 to $34, with prices that are slightly lower for lunch. Major credit cards are accepted. Free valet parking is available. Take the Metro to the Foggy Bottom station.

Nectar
✉ 824 New Hampshire Ave. NW
✆ 202-298-8085

Located near the Kennedy Center and adorned with eye-catching photos of luscious produce, this chic boutique restaurant offers American cuisine from a rotating seasonal market menu, with fare such as pheasant, New York strip steak, halibut, and scallops. Breakfast and lunch are served daily, and the tuna burger is recommended. Kids will love the baked Alaska. Dinner runs between $17 and $27. Major credit card are accepted. Take the Metro to the Foggy Bottom station.

Roof Terrace Restaurant/Hors D'oeuvrerie
✉ The Kennedy Center, New Hampshire Ave.
✆ 202-416-8555

Needless to say, an excellent restaurant with fabulous Potomac views located at Rock Creek Parkway in the Kennedy Center requires a reservation—though the lighter fare Hors D'oeuvrerie doesn't accept them. On some evenings you can choose from selections on either menu. The beef is recommended, as is the fish; the appetizers are always good, and there's always a daily special. There's also a spectacular Sunday brunch that attracts a crowd.

Hours of operation are really geared around performances, so call to make sure that the restaurant is open. Entrees run $12 to $29, less for appetizers and lunch. Major credit cards are accepted. There is garage parking, but you have to pay for it. Take the Metro to the Foggy Bottom station.

CHAPTER 15

Cheap and Exotic Eats

WHAT INCREDIBLE VARIETY this city has when it comes to places to eat! Because the city has a very diverse population, there are wonderful affordable ethnic restaurants, with great Chinese fare in D.C.'s small Chinatown, as well as Greek, Japanese, Thai, and Vietnamese restaurants, and more Ethiopian restaurants than in any other American city—and kids enjoy eating Ethiopian food because they can eat with their hands.

In this chapter, you'll also find good options for inexpensive breakfast or lunch, with most meals running between $5 and $12. The majority of these places to eat are located downtown or in the Dupont Circle area.

Eating on the Cheap

There are so many wonderful restaurants, diners, cafes, and cafeterias throughout Washington, D.C., that breakfast and lunch should never put you over the top of your budget. Since you'll be on the go from morning until the sun sets, your best bet is to look for something along your route during the day and then splurge on one of the city's unique dining experiences for dinner, when you'll need to get off your feet.

There are fabulous breakfasts throughout the city, but your best bet is likely to be your hotel restaurant or a diner around the corner. Many hotels offer a continental breakfast with the hotel room price. If you are going to be in town on Sunday morning, and have the time to dine leisurely, you might want to schedule a Sunday brunch, as the city hosts a phenomenal variety of truly unique brunch experiences.

💼 TRAVEL TIP

There are many unique and exotic options listed in this chapter, but there are days when you may prefer to stop at the nearest fast-food chain restaurant. If you're looking for a Burger King or McDonald's, ask your hotel concierge for the one closest to you.

You will most likely eat lunch on the go, and if you are touring one of the city's major museums, you should consider eating in either their restaurant or cafeteria. They all offer a good variety of kid-pleasing menu items, and some are truly exceptional dining experiences, such as the Corcoran Gallery or the restaurant in the National Gallery of Art. Because of security concerns, it is now almost impossible to bring food into a museum or interior in a knapsack, as all bags must be checked when you enter.

Downtown D.C.

Cheap Eats

Fado Irish Pub
⊠808 7th St. NW
☏202-789-0066

If you're touring Chinatown or the MCI Center, this is a good bet. The menu features such Irish staples as corned beef and cabbage, and there are some interesting deviations such as oysters, mussels, and salmon, plus a wide selection of Irish beer and whiskey. Entrees are very reasonably priced, with most under $10. Major credit cards are accepted. Take the Metro to the Gallery Place station.

Full Kee
✉509 H St. NW
☎202-371-2233

This is one of the best little Chinese restaurants in town, with a daily menu of specialties (featuring a lot of fish and shellfish in the summer) that includes such unique fare as Hong Kong wonton soup (eight wontons stuffed with shrimp in a spicy broth) and wonderful casseroles of pork and tofu or oysters. Most entrees are $5 to $12. The restaurant accepts cash only. Take the Metro to the Gallery Place station.

👫 JUST FOR PARENTS

Any one of the lounges in any of the six Kimpton Hotels—Helix, Hotel George, Hotel Monaco, Madera, Rouge, and Topaz—offers a great happy hour, where signature drinks are half price (usually $5) and there's always great food on the menu as well, also at half price. Kimpton happy hours are offered every day from 5:00 to 7:00 P.M.

Go-Lo's
✉604 H St
☎202-437-4656

After viewing Ford's Theatre and Petersen House, you might want to dine in a bit of history. Conspirators met here in Mary Surratt's boarding house to plan the kidnapping of President Lincoln. There is a landmark plaque on the building.

Entrees run $7 to $16 and include Hunan and Szechuan options, including the popular Kung Pao preparation, with an assortment of soups, combo platters, and family-style meals. The duck and the Chilean sea bass are specialties of the house. American

Express, MasterCard, and Visa are accepted. Take the Metro to the Gallery Place station.

Jordans Restaurant
✉ 1300 Pennsylvania Ave
✆ 202-589-1223

Sometimes kids really want to go to a celebrity restaurant, and if you don't want to lay out the big bucks for dinner, lunch here is affordable (be aware, however, that it is only served until 2:30 P.M.). Since this is a hotspot, make a reservation, so your kids aren't disappointed. There are burgers, salads, and sandwiches on the menu, running at about $8 to $13. Major credit cards are accepted. Take the Metro to the Federal Triangle station.

The Wright Place Cafeteria
✉ Independence at 4th St. NW

When you tour the National Air and Space Museum, stop at the Wright Place Cafeteria. Recently remodeled and taking up a large space on the first floor of the museum, this cafeteria offers McDonald's, Boston Market, and Donato's Pizza. The McDonald's Happy Meal has a little space shuttle in it. Credit cards are accepted. Take the Metro to the Smithsonian station.

National Museum of Natural History Cafeteria
✉ 10th St. and Constitution Ave. NW

There's a new cafeteria at the museum, which has many child-pleasing meals (hamburgers, pizza), as well as homemade soups, hot food, and personally prepared sandwiches, desserts, coffee, and tea. Meals run $5 to $12. Major credit cards are accepted. Take the Metro to the Smithsonian station.

National Museum of American History
✉ 14th Street and Constitution Ave

You'll find a wonderful old-fashioned ice cream parlor and three other restaurants in the museum, so you don't have to leave the premises for lunch or dinner. Meals are under $10. Major credit cards are accepted. Take the Metro to the Smithsonian station.

Old Ebbitt Grill

✉675 15th St.

✆202-437-4801

Because of its location, this is a great place to catch a sit-down meal, especially if you are touring the White House. Kids can eat crab cakes or clam chowder, and the sandwiches are generous. Lunch runs $8 to $13. This is one of the few restaurants downtown that serves breakfast ($4 to $7), and Sunday brunch is $6 to $16. Major credit cards are accepted. Take the Metro to the McPherson Square or Metro Center station.

═FAST FACT

Old Ebbitt Grill has been a Washington watering hole and business lunch spot for years. It's where many visiting celebrities can be seen. Clint Eastwood, the Rolling Stones, and President Clinton have been spotted here occasionally.

Ollie's Trolley

✉425 12th St. NW

✆202-347-6119

A neighborhood institution and a real kid-pleaser, Ollie's Trolley is a restaurant shaped like an old trolley. Everyone comes for the ten-ounce burger with unique herbs and spices on a sesame bun, as well as Ollie's fries with special spices and the excellent milk shakes; other sandwiches are available. Most sandwiches and combo meals are under $5. The restaurant accepts cash only. Take the Metro to the Federal Triangle station.

Planet Hollywood

✉1101 Pennsylvania Ave. NW

✆202-783-7827

This is actually the perfect lunch spot, so it's often crowded. The kids' meals are a bargain at $6.99, with a souvenir glass to go. Servers are friendly and very comfortable with families. Major credit cards are accepted. Take the Metro to the Federal Triangle station.

TGI Friday's
✉1201 Pennsylvania Ave. NW at 12th St.
✆202-628-8443

Across the street from the Federal Triangle Metro stop, this often very crowded restaurant offers very basic lunch items of the Tex-Mex variety—also hamburgers, chicken fingers, and so on. It is kid-friendly with a good and inexpensive kids' menu. Entrees run $7 to $15, less for lunch and appetizers, from which you can easily make a meal. Most major credit cards are accepted. Take the Metro to the Federal Triangle station.

Tony Cheng's
✉619 H St. NW
✆202-842-8669

This well-known two-story restaurant offers lunch and dinner specials for as little as $5 and a "Mongolian grill" (all-you-can-eat barbeque) for $14.95 in the downstairs dining area. Also featured are dim sum and exotic seafood specialties. Chef and owner Tony Cheng is usually on the premises, and you can see pictures of him with presidents of the past thirty years, from Carter to Bush. American Express, MasterCard, and Visa are accepted. Take the Metro to the Gallery Place station.

Waffle Shop
✉512 10th St. NW
✆202-638-3430

A neighborhood institution for more than fifty years, this counter-service, cash-only all-day breakfast spot is a real find. Steak and eggs, huge pancakes, and eggs with sausage and bacon are all about $5, and meals can be served with delicious grits. Lunch is served as well, also at extremely reasonable prices. Be prepared to wait a bit on weekends, but it's worth it. This is a great location for breakfast and/or lunch while you're visiting Ford's Theatre and the Petersen House, which is on the block. Take the Metro to the Metro Center station.

🧳 TRAVEL TIP

Legal Seafoods is considered one of the best kids' meals in town, because they offer a great fish selection on the kids' menu (including a one-pound lobster), as well as the usual kids' fare of burgers and chicken tenders. TGI Fridays and Planet Hollywood also have good kids' meals at an affordable price, as does the Austin Grill.

Moderate Options

Bombay Club
✉815 Connecticut Ave. NW
☎202-659-3727

The Clintons often dined at this very popular upscale Indian restaurant. The setting is very British colonial, with ceiling fans and wicker chairs. The food is often very hot and spicy, but it's well done, and many of the seafood entrees are unique to this restaurant. Entrees run $8 to $20, but there's a pre-theater *prix fixe* meal, as well as a Sunday brunch. Major credit cards are accepted. Take the Metro to the Farragut West station.

Café Atlántico
✉405 8th St. NW
☎202-393-0892

A popular Latin three-level restaurant and nightclub, this place is usually packed, so make a reservation. The décor is colorful with artwork on the walls. The restaurant has a number of signature drinks to choose from, and your server will make guacamole at your table right in front of you. There are many great appetizers on the menu, and many people make a meal out of them. You can also choose the tasting menu. Desserts are rich and creative.

Entrees run $8 to $20; lunch is less expensive, and the appetizers start at about $5. Most major credit cards are accepted. Take the Metro to the National Archives station.

El Catalán

✉ 1319 F St. NW, at 14th St.

☎ 202-628-2299

A wonderful mix of Spanish and French cooking, the restaurant is named after the region in Spain where the two cuisines (and languages) meet. The interior features murals, ironwork, and Spanish tiles. Of course, there's a wide selection of tapas, and the homemade soups are excellent, as are the seafood and meat dishes. Jacket and tie are suggested at dinner. Entrees are $13 to $36, but many guests make a meal of the tapas. Most major credit cards are accepted. Complimentary parking is available during dinner. Take the Metro to the Metro Center station.

Jaleo

✉ 480 7th St. NW

☎ 202-628-7949

This popular tapas bar is named after a John Singer Sargent painting of a Spanish dancer, El Jaleo, which is re-created on the back wall. The sangria is refreshing, and the tapas selection is wide— Spanish cheeses, sausages, gazpacho, the traditional torta omelet, and lots more. There is also paella for two. A meal for one (two tapas with a half carafe of sangria) should run about $20. Homemade bread, Spanish olive oil, and a dish of olives are served with your meal. Major credit cards accepted. Call for reservations as this place is popular with the locals (also right next door to the National Shakespeare theater), and you might have to wait up to an hour without a reservation in the summer months. It's a great restaurant for kids who like to eat, because they can choose from the various tapas for a main meal. Take the Metro to the Metro Center station.

Zaytinya

✉701 9th St. NW

✆202-638-0800

A marvelous upscale Greek restaurant that is surprisingly afford-able, with a soothing blue-and-white interior. This a great restaurant to take children with an adventurous palate.

Make a meal of the appetizers and desserts, as they are all deli-cious, and prices run between $4 and $8. Main courses are $14 to $25. Have the dessert wine from Samos—it's surprisingly sweet and strong. Major credit cards accepted. Take the Metro to the Gallery Place/Chinatown station.

Capitol Hill

Cheap Eats

Al Tiramisu

✉2014 P St. NW

✆202-467-4466

This is a good Italian restaurant that has a variety of pastas, as well as seafood and meat and fish. Major credit cards are accepted. Take the Metro to the Dupont Circle station.

Market House

✉225 E. 7th St. NW

✆202-547-8444

Eastern Market is an indoor/outdoor marketplace that thrives with arts and food vendors on the weekend. Inside the south hall of the marketplace is the Market House, a great sit-down diner where you can get fabulous blueberry buckwheat pancakes or egg sandwiches for less than $5. Lunches of crab cakes and soft shell crab sandwiches are also served. The Market House is popular with the locals, so be prepared to wait about half an hour. The restaurant accepts cash only. Take the Metro to the Union Station station.

Monocle
✉107 D St. NW
📞202-546-4488

If your kids like crab cakes, this is the place for them. There's also a good selection of sandwiches and salads. Lunch runs between $7 and $12. Major credit cards are accepted. Take the Metro to the Union Station station.

👫 JUST FOR PARENTS

The Morrison-Clark Inn seats only about forty diners in its Victorian living-room-turned-restaurant. There are white marble fireplaces, beautiful crystal chandeliers, and candles, as well as creative and delicious food.

Oodles Noodles
✉1120 19th St. NW
📞202-293-3138

There's always a big lunch crowd for this pan-Asian noodle shop featuring all sorts of noodle dishes, as well as curries and teriyaki. Prices run from $8 to $12. Major credit cards are accepted. Take the Metro to the Dupont Circle station.

Pizzeria Uno
✉Union Station
📞202-842-0438

Home of the Chicago deep-dish pizza, Pizzeria Uno also features hot wings and appetizers that can make a meal, as well as burgers, sandwiches, and salads. Kids' menu prices run about $5. Major credit cards are accepted. Take the Metro to the Union Station station.

Union Station Food Court
✉Union Station

Located on the lower level of Union Station, the food court is an entire floor of fast-food establishments that offer everything from sushi to quiche and sauerbraten. Most meals are around $5. Take the Metro to the Union Station station.

Moderate Options

Lebanese Taverna
✉2641 Connecticut Ave. NW
✆202-667-5350

A mainstay of the Woodley Park dining zone since it opened more than twenty years ago, the Lebanese Taverna is a very popular Lebanese restaurant, and it is usually packed on the weekends (reservations are only accepted until 6:30 P.M.). The interior is decorated with prints of Old Lebanon and prayer rugs; Lebanese music plays in the background.

The big hit on the menu is the demi mezze, where you are given a sampling of a dozen appetizers, such as humus, baba ganoush, spinach pies, and more. There are also homemade pitas cooked in the wood-burning oven and a wonderful selection of main courses, such as kabobs, falafel, fish, and vegetarian dishes. Meals run from $10 to $16. Free parking is available at a nearby garage. Most major credit cards are accepted. Take the Metro to the Woodley Park station.

Meskerem
✉2434 18th St. NW
✆202-462-4100

Some say that this is the best Ethiopian restaurant in the city. Its spicy fare of lamb, chicken, beef, and vegetables is served with the traditional Ethiopian bread (*injera*) by a staff dressed in Ethiopian clothing. Ethiopian wine and beer is served, and live Ethiopian music is performed after 11:30 P.M. on Friday and Saturday nights. Meals run from $8 to $15. Major credit cards are accepted. Take the Metro to the Woodley Park station.

Adams Morgan/Woodley Park

Cheap Eats

Julia's Empanada
✉2452 18th St. NW
☎202-328-6232

Julia's is a great little lunch place where you can get a variety of meat or vegetable empanadas for about $3 each. Soups are sometimes offered as well. The restaurant accepts cash only. Take the Metro to the Woodley Park station

💼 TRAVEL TIP

Julia's Empanada has three other locations in the city: ✉1000 Vermont Ave. NW (☎202-789-1878); ✉1221 Connecticut Ave. NW (☎202-861-8828); and ✉1410 U St. NW (☎202-387-4100).

Pasta Mia
✉1790 Columbia Rd. NW
☎202-328-9114

Pasta Mia is another good Italian restaurant that serves healthy portions of pasta (thirty menu items to choose from) and wonderful Italian bread. Almost all offerings here are under $10, and some lunch entrees are even less. Only MasterCard and Visa are accepted. Take the Metro to the Woodley Park station.

Peyote Cafe/Roxanne
✉2319 18th St. NW
☎202-462-8330

Housed in an Adams Morgan brownstone, Peyote Cafe is a small, fun Santa Fe–style Mexican restaurant with brightly colored walls and a good menu of tacos and cheese pizza (a real kid-pleaser) as well as more exotic fare, such as chili-grilled shrimp, from Roxanne, the upscale restaurant upstairs. Lunch entrees are $7 to $11. Most major credit cards are accepted. Take the Metro to the Woodley Park station.

Georgetown

Cheap Eats

Austin Grill

✉2404 Wisconsin Ave. NW

✆202-337-8080

Austin Grill is part of a chain that features good Tex-Mex fare, and the emphasis here is on chili and ribs. This is a kid-friendly restaurant with a good kids' menu featuring burgers, tacos, enchiladas, and nachos, all under $5, drink included. Major credit cards are accepted.

Bistro Francais

✉3124–28 N St.

✆202-338-3830

This charming French bistro offers terrific *prix fixe* meals for $13.95 that include wine, salad or soup, a selection of main courses, as well as four choices of fruit tart for dessert. Weekend brunches include all-you-can-drink champagne with a choice of an omelette, steak and eggs, eggs benedict, and so on. There are also post- and pre-theater dinner specials. The restaurant is open until 3:00 A.M. on weekdays and 4:00 A.M. on weekends, so it is a popular late-night dining spot. Major credit cards are accepted.

Bistrot Lepic

✉1736 Wisconsin Ave. NW

✆202-333-0111

A Georgetown favorite for both the authentic French bistro food and the quirkiness of the tiny restaurant, Bistrot Lepic is often crowded, even for lunch. The food is the kind of bistro fare you might actually find in a Parisian restaurant—plenty of kidney, liver, even pig's feet, as well as salmon, tuna, and lamb. The desserts are quite good too. Lunch is $7 to $12. Major credit cards are accepted.

≡FAST FACT

It seems as if D.C. has more Ethiopian restaurants than any other American city, and that might be the case. According to D.C.'s tourist office, Washington, D.C., was very open to Ethiopian refugees after the fall of Haile Selassie's regime in the 1980s, and many of these immigrants set up family-run restaurants, which have become quite well known.

Café Deluxe
✉Wisconsin Ave. NW
☏202-686-2233

Ask Washingtonians what their favorite restaurants are, and after they try to impress you with the fact that they've been to the latest hotspot, they will all mention Café Deluxe. It's always packed and full of lively energy. The food is consistent and never expensive. The interior is fairly plain, with white tablecloths and simple white plates—a step up from a diner—but the beef and tuna burgers are excellent, and so is the meatloaf. The desserts are homemade, as are the soups. Meals run $7 to $16. Most major credit cards accepted.

Clyde's of Georgetown
✉3236 M St. NW
☏202-333-9180

Founded in 1963 as a faux-Victorian pub for Georgetown University students, this has become a popular chain of local restaurants (including the venerated Old Ebbitt Grill and several other Clyde's locations) where you can always get good American saloon food. The standard selection includes a juicy burger, buffalo wings, crab cake sandwich, hearty soups, and a surprisingly excellent cheese platter that pairs blackberries with your four cheese selections. Most people order from the appetizer menu, which is varied and creative. Of course, there's a wide selection of beers on tap and a good wine list.

Weekend brunches have become a tradition (especially because this restaurant is located in the Shops at Georgetown Park). Meals run from $10 to $17, and lunch is less expensive. Validated parking is available in the nearby mall. Major credit are cards accepted.

Shops at Georgetown Park Food Court
✉On M St.

There are a dozen or so fast-food establishments located here, offering pizza, Philly cheese steaks, pretzels, ice cream, gyros, and other light fare, all reasonably priced.

Myth.com
✉3243 M St. NW
☎202-625-6984

At this cybercafe and restaurant, you can partake of a wide selection of coffees, teas, and fruit drinks, as well as a killer hamburger, all while you check your e-mail. Internet usage is free to students and faculty with I.D. cards; otherwise, fees run $2.50 for fifteen minutes, or $10 an hour). Major credit cards accepted.

Dupont Circle

Cheap Eats

Helix Lounge
✉1430 Rhode Island Ave. NW
☎202-462-9001

One of the restaurant lounges in the Kimpton Hotel chain, this small, hip lounge offer great burgers and a terrific array of hearty appetizers. You could actually order a few appetizers and feed the whole family. Every day there's a happy hour from 5:00 until 7:00 P.M., when burgers are only $5. Wonderful creative drinks are available too, even for kids. Have them ask for the fruitini, which is mixed fruit juices and 7-Up served in an adult martini glass. Preteens and teens will love the beaded curtains and the flashing lights. This place is very older-child-friendly. Major credit cards are accepted. Take the Metro to the Dupont Circle station.

Kramerbooks & Afterwords
✉ 1517 Connecticut Ave. NW at Q St.
✆ 202-387-1400

This is a good restaurant, and it's located in one of the late-night bookstores and cybercafes in town (with a free fifteen-minute e-mail check available). The menu is pages long, featuring a variety of dishes from vegetable chili to lamb chops to quesadillas, with a wide selection of beers. Sunday brunch (served all day) is very popular here. Entrees run $7 to $11. Major credit cards are accepted. Take the Metro to the Dupont Circle station.

💼 TRAVEL TIP

With so much to see and do in the city, you don't want to be walking through the streets looking for a good or affordable place to eat when the museum closes at 4:45 P.M. So it's a good idea to plan your meals in conjunction with your sightseeing, and if a place is highly recommended, make a reservation just in case. (During the summer, keep in mind that restaurants are packed.)

Luigi's
✉ 1132 19th St. NW
✆ 202-331-7574

Great pizza with lots of options for toppings in a restaurant with red-and-white checked tablecloths that has been in existence since

1943. Great pasta is offered here, too—including cheese ravioli, lasagna, and manicotti. Meals run from $5 to $14. Kids' pasta selections are all under $5. Major credit cards are accepted. Take the Metro to the Dupont Circle or Farragut North stations.

Teaism
✉800 Connecticut Ave.
✆202-835-2233

This wonderful Asian restaurant serves a wide selection of personal potted teas, ice creams (green tea and ginger are first rate), and meals, including Japanese bento boxes, kebobs, curries, salads, and even an ostrich burger. Most meals are under $5, except for the ostrich burger. Most credit cards are accepted. Take the Metro to the Dupont Circle station. Another brunch is located nearby, at ✉2009 R St. (✆202-667-3827).

Topaz Bar
✉1733 N St. NW
✆202-393-3000

Another of the restaurant/bars in the Kimpton Hotel chain, Topaz Bar offers a pan-Asian appetizer spread that can serve as a meal (half-price every day between 5:00 and 7:00 P.M.). The chicken satay and the spring rolls are delicious, and there are some kicky signature drinks. Because this is a bar atmosphere, it is inappropriate for younger children. Major credit cards are accepted. Take the Metro to the Dupont Circle station.

Zorba's Cafe
✉1612 20th St. NW at Connecticut Ave.
✆202-387-8555

This inexpensive Greek restaurant is located on Dupont Circle's main drag. It features a wonderful selection of fast Greek food, from dips to fried cheese to a souvlaki plate and baklava for dessert. Entrees start at around $5. Some credit cards are accepted. Take the Metro to the Dupont Circle station.

Moderate Options

Athens Taverna
✉ 1732 Connecticut Ave. NW
☎ 202-667-9211

This moderately priced Greek restaurant features a good selection of food and seafood, including a three-entree combo plate of stuffed grape leaves with lemon sauce, moussaka (eggplant with custard), and pastitsio (a sort of Greek lasagna), as well as an excellent retsina wine. Galatobutiko (literally "milk and butter," a rich Greek dessert made of sugared farina wrapped in phyllo dough) is on the dessert menu. Entrees run $9 to $20. Major credit cards are accepted. Take the Metro to the Dupont Circle station.

Buca di Beppo
✉ 1825 Connecticut Ave. NW
☎ 202-232-8466

Family-style, large portions of Southern Italian cuisine are this restaurant's claim to fame, as it was designed to resemble a 1950s supper club. Platters of pasta, oversized pizza, and standards such as chicken cacciatore are featured on the menu. Entrees run $16 to $20, but they are meant to be shared. Most major credit cards are accepted. Take the Metro to the Dupont Circle station.

≡FAST FACT

Although hotel restaurants are a good bet for breakfast, some of the better or more unique (and filling) breakfasts can be found at the Waffle House downtown, where you can sit at a counter and order filling breakfasts of eggs and bacon, or pancakes, waffles, and even steak and eggs, all for under $5.

Gabriel
✉ 2121 P St. NW
☎ 202-956-6690

Gabriel is an upscale Spanish restaurant located in the Radisson Barcelo Hotel. The emphasis here is on European, as opposed to Latin American, cuisine. There's a wonderful selection of tapas and some delicious Spanish dishes, such as roast pig, and exquisite desserts. As in all tapas restaurants, you can get away with making a meal out of two tapas selections. Dinner can run you as little as $12, but entrees are $15 to $22. Gabriel's is also known for its sumptuous Sunday brunch. Major credit cards are accepted. Complimentary valet parking is available. Take the Metro to the Dupont Circle station.

Levante's
✉ 1320 19th St. NW
☎ 202-293-3244

This upscale Mediterranean restaurant (Turkish cuisine via Europe) has an outdoor patio and features a terrific appetizer plate of fried cheese, salad, and dolmathes (stuffed grape leaf rolls); they also offer a terrific spinach pie. Entrees run $6 to $16.50. Most major credit cards are accepted. Take the Metro to the Dupont Circle station.

Foggy Bottom/West End

Cheap Eats

Moby Dick's House of Kabob
✉ 1070 31st St. NW
☎ 202-333-4400

A very popular restaurant with the locals, this is the third branch of a chain that started in the suburbs. It features Persian food, mainly kabobs and grilled meat, laced with a secret house seasoning. There's hardly any seating, but it's always crowded. Only cash is accepted. Take the Metro to the Cleveland Park station.

Nam Viet
✉ 3419 Connecticut Ave. NW at Macomb St.
☎ 202-237-1015

This is one of the older and best Vietnamese restaurants in town. Everyone recommends the pho (beef noodle soup) and the fresh crispy fish, as well as the spring rolls and the shrimp toast. Entrees run $7 to $14. Most major credit cards are accepted. Take the Metro to the Cleveland Park station.

Moderate Options

Circle Bistro
✉One Washington Circle, NW
✆202-293-5390

Located near the Kennedy Center and Georgetown, this stunning American bistro with a Mediterranean flair serves up signature dishes including Moroccan-style lamb with figs, caramelized plantains and couscous, curried veal with grilled papaya and pineapple, ravioli with lobster and jumbo lump crabmeat, and vegetable strudel with zucchini, squash, eggplant, and peanut essence.

The sunset menu offers three courses for $28. The lounge, with its oversized sofas and widescreen TV, features tempting cheese and chocolate fondues, a favorite among kids who can handle a skewer. Also available are sandwiches and appetizers. Dinner runs $15 to $21, but the appetizer portions are large enough for smaller appetites. Several items are offered at $1 apiece during the 5:00 to 7:00 P.M. happy hour. Major credit cards are accepted. Take the Metro to the Foggy Bottom station.

🧳 TRAVEL TIP

For authentic Chinese food, visit D.C.'s small Chinatown (along H and 7th Streets). Full Kee (✉509 H Street, NW) is a local favorite, and the food is extremely authentic. Go-Lo's (✉605 H St.), the former site of the boarding house where President Lincoln's end was plotted, has a wonderful assortment of Hunan and Szechuan entrees, and Tony Cheng's (✉619 H St. NW) has hosted just about every president in the last thirty years—and Cheng has a picture on the wall to prove it.

U Street Corridor

Cheap Eats

Ben's Chili Bowl

✉ 1213 E St. NW

☎ 202-667-0909

Ben's may be off the beaten path, but the restaurant is a D.C. landmark nonetheless. This seventy-year-old restaurant was made famous on the *Cosby Show* in the late 1980s, and people have been lining up for Ben's delicious and ample chili dogs (with or without cheese and onions) for years. There are chili burgers, and just plain chili as well; vegetarian chili is also available. Almost everything is $5 or less. Only cash is accepted. Take the Metro to the U Street station.

Love Cafe

✉ 1501 U St. NW

☎ 202-667-5221

Owner Warren Brown told his story of making cakes from scratch and selling them in a tiny U Street storefront on the *Oprah Winfrey Show,* and before you know it, everyone in Washington, D.C., was going to the Love Cafe for these delicious cakes. The original storefront is closed now, and there is a sit-down pastry shop where every cupcake combination known to man is available for a mere $2. Buy some on your way out of town, and they'll pack them for you. Take the Metro to the U Street station.

Brunches and Afternoon Teas

Afternoon tea and Sunday brunch are also a big dining to-do in this town, and some of these are spectacular or at least unique: The National Cathedral's afternoon tea is legendary, and the Sunday brunch at the Smithsonian Castle is a unique experience. Here are a few suggestions.

Best Brunches

Washingtonians love Sunday brunch, so you'll find it offered at most hotel restaurants and most of the chain restaurants. Of course, not all brunches are equal. Some are opulent food extravaganzas that offer everything but the kitchen sink, including unlimited champagne; others are so quirky they seem like something out of *Alice in Wonderland.* The following is a list of the standouts in town:

- **Bistro Francais** in Georgetown offers a moderately priced brunch with a selection of eggs or French fare and all the champagne you can drink for $15.95.
- **Bombay Club** offers a sumptuous buffet that includes an array of Indian dishes, as well as a carving station, for $16.50.
- The Corcoran's gospel brunch in the **Corcoran Gallery's Café des Artistes** features gospel music as you dine in the museum's atrium drinking mimosas. The $18.95 brunch includes your museum entry fee.
- **Clyde's of Georgetown** is a popular brunch spot (priced from $7 to $11) with a nice selection of omelets, steak and eggs, and so on. Its sister restaurant, the **Old Ebbitt Grill** downtown, has a much fancier brunch menu (from $6 to $13).
- **Gabriel** in the Hotel Radisson Barcelo is packed on Sundays with locals and tourists who come for the extravagant array of food. Everything from salads to quesadillas, with a carving station offering beef, lamb, and suckling pig, plus a fabulous selection of desserts, all for $17.95.
- **Kramers & Afterwords** offers Sunday brunch all day in a very affordable price range, so it is a popular Sunday destination in the Dupont Circle area.
- **Roof Top Terrace** at the Kennedy Center is one of the best brunch deals in town with a lavish buffet of pasta, smoked meats, omelets made to order, and desserts, as well as your choice of a drink, for $25.95.

- The **Morrison-Clark Hotel Restaurant** offers an exquisite upscale brunch with unlimited champagne for $29.95.
- **Perry's,** in the Adams Morgan area, is the most creative Sunday brunch in town. Take in the funky, funny drag show while you eat from a buffet of pasta, breakfast meats, bagels, dessert, and coffee for $15.95. Alcoholic drinks are additional. The crowd is mixed, and you'll even see some couples with baby carriages.

≡FAST FACT

The brunch offered at Castle Common in the Smithsonian is your chance to eat in this wonderful old building and then rush out to see the sights on the Mall. Sunday brunch offers a "noble feast" of carved meats, omelets, and the famous spiced shrimp buffet for $18.95 for adults, and $8.95 for children. Reservations are recommended because this is such a popular brunch spot (☎202-357-2957).

Afternoon Tea

Afternoon tea is a big deal in this town. You'll find it offered at most of the better hotel restaurants. There are a handful of truly stellar afternoon tea experiences in the city, and if you like a late lunch or a little something before dinner, you should really try to fit them into your schedule.

Tea at the **National Cathedral** is grand, and you really should make a reservation because it's also very popular with tourists and regulars. It is served on Tuesdays and Wednesdays only at 1:30 P.M. and costs a flat $15, for which you are offered a selection of tea sandwiches, pastries, scones, a selection of delicious desserts, and tea. A tour of the cathedral comes with the tea.

Coeur de Lion, in the elegant Henley Park Hotel in the downtown area, serves a wonderful afternoon tea in its dining room from 4:00 P.M. to 6:00 P.M., with a wide selection of pastries and scones.

Other hotel restaurants that feature afternoon tea include the **Lafayette** in the Hay-Adams Hotel, **Melrose** in the Park Hyatt, **Seasons** in the Four Seasons Hotel, and at the lobby lounge of the Westfield Marriott in Chantilly, Virginia (near Tyson's Corner).

CHAPTER 16

Where to Stay Under $100

THERE ARE HUNDREDS OF HOTELS in Washington, D.C., from those that cater to the family, to some of the most luxurious suites in the nation, to those for people on a very tight budget, to international business people.

This chapter features the budget hotels—under $100 if you get a special, otherwise, they may be higher. Remember that sometimes it's worth it to pay a little more for location. Otherwise, you'll be paying to park the car all day and/or paying Metro fares for the whole family, when you could have been just walking from a downtown hotel.

The hotel reviews are organized by location, beginning with the downtown and Capitol Hill hotels; nearby Metro stops are included.

How to Save

There are many ways to cut the cost of your hotel stay. See if you can use Automobile Association of America (AAA) and the American Association of Retired Persons (AARP) discounts, which are usually around 10 percent. You can also look for hotels that offer free continental breakfast or even have kitchenettes. There are often discounts for business travelers, as well as summer and weekend specials and family rates, so ask for the lowest rate when you call for reservations.

≡FAST FACT

The average hotel room runs about $150 for double occupancy, according to a 2003 article in the *Washington Post*. Hotel taxes are another $15 a night, and parking charges can be as high as $25 a night.

Always try the variety of Internet travel search engines that offer hotel rooms (some offer discounts too), as they often have the best rates available and make a deluxe hotel very affordable for the family. The following is a good selection of travel-related sites.

Washington, D.C., Convention and Visitor's Association
✍*www.washington.org*

This site offers searchable hotel listings prepared by the D.C. Convention and Visitor's Association. The information here is organized by price and location, offering listings from hotels, bed and breakfasts, hostels, and even campgrounds. It has a special weekend-rate search engine too.

Fodors.com
✍*www.fodors.com*

The travel guide site offers a similar hotel index that you can use to search by name or category, as well as its own list of best hotels.

Priceline
✍*www.priceline.com*

This travel auction Web site will book you a discounted hotel room in D.C., but you can't see where it is when you place the bid. They say that all their hotels are members of major chains, and you can probably get a very good rate this way (you set the price and see what comes in), but just be aware that there are parts of downtown Washington that you have to take a cab to once the sun sets.

Expedia.com

✑*www.expedia.com*

This site will give you a listing of hotels by location and price, and you can even see photos, but make sure you look the hotel up elsewhere, as sometimes they are adjacent to seedier parts of town.

Orbitz

✑*www.orbitz.com*

This travel Web site also has a hotel search engine with hotel photos, but double-check the listing.

TripAdvisor

✑*www.tripadvisor.com*

A great Web site that will give you travelers' reviews as well as the best price on the Web for any hotel you are searching for.

Travelocity

✑*www.travelocity.com*

Another good Web site if you know the neighborhood where you want to stay and/or hotel you want to stay in.

Washington Post

✑*www.washingtonpost.com*

Among the many services offered by the newspaper is a search engine that lists hotels by neighborhood and price.

Preferred Hotels and Resorts Worldwide

✑*www.preferredhotels.com*

Offered by Travelweb, this site functions as a reservation system for the hotel industry.

Holiday Inn and Radisson Hotel

www.holidayinn.com

www.radisson.com

These hotel chains also have Internet sites, and you can sometimes find good packages and last-minute deals there.

TRAVEL TIP

If you're looking for a kid-friendly hotel, here's something to consider. Red Roof Inn in Chinatown has in-room pay-per-service Nintendo game systems. Loew's L'Enfant Plaza offers free meals and a welcoming gift to every child under the age of 12. Washington Plaza has a pool and family-oriented activities all summer long.

Downtown D.C.

Holiday Inn Capital at the Smithsonian

✉550 C St. NW

✆202-479-4000

Location, location, location. This 529-room hotel is a block away from the Smithsonian's National Air and Space Museum, the most popular museum in the Smithsonian Institution, as well as the other Smithsonian museums and the National Archives. Rooms are designed in traditional hotel-chain style, with hair dryers and irons available. There's a rooftop pool and a health club. On-site dining includes Smithson's Restaurant, the Shuttle Express Deli, and a lobby bar for cocktails. Published room rates are as much as $169 per night, but Internet specials often list rooms for $79.95, so ask how you can get a room at that price. Parking is an additional $18 per night. All major credit cards are accepted. This hotel is convenient to the L'Enfant Plaza Metro station.

Days Inn Premier

✉ 1201 K St. NW

☎ 1-800-562-3350

Near the Convention Center and family-friendly, this eight-story hotel has a rooftop pool, which is always popular with kids. Rooms are fairly standard, with hair dryers, satellite television and pay-per-view movies, and coffeemakers. There is a fitness center on the premises. Room rates run $99 to $125 on weekdays, $79 to $99 on weekends, but there are a number of supersaver packages, so ask for the best price when you call. Parking is an additional $14. Major credit cards are accepted. This hotel is convenient to the McPherson Square and Metro Center Metro stations.

Lincoln Suites Downtown

✉ 1823 L St. NW

☎ 1-800-424-2970

This is an all-suite, ten-story hotel with ninety-nine suites. Many guests stay for weeks or longer when doing business in the city because it is only five blocks from the White House and central to most of the capital's attractions. About one-third of the suites feature full kitchens; others have microwaves and refrigerators. Other amenities include a wet bar, hair dryer, complimentary milk and cookies in the evening, and continental breakfast in the morning. There are two restaurants on site. Samantha's features traditional American food, and Beatrice is an Italian restaurant. Suites are $99 to $159. Major credit cards are accepted. Parking is an additional $9 per day in the adjoining garage. This hotel is convenient to the Farragut North and Farragut West Metro stations.

Braxton Hotel

✉ 1440 Rhode Island Ave. NW at 14th St.

☎ 1-800-350-5759

This sixty-two-room hotel is decorated with a hodgepodge of themed antiques, which certainly has its own unique charm. A free continental breakfast is offered in the dining room, with twenty-four-hour coffee and tea available. Room rates are $50 to $79 for a single room, and $65 to $89 for a double. Parking is an additional $7 per night. Most major credit cards are accepted, excluding American Express. This hotel is convenient to the McPherson Square Metro station.

≡FAST FACT

Here's some D.C. trivia: The classic movie *Mr. Smith Goes to Washington* was filmed at the Hotel Washington. And did you know that Albert Einstein once lived at the St. Regis Hotel (now the Sheraton-Carlton)?

Red Roof Inn
✉500 H St. NW
✆1-800-THE-ROOF

A ten-story hotel in the heart of the capital's Chinatown, right across the street from one of the best Chinese restaurants (Full Kee), the Red Roof is also within walking distance to many of the city's major attractions, such as the MCI Center, Ford's Theatre, and the Convention Center. Rooms are spacious and decorated in contemporary hotel decor, with pay-per-view movie service, as well as Nintendo for children. The hotel's restaurant serves an inexpensive breakfast and lunch, and there is a washer/dryer on the premises, as well as a health club and sauna. Weekday rates are $97.99 to $120 for a double, and weekend rates are $70 to $102. Outdoor parking is $9.50 per day. Major credit cards are accepted. This hotel is convenient to the Gallery Place Metro station.

Swiss Inn
✉1204 Massachusetts Ave. NW
✆202-371-1816

This is an affordable hotel in a former brownstone within walking distance to almost everything you'll need, but it's a small hotel, so book in advance. Rooms are simple but nicely decorated with a kitchenette in each room. Pets are allowed. Room rates are $69 to $119. Most major credit cards are accepted. Parking is free on weekends, and the fee is $8.50 during the week. This hotel is convenient to the Metro Center Metro station.

Travelodge City Center Hotel
✉ 1201 13th St. NW at M St.

☎ 202-682-5300

This hotel offers fairly standard hotel accommodations at a central, if somewhat urban, location. There is a free continental breakfast and a coffeemaker in each room. Room rates are $79 for a single room, and $89 for a double. Parking is an additional $11 to $21, depending on the size of the vehicle. Major credit cards are accepted. This hotel is convenient to the McPherson Square Metro station.

Capitol Hill

Capitol Hill Suites
✉ 200 C St. NW

☎ 1-800-424-9165

The location of Capitol Hill Suites on the House of Representatives side of the Capitol makes this a regular haunt of congresspeople, whose recent photos adorn the lobby walls. This is an all-suite hotel with 152 rooms, most of which have kitchens and dining rooms, so it is also a good family place to stay. There is no on-site restaurant, but there is a food court as well as many nearby restaurants, which the hotel staff will gladly inform you about. Amenities include a continental breakfast, washer and dryer on premises, and use of a nearby health club. Suite rates are $89 to $199, with a $20 surcharge for extra adults. Parking is an additional $15 per night. Major credit cards are accepted. This hotel is convenient to the Capitol South Metro station.

Adams Morgan/Woodley Park

Windsor Park Hotel

✉ 2116 Kalorama Rd. NW at Connecticut Ave.

☎ 202-483-0770

This charming forty-three-room hotel is furnished with antiques and dried flowers, giving it a Victorian feel. Hotel amenities include a minibar, free newspaper delivery, and a continental breakfast buffet in the Tea Room. Room rates are $98 for a single room and $108 for a double. Parking is available on the street. Major credit cards are accepted. This hotel is convenient to the Woodley Park Metro station.

🧳 TRAVEL TIP

Because Washington, D.C., is the nation's capital and so many business travelers come to the city to try to work with the government agencies around town, hotel rooms are usually more expensive during the week than during the weekend. Rates are also lower during the summer when Congress isn't in session.

Adams Inn

✉ 1744 Lanier Place NW

☎ 1-800-578-6807

This hotel, located between Calvert Street and Ontario Road, is composed of three turn-of-the-twentieth-century townhouses that have been combined to make a total of twenty-five rooms, some of which do not have bathrooms of their own. This is a charming Old-World inn furnished in a faux Victorian style. In keeping with that décor, the rooms do not have televisions or phones, but there is a pay phone in the lobby and the hotel will take messages for you. There is also a communal television room and a refrigerator and microwave for guest use. There is a washer/dryer for guest use, and a free continental breakfast is offered in the morning.

Room rates are $65 for a double without a bathroom, $70 to $95 for rooms with a bathroom. Weekly rates are available. Major credit cards are accepted. Parking is an additional $7 per night. The closest Metro stop is Woodley Park, but it's a hike.

Kalorama Guest House

✉ 1854 Mintwood Place NW

✆ 202-667-6369

The Mintwood Place location, between 19th Street and Columbia Road, is composed of four townhouses. Another branch is located on 2700 Cathedral Avenue NW at 27th Street and is housed in two townhouses.

Though small by hotel standards, these charming inns both offer a great location for a great price. They are a good option if you don't mind sharing a bathroom (this is actually perfect for families or friends traveling together, although it's not ideal for very young children) and not having a television or phone in your room. There is a communal television room for those who just can't live without TV, and a phone in the lobby where you can make free local calls (the inn will take messages for you). There is a free continental breakfast in the morning and a snack and drinks on Friday and Saturday afternoons. Room rates are $60 to $90 for a double with a shared bathroom, $65 to $105 for a double with bathroom. Parking is an additional $10. Major credit cards accepted. This hotel is convenient to the Woodley Park Metro station.

Dupont Circle

Hotel Tabard Inn

✉ 1739 N St. NW

✆ 202-785-1227

This small hotel (sixty-two units) is made up of three Victorian townhouses. It retains much of the charm of its original architecture, such as bay windows in several rooms, and a beamed ceiling and working fireplace in the lounge. The on-site restaurant is known for its Sunday brunch, and is popular with Washingtonians. Rooms are quirky but nice, although some do not have bathrooms of their own. A free continental breakfast is available to guests.

Room rates are $90 to $100 for rooms with a shared bathroom, $114 to $165 with bathroom, but there are summer specials. Major credit cards are accepted. Valet parking is $14; self-parking is an additional $10 per night. This hotel is convenient to the Dupont Circle Metro station.

Normandy Inn
✉2118 Wyoming Ave. NW
✆1-800-424-3729.

This is a lovely small hotel (seventy-five rooms) near Connecticut Avenue in the midst of Embassy Row, so many travelers are here on foreign affairs business. The hotel has a European air (it's run by an Irish company) and serves coffee and tea all day long in the appropriately named Tea Room, as well as afternoon cookies. The Tea Room is also where the complimentary continental breakfast is served every morning. In-room amenities include a small refrigerator and a coffeemaker, and the hotel charges $79 to $155 for a double room. Parking is an additional $10. Major credit cards are accepted.

Dupont Circle Metro Station Swann House
✉1808 New Hampshire Ave. NW
✆202-265-7677

This eleven-unit inn is housed in a mansion built in 1883, and each room is uniquely and handsomely decorated. Most have working fireplaces. The main floor features high ceilings, original woodwork, and a sunroom where a continental breakfast of home-made pastries is served daily. The hotel has an outdoor swimming pool set in a garden. Room rates are $110 to $235. Credit cards accepted are MasterCard and Visa only. This hotel is convenient to the Dupont Circle Metro station.

Embassy Inn

✉ 1627 16th St. NW

☎ 1-800-423-9111

This thirty-eight-room hotel in a four-story townhouse is on a nice block with other turn-of-the-twentieth-century townhouses between Q and R Streets. Much of its interior architecture is original, which is why the sinks are in the bedroom and some interior rooms have no windows. Amenities include a free continental breakfast, evening sherry, and snacks. Room rates are $79 to $110 on weekdays, with weekend rates being much cheaper. Street parking only is available. Major credit cards are accepted. This hotel is convenient to the Dupont Circle Metro station.

≡FAST FACT

An all-new Embassy Suites hotel is set to be opened in the fall of 2005 on 10th Street and K NW, within walking distance of the new Convention Center. It will offer 383 guest suites, as well as a pool and health facility.

Windsor Inn

✉ 1842 16th St. NW at T St.

☎ 1-800-423-9111

This hotel is operated by the same management as the Embassy Inn and offers some of the same amenities, such as free continental breakfast and afternoon snack and sherry. The forty-seven-room hotel is composed of two buildings, with two separate entrances, that sit side by side. Hotel rooms are nicely laid out and a handful have fireplaces. Most rooms have tubs and showers, but six rooms have showers only, so ask when you call for your reservation. Room rates are $79 to $125 for a double room on weekdays, with weekend rates being cheaper. Parking is available on the street only. Major credit cards accepted. This hotel is convenient to the Dupont Circle Metro station.

Foggy Bottom/West End

Allen Lee Hotel
✉2224 F St. NW at 23rd St.

☎202-331-1224

This is a real find—a nice, clean, safe, and very inexpensive hotel near a Metro stop. Many of the people who stay here are prospective George Washington University students or their visiting parents. The hotel is also within walking distance to the Kennedy Center.

There are only eighty-five rooms available, so book early. Room rates are $45 to $74 for a single room and $62 to $74 for a double, but there are common bathrooms for the less expensive rooms. Triples and quads are also available. Parking is on the street only, although there is parking in a nearby lot for $10. MasterCard and Visa are the only credit cards accepted. This hotel is convenient to the Foggy Bottom Metro station.

The River Inn
✉924 25th St. NW

☎202-337-7600

The River Inn is located between K and L Sts., within walking distance to the Kennedy Center and to Georgetown (a long walk). This is a very affordable hotel offering guests fully stocked kitchens and microwave ovens. The newly opened DISN restaurant serves up American classics with a fresh twist at affordable prices. Hotel amenities include a free continental breakfast, health club, and newspaper delivery. Rooms rates are $99 for a single room and $150 for a double. Major credit cards are accepted. Parking is an additional $12 to $15. This hotel is convenient to the Foggy Bottom Metro station.

Georgetown

Georgetown Suites

✉1000 29th St. NW

✆1-800-348-7203

This seventy-eight-unit, all-suite hotel in the heart of Georgetown (between K and M Streets) offers a living room, dining area, and fully stocked kitchen in all suites. In-room amenities include a hair dryer, iron, and writing area. Hotel amenities include a free continental breakfast, fitness center, washer and dryer, and an outdoor barbecue grill for guest use. Room rates are $139 for a double room on weekdays, $99 for a double on weekends, and more for larger suites. Parking is an additional $15. There is no convenient Metro service.

═FAST FACT

Georgetown Suites has a sister hotel with an additional 136 suites (same phone number and rates). The address is ✉1111 30th Street NW, just down the street (also between K and M Streets).

Holiday Inn Georgetown

✉2101 Wisconsin Ave. NW

✆1-866-260-0402

This Holiday Inn location is at the very edge of Georgetown, so it's only a mile from the nearest Metro station, and there's a free shuttle going between the station and the inn. This 296-room hotel offers an outdoor pool, restaurant and bar on premises, a fitness center, and even a washer and dryer on the premises, which can be a real plus when traveling with kids. Amenities include daily newspaper, coffee machine, and Nintendo in most rooms. Rates vary, but during the winter you can get a double room for $69.95, while rates may go up to $95.95 at other times. Major credit cards are accepted.

CHAPTER 17

Moderately Priced Hotels ($100–$150)

THIS CHAPTER FEATURES the moderate family hotels, which Washington, D.C., really seems to specialize in. When traveling with a family, remember that how close your hotel is to the attractions you want to see is a consideration if your children need to nap or take a midday pool break. Also check to see if the hotel has pay-per-view movies and Nintendo or a game room, as well as a pool.

TRAVEL TIP

The six newly renovated hotels in the Kimpton chain are always an affordable and fun choice for family stays. Most of them run about $125 per night, and they are pet-friendly as well.

Downtown D.C.

Governor's House Hotel
✉ 1615 Rhode Island Ave. NW
☏ 202-296-2100
A 146-room hotel built in the refurbished home of a former governor of Pennsylvania, Governor's House Hotel has just undergone

a multimillion-dollar renovation. This elegant hotel is within walking distance of many of the city's popular attractions. The on-site restaurant, The 17th Street Bar & Grill, features traditional American fare. The hotel has a fitness center and a pool. There are also deluxe accommodations in the top two floors that include a coffeemaker, wine, and flowers in each room.

Rates start at $145 and go up from there, but in the summer the hotel has an $89 special rate (ask for the *New York Times* rate). Parking is an additional $14 (Friday and Saturday) or $20 (Sunday through Thursday) per night. This hotel is convenient to the Farragut North Metro station.

Henley Park

✉926 Massachusetts Ave. NW

✆1-800-678-8946

Once an elegant apartment building, the Henley Park is now a ninety-six-room hotel with 118 gargoyles on its façade (including the faces of the architect and his wife). The rooms are large and nicely decorated, with a fax machine in most rooms, as well as a bathrobe, coffeemaker, hair dryer, and iron. Other hotel amenities include free newspaper, nightly turndown service with chocolates, and a free limousine service in the morning. The hotel restaurant, Coeur de Lion, is one of the best hotel restaurants in the city, and nightly hors d'oeuvres are served in the jazz club, Marley's Lounge, with dancing on weekends. There is also a fireside afternoon tea in the hotel's lobby, which has stained-glass windows and original Mercer tiled floors.

The hotel is within walking distance to the National Gallery, Ford's Theatre, the National Museum of Women in the Arts, and Chinatown. Published rates are $165 for a single and $225 for a double, but there is a $99 summer rate (mention the *New York Times* rate). Major credit cards are accepted. The closest Metro station is Metro Center (about five blocks away).

Hotel Helix

✉ 1430 Rhode Island Ave. NW

✆ 202-462-7777

This is a great hotel for families with teens and preteens. It's unbelievably hip, with a giant painting of Magritte's businessman in a bowler hat on the outside of the building. Part of the Kimpton chain, there's a great lounge that serves terrific burgers and a half-price happy hour on both food and terrific martinis—try the Ding-dongtini, which has a Ding Dong floating in it!—every day from 5:00 to 7:00 P.M. An outdoor patio is open in the summer. Rooms are stylish, with green gauze canopies over the bed with faux fur bed-spreads, and a large-screen television, Nintendo, and a CD player in every room. Amenities include the fabulous Aveda soaps and shampoos.

🚶 JUST FOR PARENTS

Although there is plenty of nightlife in Washington, most of the better hotels have highly recommended lounges where you can hear piano and/or jazz, and some even have dancing. Among those that stand out are the Hilton Tower, Grand Hyatt, Henley Park, Westin Fairfax, One Washington Circle Hotel, and the Washington Plaza Hotel.

There's a continental breakfast in the morning with bagels and cereal. Room rates are about $125, slightly more for a king and more for the bunk suite, but there are always specials. There are terrific "bunk bed" suites that have a second room for the kids, but these are limited, so reserve ahead. All Kimpton hotels are pet-friendly, for an additional $15 per night. Parking is an additional $22 per night. All major credit cards accepted. This hotel is convenient to the McPherson Square Metro station.

Holiday Inn Downtown
✉ 1155 14th St. NW
✆ 1-800-HOLIDAY

Five blocks from the White House, this fourteen-story hotel is very family-friendly, with a kids-eat-free promo that is just one of the chain's many extra perks. The hotel features a rooftop pool and sun deck, a fitness center next door, as well as washers and dryers. The restaurant offers breakfast and dinner buffets. Room rates are $130 to $170 on weekdays and $100 to $170 on weekends. Inquire about summer rates. Valet parking is $18 per night. This hotel is convenient to the McPherson Square Metro station.

Hotel Harrington
✉ 416 11th St. NW
✆ 202-628-8140

Almost ninety years old, this hotel has a great location and tradition. Good rooms, centrally located at an affordable price, it's been serving traveling families for generations. Right near the MCI Center and the ESPNZone, it offers adjoining family rooms for $135 to $145. Doubles are $100 to $125, and parking costs $8.50 a day. Major credit cards are accepted. This hotel is convenient to the Gallery Place Metro station.

Lincoln Suites Downtown
✉ 1823 L St. NW
✆ 1-800-424-2970

This is an all-suite, ten-story hotel with ninety-nine suites. Many guests stay for weeks or longer when doing business in the city because it is only five blocks from the White House and central to most of the capital's attractions. About one-third of the suites feature full kitchens; others have microwaves and refrigerators. Other amenities include a wet bar, hair dryer, complimentary milk and cookies in the evening, and continental breakfast in the morning. There are two restaurants on site. Samantha's features traditional American food, and Beatrice is an Italian restaurant. Suites are $99 to $159. Major credit cards are accepted. Parking is an additional $9 per day in the adjoining garage. This hotel is convenient to the Farragut North or Farragut West Metro stations.

Hotel Monaco

✉700 F St. NW

✆1-800-649-1202

This is a one-of-a-kind hotel, and it's very kid-friendly. The Kimpton hotel chain bought this old post office and converted it into a fun hotel. Long hallways look like something out of Tom Petty's "Alice in Wonderland" video. Rooms are large and have wonderful windows and high ceilings, and you can even request that a goldfish in a bowl be brought to your room. It's also near the International Spy Museum, Ford's Theatre, the soon-to-be-renovated National Portrait Museum, and the Museum of American Art. Some rooms have vaulted ceilings and Jacuzzis, and there's a well-equipped health club on the premises. All rooms have Nintendo and a changeable CD player, as well as the Aveda soap and shampoos. The Poste Brasserie on the premises offers a terrific selection of bistro fare, and there's a lounge at the front of the restaurant for slightly faster and less expensive fare. Rooms start at about $125 per night, but there are always specials. Parking is $22 a night. This hotel is convenient to the Metro Center station.

J.W. Marriott

✉1331 Pennsylvania Ave. NW at E St.

✆1-800-228-9290

This hotel's location is central to lots of downtown activity, such as the Convention Center and National Theater, and is two blocks from the White House. There are three restaurants on the premises, and the hotel connects to a mall with eighty shops and restaurants. The hotel has a fitness center, indoor pool, and game room. Rooms are comfortable and feature a desk area, hair dryer, iron, and toiletries. Other amenities include twice-daily maid service, nightly turndown, and morning paper.

Rates are $234 for a double on weekdays and $109 to $234 on weekends. The hotel does run a number of specials, such as its $89-per-night holiday package before Christmas, so ask for special rates. Parking is an additional $25. Major credit cards are accepted. This hotel is convenient to the Metro Center Metro station.

📼 TRAVEL TIP

The two most important elements to choosing your accommodations in D.C. should be location and price. Of course, if you are traveling as a family or visiting the city on business, there might be additional amenities that you will want (such as a pool or a fax machine). If you are not coming by car or don't plan on renting one, try to find a hotel near a Metro station.

Morrison-Clark Inn
✉ 1015 L St. NW
✆ 1-800-678-8946

This hotel was once two separate townhouses, which have been joined to create this unique inn, the only city inn to be listed in the National Register of Historic Places. From 1923 until the 1980s, the site was the Soldiers, Sailors, Marines and Airmen's Club. Some rooms are small, but they are elegantly detailed and furnished with wonderful antiques. There are transformed carriage houses on the first floor, which offer spacious accommodations, and some rooms feature fireplaces, pier mirrors, and wrought-iron ceiling medallions. Hotel amenities include a lovely continental breakfast in the hotel's dining area with scones, pastries, and cereal, nightly turndown service with chocolates, free morning newspaper, complimentary fitness center (open twenty-four hours with your room key), and a minibar in every room. The hotel restaurant is nationally acclaimed and offers fabulous Southern and American cuisine, including great desserts.

The Morrison-Clark is within walking distance to the National Gallery, Ford's Theatre, MCI Center, and the Convention Center. Published room rates are $150 for a single room and $210 for a double, but there is a $99 summer rate (ask for the *New York Times* rate). Major credit cards are accepted. The closest Metro stop is Metro Center.

Washington Plaza
✉10 Thomas Circle NW at 14th St.

✆1-800-424-1140

A little off the beaten track, but trying to be family-friendly, the Washington Plaza offers many family-oriented activities in the summer, such as Friday night poolside barbecues. Recently renovated, this large hotel (339 rooms) brings back the International style of the 1960s in its lobby furnished with Mies van der Rohe chairs. Rooms are large, with in-room coffeemakers. Other amenities include twice-daily maid service, twenty-four-hour room service, and a morning paper. There is nightly jazz in the plaza lounge, free American breakfast buffet, and a fitness center.

Published rates are $125 to $175 for a single room and $145 to $175 for a double, but the hotel offers a $99 summer rate (ask for the *New York Times* rate). Major credit cards are accepted. Parking is an additional $10 a night. This hotel is convenient to the McPherson Metro station.

Capitol Hill

Phoenix Park Hotel
✉520 N. Capitol St. NW

✆1-800-824-5419

This hotel is a block away from Union Station and two blocks from the Capitol and was once known as the Commodore Hotel. The hotel has an Irish pub, the Dubliner, on the premises and in keeping with that theme has tried to make things Irish throughout, with Irish toiletries and linens in the bathrooms and much green in the decor. The 150 rooms are comfortable and feature hair dryers and coffeemakers. Room rates are $189 to $219 for a double on weekdays, and they cost $89 and up on weekends. Parking is an additional $15. This hotel is convenient to the Union Station Metro station.

Capitol Hill Suites
✉200 C St. NW
✆1-800-424-9165

Its location on the House of Representatives side of the Capitol makes this a regular haunt of congresspeople, whose recent photos adorn the lobby walls. This is an all-suite hotel with 152 rooms, most of which have kitchens and dining rooms, so it is also a good family place to stay. There is no on-site restaurant, but there is a food court and many nearby restaurants, which the hotel staff will gladly inform you about. Amenities include a continental breakfast, washer and dryer on premises, and use of a nearby health club. Suite rates are $89 to $199, with a $20 surcharge for extra adults. Parking is an additional $15 per night. Major credit cards are accepted. This hotel is convenient to the Capitol South Metro stop.

≡FAST FACT

Two of Washington's largest hotels in the Woodley Park area (right near the zoo) have recently undergone major renovations, making them more business- and family-friendly: The Marriott Wardman Park Hotel and the neighboring Omni Shoreham. The Omni is also one of the two "haunted" hotels in the city.

Dupont Circle

Hotel Madera
✉1310 New Hampshire Ave. NW
✆202-296-7600

The Hotel Madera is a lovely, peaceful hotel a little off to the side in downtown Washington near the Heurich House. There's an utterly fabulous restaurant on the premises, so be sure to make a reservation to dine at Firefly, where the décor is that of a summer evening. Rooms are decorated in a rich brown-and-gold hue, there's a free wine-tasting every night at 6:00, and half the rooms have a balcony with a splendid view of the city's rooftops. Order room service in the morning and drag a chair out there. As in all Kimpton hotels, there's a large television, Nintendo, two phones, a dataport, free daily newspaper, and the Aveda soaps and shampoos provided in each room. The Hotel Madera is also pet-friendly. Rooms start at about $125, but there are always specials, and be sure to check the Internet for deals. Parking is $22 per night. All major credit cards are accepted. This hotel is convenient to the Dupont Circle Metro station.

Topaz Hotel
✉ 1733 N St. NW
✆ 1-800-775-1202

This site was once "The Little White House" when it was Teddy Roosevelt's private residence. Now it is one of the coolest hotels in D.C., as part of the hip Kimpton hotel chain. Every room in the hotel is decorated in turquoise and chartreuse, and the beds have canopy linens and pillows that are both plush and stylish. All rooms have a twenty-five-inch television and a dataport, as well as a CD player and a tea maker. There are specialty rooms for yoga and fitness (with equipment in the room), but every guest gets some healing stones on their pillow before bed. This is a great choice for a mother/daughter getaway. Amenities include an array of Aveda hair and soap products and a morning paper.

Prices run about $125, more for specialty rooms, but ask for weekend specials. Free high-energy drinks are served in the morning. There's a great bar lounge with a terrific happy hour that offers appetizers and drinks for only $5 from 5:00 to 7:00 P.M. every night. Parking is $25. All major credit cards are accepted. This hotel is convenient to the Dupont Circle Metro station.

Rouge
✉ 1315 16th St. NW
✆ 202-232-8000

This is the red hotel in the Kimpton chain, with rooms decorated in rich red velvet and leopard fabrics. Most rooms have an ottoman too, which kids love when sitting in front of the large television or playing Nintendo. Kids also love the oversize zebra bathrobes (which can be purchased). A good location off of Dupont Circle, near Embassy Row, the hotel's rooms are spacious, with desk work areas and a funky decor. Some rooms have balconies; others have kitchenettes. There is a lounge on site. Amenities include the Aveda soaps and shampoos, daily newspaper delivery, and a minibar in the room.

Room rates are about $125, more for suites and specialty rooms, such as the Chill room, which offers two TV/entertainment stations, so the kids can play while the parents relax. There are low summer rates and Internet specials, and Rouge is pet-friendly. Parking is $22 extra a night. Major credit cards are accepted. This hotel is convenient to the Dupont Circle Metro station.

🧳 TRAVEL TIP

If you prefer cooking to restaurants, kitchenettes can be found at the Lincoln Suites Downtown, Doubletree Guest Suites, The River Inn, the Georgetown Dutch Inn, and Georgetown Suites.

Foggy Bottom/West End

Hotel Lombardy
✉ 2019 Pennsylvania Ave. NW at 21st St.
✆ 1-800-424-5486.

This was once an elegant apartment building and has been recently refurbished into an elegant ten-story hotel (with a handful of apartmentlike suites available for rental). The hotel still has an elevator operated by a human being. The rooms are individually decorated and have retained some of the apartment building flavor, such as crystal doorknobs and breakfast nooks. Hotel amenities include a coffeemaker, hair dryer, and complimentary newspaper. There's a very good restaurant on the premises, Cafe Lombardy, as well as The Venetian Room, which is a more elegant dining area.

The location of the hotel puts it within walking distance of both the White House in one direction and Georgetown in the other. Room rates vary wildly. In the summer you can get a room for $99 a night (ask for the *New York Times* rate), but the list price is $120 to $155 for a single and $140 to $175 for a double. All major credit cards are accepted. Parking is an additional $20 per night. This hotel is convenient to the Foggy Bottom Metro station.

Hotel St. James
✉950 24th St. NW at K St.
✆1-800-852-8512

This 195-room suite hotel was once a Catholic all-girls school. Each suite has two televisions, a dual-line phone, and a fully stocked kitchen. There is no restaurant on the premises, but you can order from room service. A continental breakfast is served in the morning. There is a small pool on site, as well as a health club. The hotel is within walking distance to Georgetown. Quoted rates are $185 for a single room and $205 for a double, but the hotel offers a $99 rate in the summer (ask for the *New York Times* rate). Parking is an additional $20 per night. All major credit cards are accepted. This hotel is convenient to the Foggy Bottom Metro station.

State Plaza Hotel
✉2117 E St. NW
✆1-800-424-2859

This all-suite hotel is located about five blocks from the White House and the Mall. From one of its two towers (which are connected through the garage) you can see the Mall and the

Washington Monument. From the north tower, you can see down-town Washington. The restaurant is in the north tower, which serves three meals a day, and there are complimentary hors d'oeuvres during happy hour. The hotel has a fitness center and offers free coffee, local phone calls, and morning newspaper. All rooms have kitchens; one-bedrooms have a dining area.

Room rates are $125 to $150 for an efficiency and $175 to $225 for a one-bedroom. In the summer, the hotel offers a $99 rate (ask for the *New York Times* rate). Parking is an additional $20 per night. All major credit cards are accepted. This hotel is convenient to the Foggy Bottom Metro station.

Wyndham City Center Hotel
✉ 1143 New Hampshire Ave. NW at M St.
✆ 202-775-0800

This hotel is the site of a former private hospital, recently ren-ovated, and its 352 rooms are spacious and have some interesting decorative features. Rooms feature a coffeemaker. There is a fitness club on the premises and a good restaurant, Shula's Steakhouse. Room rates are $129 for a single or a double room. Parking is an additional $26 per night. Major credit cards are accepted. This hotel is convenient to the Foggy Bottom Metro station.

═FAST FACT

Marriott Wardman Park and the Omni Shoreham both have fabulous pools for kids, are located near the zoo, and have extensive grounds featuring a host of outdoor activities. Days Inn has a rooftop pool, as does the Holiday Inn Capital.

One Washington Circle Hotel
✉ 1 Washington Circle NW
✆ 1-800-424-9671

This is an all-suite hotel with a variety of suite sizes and is said to be where President Nixon stayed when hiding out in town after the Watergate scandal. All suites include a kitchen, dining area, and a terrace. The on-site restaurant, Circle Bistro, serves wonderful creative Mediterranean food. Suite rates are $135 to $165 on weekdays for smaller suites, though sometimes there are weekend specials; larger suites are more expensive. Valet parking is $20 per night. Major credit cards are accepted. This hotel is convenient to the Foggy Bottom Metro station.

Georgetown

The Georgetown Dutch Inn
✉ 1075 Thomas Jefferson St. NW
✆ 1-800-388-2410

This small, forty-seven-unit inn offers spacious one- and two-bedroom apartmentlike suites with fully stocked kitchens. In-room amenities include three phones. The hotel offers a free continental breakfast in the lobby and use of a nearby health club. Room rates are $125 to $195 for a double room on weekdays and $105 to $115 on weekends, more for larger suites. Major credit cards are accepted. Limited free parking is available. There is no Metro service convenient to the hotel.

CHAPTER 18

In Style—
Luxury Hotels

WASHINGTON HAS some of the most historic hotels in the country. You can actually stay in rooms where presidents and royalty have slept and partied, as well as famous rockers like U2 and the Rolling Stones.

It is a city that has been putting out the red carpet for over 200 years, and many of its best hotels have both stories and traditions of their own. Some even have books about them (the Mayflower) and a museum (the Willard). You could actually have a wonderful time just touring the city's best and oldest hotels (and you can, if you go to the Historic Hotels of America's Web site and request a tour of their D.C. properties, *www.historichotels.org*).

The most luxurious of these hotels also feature fabulous restaurants, antiques, and wonderful art. While the average hotel room in Washington will run about $150, these luxury accommodations can start there and go up to thousands of dollars for a presidential suite.

TRAVEL TIP

Remember that even the most expensive hotels have special rates during the summer, so you may be able to stay at a first-class hotel for half-price if you ask for a summer rate.

Downtown D.C.

Grand Hyatt Washington
✉ 1000 H St. NW
☎ 1-800-233-1234

This is a luxurious mega-hotel with 900 rooms. The lobby alone is stupendous, with a glass-enclosed atrium that is twelve stories high and features fountains and a waterfall; a baby grand piano floating on its own island in a "lagoon" surrounded by a bar; and two floors of shops and restaurants. The hotel is across the street from the Convention Center and near the MCI Center. Rooms are large but relatively standard with hair dryers, cable TV, and a basket of toiletries. The health club is two stories high, with a lap pool and sauna.

Room rates are $290 for a double room on weekdays and $119 to $139 on weekends. For an additional $20 you can get the business plan, which includes a large desk, fax machine, and coffeemaker. There are a number of special packages available (such as the winter holiday package), so ask for specials when you make your reservations. Parking is an additional $20 for self-parking and $26 for valet. Major credit cards are accepted. This hotel is convenient to the Metro Center Metro station.

Hay-Adams Hotel
✉ 16th & H Sts. NW
☎ 1-800-678-8946

This hotel was built on the former land of John Hay and Henry Adams, two prominent Washington social and political bigwigs whose homes faced Lafayette Square and were across the street from the White House. When the hotel opened in 1927, such luminaries as Charles Lindbergh and Amelia Earhart stayed here. *W* magazine said of the recent restoration, "This is as close as one gets to staying at the White House, short of being invited by the president."

Rooms on the fifth through eighth floors on the H Street side have spectacular views of the White House with the Washington

Monument behind it. Some rooms have fireplaces. Hotel amenities include bathrobes, nightly turndown service, daily newspaper, and health club privileges. Rumor has it that the ghost of Hay's wife haunts the hotel's fourth floor.

The hotel's restaurant, The Lafayette, overlooking the White House and Lafayette Square, offers contemporary American cuisine as well as afternoon tea. Off the Record, a wine and champagne bar, serves cocktails and light fare. Room rates are $265 to $825, and suites run higher. Major credit cards are accepted. This hotel is convenient to the Metro Center Metro station.

═FAST FACT

The Renaissance Mayflower Hotel, built in 1925, has so much Washington, D.C., history that a book has been written about it, which you can buy in the hotel lobby gift store. It has been the site of many inaugural balls and the makeshift home of most of our presidents while they waited to occupy the White House. Here, Franklin Delano Roosevelt wrote his famous words, "The only thing we have to fear is fear itself."

Hotel Washington
✉515 15th St. NW
✆1-800-424-9540

This elegant hotel is right across the street from the White House. Its lobby features green velvet chairs that you can sit in to look out over the White House and the Treasury Building. Its 350 rooms are mostly small but are furnished in Colonial-style antiques (some rooms feature four-poster beds). The rooftop deck offers dinner and drinks and a stupendous view of the city, which you can always take in even if you are not staying here.

Rooms run from $174 to $260 for a single room. However, in the summer, when Congress is not in session, the hotel runs a super family sale for $106 per night (ask for the *New York Times* rate or the Family Plan). All major credit cards are accepted.

Parking is an additional $20 per day in the on-site garage. This hotel is convenient to the Metro Center Metro station.

💼 TRAVEL TIP

During the summer months, when Washington empties its hotel rooms of lobbyists because the House and Senate are on vacation, some of the best hotels in the city offer incredibly reduced rates. These include Hotel Washington, Hotel Lombardy, Henley Park, Governor's House, and Morrison-Clark.

The Jefferson
✉ 16th & M Sts. NW
📞 1-800-235-6397

Now under Loews' Management, this former luxury apartment building was built in 1923 and was a hotel for military personnel during World War II. In 1986, it was restored and transformed into a 100-room hotel, which is now a popular hotel for dignitaries and celebrities. Both the lobby and some rooms feature some genuine Jefferson artifacts (on loan from Monticello), such as signed documents and letters, as well as a bust of Jefferson in the lobby and Jefferson prints in the restaurant.

Hotel amenities include fax machines, nightly turndown service with Godiva chocolate, morning newspaper, VCRs, CD players, bathrobes, and a health club with a pool across the street. Some rooms have fireplaces and four-poster beds. The Restaurant at the Jefferson features American cuisine, as well as an afternoon tea, and an excellent Sunday brunch. It is located four blocks from the White House. Published hotel rates are $159 to $339 for a single or a double room. Parking is an additional $20. Major credit cards are accepted. This hotel is convenient to the Metro Center Metro station.

Loew's L'Enfant Plaza Hotel
✉ 480 L'Enfant Plaza SW — 269⁰⁰ park included
📞 1-800-235-6397

This posh hotel is located a hop, skip, and a jump from the Mall, and it has a reputation for catering to visitors traveling with pets. (Being able to take your dog for a run on the Mall is a real treat.) It's also quite child-friendly, offering free meals in the hotel restaurant for children under 5 and a welcoming gift to all children under the age of 12. The hotel has a year-round rooftop pool and a fitness center and offers a complimentary continental breakfast.

Room rates are $189 to $229, but there are occasional specials. Parking is an additional $20 a night. Major credit cards are accepted. The L'Enfant Plaza Metro station leads you right into the hotel.

Renaissance Mayflower Hotel
✉ 1127 Connecticut Ave. NW
✆ 1-800-678-8946

The Mayflower is one of the most historic and luxurious hotels in the city and offers 660 deluxe guest rooms. It was where Calvin Coolidge held his 1925 inauguration for 1,000 people, which was also the hotel's grand opening. It was designed by Warren & Wetmore, the same architectural firm that designed New York's Grand Central Station, and it is almost as big, taking up most of the block. Franklin Delano Roosevelt lived at the Mayflower between his election and inauguration; John F. Kennedy used to stay here when he was a congressman; and Jean Harlow was so fascinated by the switchboard that she played operator-for-a-day when she visited.

When it opened its doors, the Mayflower boasted more gold leaf than any other building in the city except the Library of Congress and was one of the capital's first air-conditioned buildings. Forty-six-thousand square feet of Italian marble was used to create the hotel's bathrooms. A recent renovation uncovered a sixty-foot skylight that had been blacked out during World War II, as well as murals painted by Edward Lanning.

Hotel amenities include bathrobes, morning newspaper, your own pot of coffee with wake-up call, a small television in the bathroom, and a fitness center. The hotel is so historic that there's a coffee-table book about it on sale at the gift shop. Published room rates are $170 to $500 for a single room and $179 to $575 for a double; rates run higher for suites. In the summer, the rates drop to as low as $129, with free breakfast—ask for the leisure rate. Major credit cards are accepted. Located four blocks south of the White House, this hotel is convenient to the Metro Center.

The St. Regis
✉ 923 16th St. NW
☎ 202-638-2626

Now under Starwood Management, this ornate hotel is a favorite of celebrities of all sorts, from Queen Elizabeth to the Rolling Stones when it was The Sheraton Carlton. Designed to look like an Italian palazzo, the St. Regis' lobby features chandeliers and Empire furniture. Rooms are on the smallish side, but they are elegantly furnished, with desks set aside in alcoves, and marble bathrooms stocked with everything from cotton balls to mouthwash. There's also an umbrella tucked away inside the closet. Other amenities include bathrobes, hair dryers, personal safes, coffee with wake-up call, nightly turndown, and fitness club. The St. Regis Library Lounge and Restaurant is book-lined, features a working fireplace, and allows cigar smoking, something very hard to find in the city anymore.

Room rates are $225, single or double. Major credit cards are accepted. Parking is an additional $22 per day. The St. Regis is within walking distance to the White House. This hotel is convenient to the Farragut West and McPherson Square Metro stops.

Willard Intercontinental
✉ 1401 Pennsylvania Ave. NW
☎ 1-800-327-0200

This is one of the best hotels in D.C. because of its location near the White House, its fabulous restaurant, its luxurious rooms, and its historical importance. Most U.S. presidents have stayed or dined here, from Lincoln to Clinton. Julia Ward Howe wrote "The Battle Hymn of the Republic" at the Willard in the same room that Martin Luther King Jr. later penned his "I Have a Dream" speech. Management is currently installing a photographic museum on the history of the hotel, with startling photos of how it was left abandoned in the 1980s and transformed to its current luster.

≡FAST FACT

President Grant was known to smoke cigars and sip brandy in the lobby of Willard Intercontinental, where he was constantly sought out by those wanting something from him—and this is how the word "lobbyist" came into being.

The Willard was designed by the same architect who built the Plaza Hotel in New York. The lobby features seals of the forty-eight states on the ceiling, as well as chandeliers, marble columns, and gilt trim. Rooms are large and decorated in Empire or Federal style and feature an in-room safe, minibar, hair dryer, scale, and a television speaker in the marble bathrooms. Other amenities include twice-daily maid service, nightly turndown service, and a choice of newspaper delivery. The Willard Room is a beautiful restaurant that features exquisite cuisine and fabulous desserts. The Round Robin Bar has been a popular drinking place for two centuries, with such noted guests as Mark Twain, Walt Whitman, and Nathaniel Hawthorne. There is also the café Espresso, which offers coffees and pastries, and the Nest Lounge, which plays live jazz on weekends.

Room rates are $400 to $440 for a double on weekdays and $199 on weekends, but the hotel does offer a 50 percent discount to people over 65, and there are always specials. Parking is $20 additional per night. Major credit cards are accepted. This hotel is convenient to the Metro Center station.

Capitol Hilton
✉ 16th & K St. NW
☎ 202-393-1000

This is a mega-hotel (549 rooms) that is popular because of its location two blocks from the White House. It underwent a major renovation in the early 1990s, and most rooms feature three phones and a small television in the bathroom. The Tower floors (ten through fourteen) offer extra amenities such as complimentary breakfast, afternoon tea, and hors d'oeuvres; cocktails are extra. There are three restaurants on the premises: Fran O'Brian's, which used to be Trader Vic's and is now named after a former Washington Redskin, offers steak and seafood; Twigg's Grill, a more elegant eatery; and just Twigg's, which is less expensive.

Room rates are $127 to $275 for a double, and you add $30 for Tower units. Major credit cards are accepted. Parking is $22 additional per day. This hotel is convenient to the Farragut West, Farragut North, and McPherson Square Metro stations.

📰 TRAVEL TIP

In addition to hotels, Washington has many wonderful small inns and bed and breakfasts. You can receive a list of sixty-five bed and breakfasts by calling the Bed & Breakfast League/ Sweet Dreams and Toast at ☎ 202-363-7767. Another option is to contact Bed & Breakfast Accommodations Ltd., by phone at (☎ 202-332-3885, or on the Web at ⟞ www.bnbaccom.com).

Renaissance Washington
✉ D.C. Hotel, 999 9th St. NW
☎ 202-898-9000

This another mega hotel (800 rooms) that caters to Washington business travelers visiting the nearby Convention Center. It is also within walking distance to D.C.'s Chinatown and the MCI Center. Rooms are spacious with work areas and a dataport. Hotel amenities include coffeemakers, bathrobes, and free morning newspapers.

There is a health club on the premises with an indoor pool. The hotel has three restaurants: Florentine, which serves American food; Caracella, which serves Italian food, and Plaza Gourmet, which is a New York–style deli.

Rooms run $174 to $274 for a single or double. Parking is an additional $20 per day. All major credit cards are accepted. This hotel is convenient to the Metro Center.

The Madison
✉15th and M Streets
☎202-862-1600

Having just completed a ten-month and $40-million renovation, The Madison has recently set out to claim its original place along the stellar hotels of D.C. Opened in 1963, with the President and Mrs. Kennedy in attendance, it was one of the Camelot hangouts, and considered one of the most stylish hotels of the early '60s. The current renovation is a combination of classic styles—Federalist, Georgian, and American Empire, with contemporary flair. The 353 rooms feature 300-count Egyptian cotton sheets, CD players, and a heated towel rack in the bathroom. There is a fitness center on the premises, as well as two restaurants, the highly praised Palette and the PostScript Bar.

Listed room rate is $175 per night, but check the Web for specials as well as weekend packages. Major credit cards are accepted. Parking is available. This hotel is convenient to the Metro Center Metro station.

Capitol Hill

Hyatt Regency Washington on Capitol Hill
✉400 New Jersey Ave. NW
☎202-737-1234

This mega-hotel (834 rooms) is located between First and D Streets and is the perfect location for travelers who need to be within walking distance of the Capitol, the Supreme Court, or the

House or Senate, which is one of the reasons the rooms are so pricey. The hotel offers a business plan, which includes free membership to its health club with a heated pool, free local phone calls, morning newspaper, and a continental breakfast at the Park Promenade restaurant. There are two other restaurants in the hotel: The Capital View Club, which features a stellar rooftop view of the city, and the Spy's Eye Lounge, which has a big television screen and a nightly happy hour.

Rooms are $240 for a single and $270 for a double room. Parking is an additional $22 per day. All major credit cards are accepted. This hotel is convenient to the Union Station Metro station.

Holiday Inn on the Hill
✉415 New Jersey Ave. NW
✆202-638-1616

This hotel is down the street from the Capitol, near the Library of Congress and the Folger Shakespeare Library. Rooms are large with work areas, hair dryers, minibars, and coffeemakers. There is a rooftop pool, a fitness club, and sauna. The Senators All-American Sports Grille features memorabilia from the now-defunct D.C. baseball team. Room rates are $125 to $225 per night. Parking is an additional $20 per night. All major credit cards are accepted. This hotel is convenient to the Union Station Metro station.

Hotel George
✉15 E St. NW
✆1-800-576-8331

Recently taken under the Kimpton hotel chain banner, this is an old building that has been rehabbed. The Hotel George presents itself as the hip hotel for those doing business on the Hill. Posters throughout the hotel depict images of George Washington in contemporary gear, without the wig. Rooms are spacious, with desks, hair dryers, coffeemakers, irons, and a television speaker in the bathroom. The hotel restaurant, Bis, serves French bistro food. The hotel has a fitness club and steam rooms, as well as a billiard room. Other amenities include morning newspaper, nightly turn-down service, a VCR, and CD players. Room rates are $225 to $260 on weekdays and $129 on weekends, but there are occasional special rates, so ask when you call. Parking is an additional $24 per night. Major credit cards are accepted. This hotel is convenient to the Union Station Metro station.

≡FAST FACT

The Watergate Hotel is next door to the notorious apartment and office complex where the fateful burglary took place in the 1970s. The hotel itself has long been a favorite of celebrities, politicians, and performing artists.

Adams Morgan/Woodley Park

Marriott Wardman Park
✉2660 Woodley Rd. NW at Connecticut Ave.
☎202-328-2000

The former site of the Sheraton Washington, this is the largest hotel in the city, sitting on a sixteen-acre plot of land a hop, skip, and a jump away from the National Zoo. Its more than 1,000 rooms have just undergone a major renovation. Because of its size, the hotel tends to cater to convention-goers, but it's also a good place for families because of its two pools and proximity to the zoo. There are reduced rates in the summer and when the hotel is not at capacity.

Wardman Park is a former apartment building for the rich and famous—for instance, Gore Vidal and Douglas Fairbanks Jr. once lived here—and the 200-odd rooms in this section retain a bit of its earlier charm with high ceilings and intricate moldings. In-room amenities include hair dryers, complimentary Starbucks coffee and tea, irons, and morning newspaper delivery. The hotel has two outdoor pools (one of which is heated, with a sundeck), a fitness center, a number of shops and services, and its own post office.

On-site dining is available at Americus, while breakfast and lunch are served in the Courtyard Cafe. L'Espresso serves sandwiches and pastries. Room rates are $205 to $270, but there are specials all year round. Self-parking is an additional $20 per night. Major credit cards are accepted. This hotel is convenient to the Woodley Park Metro station.

[handwritten: $199⁰⁰ 10/22 - 10/24 confirm]
[handwritten: 7 7days prior cancel]

Omni Shoreham

[handwritten: 1004032699]

✉ 2500 Calvert St. NW at Connecticut Ave.

📞 1-800-843-6664

Recently renovated from top to bottom, this is another mega-hotel (860 rooms) that serves the convention crowd. Set on an eleven-acre plot of land overlooking Rock Creek Park, it's within walking distance of the National Zoo. It was built in the 1930s and has been the site of many an inaugural ball. A suite on the eighth floor is said to be haunted and bears a plaque marked "Ghost Suite." Rooms are very spacious—some have marvelous views of Rock Creek—and nicely decorated. The hotel has a brand-new swimming pool with poolside snack bar and a children's pool, fitness center, steam room and whirlpool, completely new spa facilities, and nearby jogging and bicycling paths.

The upscale restaurant serves elegant meals and overlooks the park. There is a bar on the premises, as well as a lounge. The grounds have been completely re-landscaped, with an elliptical lawn (like the one in front of the White House but smaller) and a new formal garden with fountains, which is a popular location for weddings and parties. Room rates are $140 to $290 for a double. Parking is an additional $20. Major credit cards are accepted. This hotel is convenient to the Woodley Park Metro station.

[handwritten: Select guest # 13656368]

Dupont Circle

Washington Hilton & Towers

✉ 1919 Connecticut Ave. NW at T St.

📞 202-483-3000

This is the hotel where John Hinkley, Jr., tried to assassinate President Reagan. It has been a major stop for presidential events and continues to be one, with a new bulletproof side entrance added after the shooting. It has the largest ballroom on the East Coast and therefore has a steady stream of important shindigs from inaugural balls to society events. The more than 1,100 rooms are designed in a contemporary décor with the work of local artists on the walls. Above the fifth floor there is a panoramic city view from most hotel windows.

The hotel offers five on-site dining alternatives, from the more upscale 1919 Grill to poolside dining. In-room amenities include newspaper delivery of your choice. The hotel features a heated outdoor pool and a children's pool, tennis courts, and a health club. Room rates are $230 to $270 on weekdays and $145 on weekends; tower rooms are slightly more expensive. Parking is an additional $20 per night. Major credit cards are accepted. This hotel is convenient to the Dupont Circle Metro station.

📖 TRAVEL TIP

If you've been to D.C. before, and you would prefer a more relaxing vacation this time around, perhaps with some golfing and spa treatments, you might want to consider staying at the Westfield's Marriott resort in Chantilly, Virginia (✆703-818-0300), just twenty minutes from downtown. It's right near the new Udvar-Hazy Center, and fairly close to Tyson's Corner outlet shopping as well. It is very family-friendly, with a terrific indoor pool as well as an outdoor pool in the summer.

Westin Fairfax

✉2100 Massachusetts Ave. NW at 21st St.

✆1-800-325-3589

Vice President Al Gore just about grew up in the Westin, which has been one of the places to stay in Washington for the rich, famous, and powerful since it opened in 1927. (It was once the Ritz Hotel.) It was renovated in the '90s, and rooms are elegantly decorated, many featuring armchairs and ottomans and marble tubs. Some rooms have a view of Embassy Row. Views from upper floors include the Washington Monument and Georgetown. Amenities include robes, three phones, hair dryers, and a toiletry basket, as well as morning newspaper delivery, nightly turndown service with chocolates, twice-daily maid service, and a minibar. The hotel has a fitness club with sauna.

The Fairfax Club, which serves cocktails, has a working fireplace and a piano bar. Room rates are $275 and up for a single or a double. Parking is an additional $20 to $26 a night. Major credit cards are accepted. This hotel is convenient to the Dupont Circle Metro station.

H.H. Leonard's Mansion on O St.
✉2020 O St. NW
✆202-496-2000

This very small inn, with its six suites and a five-bedroom guest house, offers one-of-a-kind lodging. It is housed in a five-story brownstone that has a number of other tenants, such as an art gallery and antiques store. Rooms are decorated in unique themes; some have fireplaces, some have whirlpools and/or kitchens, but all have interesting touches. There is an outdoor pool and exercise room. Free breakfast comes with your stay, and you can order whatever you want. Room rates run from $150 to $1,000. Parking is an additional $15. Only MasterCard and Visa are accepted. This hotel is convenient to the Dupont Circle Metro station.

Radisson Barcelo Hotel
✉2121 P St. NW
✆1-800-333-3333

This Spanish-owned, 301-room hotel occupies a former apartment building and is said to have the largest hotel rooms in

Washington. All rooms have desks, armchairs, and couches, and marble bathrooms with shaving mirrors. You can choose among 200 movies on the pay-per-view system. Other amenities include hair dryers, coffeemaker, nightly turndown service, morning newspaper, and three phones. The hotel also has a tree-lined outdoor pool and a fitness center. The on-site restaurant, Gabriel, features Spanish food as well as tapas.

Room rates are from $135 to $299; there are weekend and summer specials, so ask when you make reservations. Parking is $20 per night. Major credit cards are accepted. This hotel is convenient to the Dupont Circle Metro station.

≡FAST FACT

The Round Robin Bar in the Willard Hotel has quite a drinking history. It has been a popular drinking place for two centuries, serving such luminaries as Mark Twain, Walt Whitman, and Nathaniel Hawthorne. It is said that Washington Irving brought Charles Dickens here for a drink.

Washington Courtyard by Marriott
✉ 1900 Connecticut Ave. NW
✆ 1-800-842-4211

This 147-unit hotel is operated by the same Irish company that runs the Normandy Inn and has brought many of the same European amenities to this hotel, such as coffee and tea served all day in the lobby and cookies in the afternoon. In-room amenities include coffeemakers and hair dryers, and the hotel has an outdoor pool and a fitness center. The on-site restaurant, Claret's, serves American food, and there is a lounge, Bailey's, on the premises as well. Room rates are $89 to $190 for a double. Parking is an additional $15 per night. Major credit cards are accepted. This hotel is convenient to the Dupont Circle Metro station.

Foggy Bottom/West End

Fairmont Hotel

✉2401 M St. NW

✆202-429-2400

This 415-room hotel, formerly the Washington Monarch Hotel, has just undergone a $12-million restoration and has become a mecca for celebrities because of its state-of-the-art fitness center, which is an additional $10 per person, although the pool, sauna, steam room, and whirlpool are free to guests. The hotel was refurbished in 1999 and has a beautiful garden courtyard, which about one-third of the rooms overlook. In-room amenities include bathrobes, three phones, high-end toiletries, and in-room safes. There is twice-daily maid service and nightly turndown service. Room rates are $280 weekdays for a double and $139 on weekends. Valet parking is an additional $25. Major credit cards are accepted. This hotel is convenient to the Foggy Bottom Metro station.

Park Hyatt Hotel

✉1201 24th St. NW at M St.

✆1-800-922-PARK

Designed as a luxury hotel by the famed New York architectural firm of Skidmore, Owings & Merrill, this 224-room hotel has a wrought-iron fountain as well as a pair of large Chinese Y'ang horses in the lobby. Rooms are dotted with modern art, much of it copies of works hanging in the National Gallery. In-room amenities include marble bathrooms with oversize tubs, twice-daily maid service, weekday newspaper delivery, nightly turndown service, and an afternoon snack. The health club is excellent, with a pool and a separate kid's pool. The Melrose Restaurant is topnotch with many seafood entrees. Afternoon tea is served on the weekends. Room rates are $325 to $440. Parking is an additional $26 per night. Major credit cards are accepted. This hotel is convenient to the Foggy Bottom Metro station.

Watergate Hotel (Swisshotel Washington)

✉2650 Virginia Ave. NW

✆1-800-424-2736

This has always been one of the best hotels in Washington, legendary long before the Watergate break-in in the nearby apartment complex and the press hordes that waited for Monica Lewinsky to emerge from her mother's apartment. Its location is one of its many drawing cards, as is the view of the Potomac that it offers. Many of the performers playing at the Kennedy Center right next door have stayed here; other notable guests include Ingrid Bergman, Muhammad Ali, and Gloria Estefan.

Rooms are spacious, and the suites are reported to be some of the largest in the city. Many rooms have balconies. The hotel has an excellent health club and a heated indoor lap pool. In-room amenities include a robe, minibar, hair dryer, toiletries, nightly turn-down service, and daily newspaper delivery. There is a complimentary weekday limo service and free coffee in the morning in the Potomac Lounge, which also serves afternoon tea. The hotel restaurant, Aquarelle, is considered one of the best hotel restaurants and often offers themed happy hours, such as Japanese sushi.

Room rates are $270 to $960 for a single or double, but there are some specials. Major credit cards are accepted. Valet parking is an additional $25. This hotel is convenient to the Foggy Bottom/GWU Metro station.

Doubletree Guest Suites

✉801 New Hampshire Ave. NW at II St.

✆202-785-2000

This 105-room chain offers larger rooms to business travelers (and touring families in the summer months) with a fully stocked kitchen (with free coffee and tea) and an in-season rooftop pool. There is no restaurant on the premises, although there are many nearby. Room rates are $145 to $270 for a single, and $249 and up for a double. Parking is an additional $20 per day. All major credit cards are accepted. This hotel is convenient to the Foggy Bottom Metro station.

Doubletree Guest Suites

✉ 2500 Pennsylvania Ave. NW at 25th St.

✆ 202-333-8060

This two-room-suite hotel is a great location for families traveling to the city. It's within walking distance to Georgetown, so the rooms are furnished in a more faux Colonial decor, but there's a television in every room and a fully stocked kitchen (with free coffee and tea). On weekends there is a complimentary breakfast. Room rates are $145 to $229. Parking is an additional $20 per day. All major credit cards are accepted. This hotel is convenient to the Foggy Bottom/GWU Metro station.

≡ FAST FACT

The Jefferson, opened in 1923, is one of D.C.'s finest and most exclusive hotels. It features an exquisite collection of fine art and antiques and is home to several original documents signed by Thomas Jefferson.

Westin Grand Hotel

✉ 2350 M St. NW at 24th St.

✆ 202-429-0100

This 263-room hotel has a number of unique features, such as working fireplaces in some rooms and French doors that open up on terraces overlooking the street. It is within walking distance to Georgetown and the Kennedy Center. There is a heated outdoor pool and a good on-site restaurant, as well as a bistro that features a mahogany bar, etched-glass windows, and wallpaper designed by William Morris. Room rates are $139 to $259 for a single, $159 to $259 for a double, with suites priced at $349. Parking is an additional $16 to $23 a night. All major credit cards are accepted. This hotel is convenient to the Foggy Bottom Metro station.

Georgetown

Four Seasons Hotel

✉2800 Pennsylvania Ave.

✆1-800-332-3442

This is one of Washington's premier hotels and has been the hotel of choice for celebrities for years. The rooms are well appointed with plants and art, armchairs and desks, as well as down comforters on the beds. Rooms come stocked with a minibar, CD players, bathrobes, hair dryers, and a toiletry basket. The on-site health club is considered one of the best in the hotel business with weights, equipment, a two-lane pool, and classes in everything from yoga to Tai Chi. Other hotel amenities include twice-daily maid service, complimentary car service weekdays, and morning newspaper of your choice.

Room rates are $295 to $2,175. Major credit cards are accepted. Parking is an additional $20 per night. This hotel is convenient to the Foggy Bottom Metro station, but you still have to walk.

🌂RAINY DAY FUN

When staying at the Four Seasons Hotel, if you inform the hotel that you will be traveling with children, they will prepare a welcome gift for each child and supply child-sized bathrobes for the rooms, as well as milk and cookies before bed. The hotel concierge will also try to have age-appropriate games available.

The Latham Hotel

✉3000 M St. NW

✆1 800-528-4261

Set in the center of Georgetown, this hotel is conveniently located near all the good restaurants and nightlife, but it is quiet because it is set back from the street. There are two excellent

French restaurants on the premises—Citronelle, which is one of the more talked-about D.C. eateries, and La Madeleine. The rooms have a French country flair. In-room amenities include desks, fax machine, hair dryers, and robes. The hotel offers free newspaper delivery and nightly turndown service and has an outdoor pool and a fitness center. Room rates are $140 to $265, slightly less on weekends. Valet parking is an additional $20. Major credit cards are accepted. There is no convenient Metro service.

CHAPTER 19

Day Trips from D.C.

THE SURROUNDING TOWNS and suburbs of Washington, D.C., are as old (if not older) than the city itself. They offer a host of fascinating and interesting things to see and do, from visiting our first president's "gentleman farm" in Mount Vernon to enjoying more modern forms of entertainment like amusement parks and outlet shopping malls.

If you have a car—you can go by bus, but then you are on someone else's time schedule—and you have the time (if you are staying in the city at least five days), you should try to see Mount Vernon and the spectacular Pope-Leighey house designed by Frank Lloyd Wright on the grounds of the neighboring Woodlawn Plantation. They are both worth the trip. You have to pass through Alexandria, Virginia, to get there, so you might want to take a drive-through tour of this old Southern town as well.

Mount Vernon

✉George Washington Memorial Parkway (Rt. 1 South)
✆703-780-2000
✐*www.mountvernon.org*

Mount Vernon is vast. It was once an 8,000-acre farm; later, Washington gave his adopted granddaughter some of this land as a wedding present, and it is now home to Woodlawn Plantation (another possible destination).

Washington lived at Mount Vernon for forty-five years, from the time he was 22 until his death. He and Martha are buried on the premises. He loved this place, and over the years he tripled the size of the mansion, redesigned the grounds and outbuildings, and bought neighboring lands. The present site was purchased by the Mount Vernon Ladies Association in 1858 from Washington's descendants for $200,000 and is almost unchanged in its appearance from 1799, when Washington died.

Today, the estate is a mere 500 acres of the former president's holdings, but even at one-sixteenth of its original size, Mount Vernon is at least a half-day's touring experience, plus there's a wonderful gift shop and a Colonial restaurant nearby, so plan on making a day of this trip.

☰FAST FACT

2004 saw the launch of an $85-million renovation and public relations campaign for the first president's residence. While the estate will remain open during this construction, a new state-of-the-art orientation center, education center, and museum are being built on the grounds.

The Tour

The Mount Vernon admission includes a tour of the mansion, which Washington made the center of his estate. Restoration on the mansion is meticulous, from the color of the paint on the walls to the placement of many of the original furnishings (such as the leather chair in Washington's study that he used for the eight years he was president, and the bed he died in).

The property also includes a new forest trail where you can walk through Washington's wilderness grounds, see his cobblestone quarry, cross a footbridge, and learn about wildlife on the estate. Washington himself loved to ride around his grounds on horseback.

Washington considered himself quite a scientific farmer, and he oversaw all the plantings on his estate. (Some of his original tree plantings are still growing at the Bowling Green entrance to the estate.) At the new Pioneer Farmer site, horses tread wheat outside the restored sixteen-sided barn, and costumed workers participate in hands-on Colonial farming activities and farm animal demonstrations.

A new museum on the grounds replicates Washington's presidential office. His last will and testament and the famous bust of Washington by Houdon are also on display. There's also a display on the archeology and restoration of the site, which shows how work was done and what has been found on the site over the years.

📰 TRAVEL TIP

There are a number of activities and experiences geared toward children at Mount Vernon. Kids can learn to build a Colonial fence, play a variety of eighteenth-century games, and harness a fiberglass mule. There's also a special "treasure hunt" for kids, which you can pick up at the main gate. If you've brought a camera, there's an opportunity to have the kids dress up in Colonial garb for a picture.

Mount Vernon also is the site of the Washington Tombs (where memorial services are held on Washington's birthday and a daily wreath-laying takes place at 10:00 A.M., April through October) along with four gardens, a slave memorial (Washington freed his slaves upon his death), a greenhouse, stables, slave quarters, and the original outbuildings throughout the estate.

The gift shop is large and offers a great selection of Washington-related memorabilia, from a porcelain bust of Washington (a copy of the Houdon) to plates depicting Washington crossing the Delaware. The shop offers great gifts to take home such as Mount Vernon wine (Virginia Blush), mulled cider, Martha's cake, and Colonial toys for kids.

Where to Eat

No food is allowed on the grounds, but there is a snack bar right outside the entrance that offers a fair selection of fast food. Next door to the gift shop is The Mount Vernon Inn (✆ 703-780-0011), which serves both lunch and dinner in a Colonial setting with costumed wait staff. The food is moderately priced and features a Colonial menu. Also nearby is the Cedar Knoll Inn, which also serves lunch and dinner. The dinner menu offers a Colonial meal at a *prix fixe* for dinner for two.

Seasonal Events at Mount Vernon

Special events are held on the estate throughout the year:

October: Celebrate Virginia Archeology month with thirty-minute tours of excavation sites at 11:30 A.M. and 2:30 P.M. all month long.

December: Holidays at Mount Vernon are commemorated with a special tour that includes costumed characters and a visit to the rarely opened third floor of the mansion. Hot cider, cookies, and caroling around a bonfire are also on the program.

February: All month long there is a thirty-minute walking tour on the slave life at Mount Vernon at 10:00 A.M., 11:30 A.M., and 1:30 P.M. Weekends in February include musical presentations and storytelling. On the weekend of Washington's birthday there are always special events, and Mount Vernon is open free to the public.

Location and Hours

The best way to get from D.C. to Mount Vernon is by car. The drive is simple. Cross any of the memorial bridges and then take the George Washington Memorial Parkway (Rt. 1) going south; the road will end at Mount Vernon.

Another option is to take the Gray Line bus (✆ 202-289-1995), which leaves for Mount Vernon at 8:30 A.M. from Union Station.

Adult fare is $30; it's $15 per child. The bus will drop you off at your hotel when the four-hour tour is over. There are also evening tours in the summer.

Another option is to take a boat. *The Spirit of Washington* (✆202-554-8000) leaves from the Washington waterfront and offers a five-hour cruise at $32 for adults and $22 for children, which includes the price of admission to the estate, but this tour is only operated from March through October.

Mount Vernon is open to visitors from 8:00 A.M. until 5:00 P.M. April through August. In March, September, and October, hours are 9:00 A.M. to 5:00 P.M. From November through February, Mount Vernon is open from 9:00 A.M. to 4:00 P.M. Admission is $11 for adults and $5 for children (under 6 free); seniors are $8.50.

☰FAST FACT

Did you know that Martha Washington was the oldest of eight children? That she had been married before, and was once considered the wealthiest widow in Virginia at 26 years old? That she was a year older than her husband George? That she brought two children from her previous marriage to her union with George, and she and George never had children of their own? That they were married in her home, which was called the White House?

Woodlawn Plantation

9000 Richmond Highway, Mount Vernon, Virginia
✆703-780-4000
✑*www.woodlawn1805.org*

Woodlawn Plantation was the home of Washington's nephew, who married Washington's adopted granddaughter. Washington gave the couple the property to build their home from his holdings at Mount Vernon. William Thornton, one of the first architects of the U.S.

Capitol building, designed the Georgian-style house. You can see the Potomac from the back porch.

The house has much Washington-related memorabilia on its two floors as well as many early American works of art (two Rembrandt Peales and a Hiram Powers bust). One of the most intriguing items on display is a mourning embroidery by Anna Austin that features a woman crying over a large memorial urn; the woman disappears and reappears as an angel when you change perspective.

Pope-Leighey House

The grounds of the Woodlawn Plantation are also home to the Pope-Leighey house, one of Frank Lloyd Wright's earliest Usonian houses (designed for middle-income families), and one whose construction he personally oversaw. It was commissioned by newspaperman Loren Pope, who was so taken with a *Life* magazine profile on Wright that he wrote him a letter requesting he design him a house.

The small three-bedroom house was built in 1939 in Falls Church, Virginia (it has been moved twice by the National Trust, which now runs it), and has many of the signature Wright elements: a small utility center where the kitchen and bathroom are housed (the size of those in a small one-bedroom apartment), a cantilevered roof, horizontal lines, a repeating fret stencil pattern on the windows, and next to no closets.

Although Pope loved the house, his family outgrew it, and it was sold to the Leighey family, who lived there until the 1980s and opened it to the public in 1996. Much of the original furniture and color scheme is preserved. When the house was commissioned, its purchase price of between $6,000 and $7,000 included the furniture. During the month of December, a 1940s Christmas is on display at the house.

The Woodlawn Plantation Gift Shop

There is a gift shop in the basement that offers many wonderful Early American gifts and T-shirts (and you can see the old well, which was one of the first successful attempts at indoor plumbing). This is also a gift store in the Pope-Leighey House, so you can buy many Frank Lloyd Wright knickknacks as well, such as cups, a mouse pad, and canvas bags, with the decorative fret design from the house's windows.

≡FAST FACT

Most architects consider Frank Lloyd Wright the greatest and most influential American architect. His designs, which spanned nearly fifty years, influenced American homes to such an extent that we might not have the ranch house with its open living-room space connected to the kitchen and the carport if it were not for his vision of the American home.

Location and Hours

Woodlawn Plantation is adjacent to Mount Vernon. You can actually walk from Mount Vernon to Woodlawn, but take your car if you have one. The estate is open daily March through December, closed January and February, but it is open on Presidents' Day for 99 cents admission. Guided docent-led tours are offered on the half hour for $7.50 per person and $3 for students. You can buy a joint tour ticket to see the Pope-Leighey house as well for $13 ($5 for students). High tea is offered at the Woodlawn Plantation at 12:30 P.M. for $20, which also includes a tour.

Alexandria, Virginia

Only about a ten-minute drive or a Metro ride from downtown D.C., Alexandria is as charming as Georgetown, but with more history. It still has a lot of Colonial character, such as its brick sidewalks, cobblestone streets, and many historic homes. Washingtonians refer to it simply as Old Town.

Alexandria is a small town and is easy to walk around in. The center of the grid is the intersection of Washington and King

Streets. Many of the streets retain their original Colonial names. For information on special events and celebrations, call the Alexandria Convention and Visitors' Bureau at ☎703-838-4200, or visit its Web site, ✐*www.alexandriacity.com*. You can also drop in at its headquarters situated in the historic William Ramsay House on King and South Fairfax Street, where you can obtain a free map for a self-guided tour.

A Little History

Alexandria was named after a Scottish tobacco merchant who purchased the land in 1669. The town was founded in 1749, and one of the surveyors who helped plan the streets was 17-year-old George Washington.

Since its founding, Alexandria has always been a country retreat for prominent Washington families. George Washington had a townhouse here, and many of the upper-crust Colonial families worshipped at the English-style Christ Church (✉Cameron and N. Washington Streets), where Washington was a vestryman and had his own pew; Robert E. Lee was confirmed here.

Washington is also said to have held his last birthday party at Gadsby's Tavern (✉N. Royal and Cameron Streets, ☎703-838-4242), which features a museum and is still a restaurant where costumed wait staff serve homemade Colonial fare. Jefferson, Madison, and the Marquis de Lafayette are also said to have dined here.

Arlington House on Oronoco Street at North Street (☎703-548-8454) is another historic home in Alexandria. Lee lived here until he enrolled at West Point in 1825. He married one of Washington's great-granddaughters and lived in the Arlington House, whose grounds eventually became Arlington National Cemetery.

On the south side of Oronoco Street is the Lee-Fendell House (☎703-548-1789), where more Lee descendants lived (a total of thirty-seven over 118 years) and where there is an extensive display of Lee memorabilia.

Other historic homes in Alexandria include the Carlyle House (✉121 N. Fairfax Street at Cameron St., ☎703-549-2997), where in 1755

Major General Edward Braddock met with five Colonial governors to begin taxing the colonies in order to defend themselves against the French and the Indians. The colonists were not happy with this proposal and eventually drove him out.

🧳 TRAVEL TIP

Most historic homes in Alexandria charge a $4 tour price and are closed on Mondays. However, you can buy a group admission ticket that will get you into most of these homes for $12 for adults and $5 for children; you can purchase tickets at the Visitors' Bureau or at any one of the historic homes.

City Hall and Market Square (bounded by King, N. Royal, Cameron, and N. Fairfax Streets) is the site of a weekly outdoor market. Across the street on the south side of King Street is the Stabler-Leadbeater Apothecary Shop and Museum (✆703-836-3713) which was the second oldest drugstore in the nation until it closed in 1933. A Quaker family ran it for five generations. It is now a museum and gift shop.

The Lyceum (✉201 S. Washington Street, off Prince Street) is a museum that features changing exhibits on the history of Alexandria from the seventeenth century to the present.

The Torpedo Factory Art Center (✉105 N. Union St. between King and Cameron Streets, on the waterfront) is the shell of a former torpedo factory. Two hundred artists now show their works on the premises; an exhibition of Alexandria archeology lets visitors see archeologists at work in their lab.

The Black History Resource Center (✆703-838-4829) is housed in the former Robinson Library, once a segregated library for Alexandria's black community. America's first sit-in against segregation was staged in Alexandria in 1939 to protest the exclusion of blacks from Alexandria's public libraries, which led to the creation of the Robinson Library in 1940. The center, located at ✉603 N. Alfred Street, presently displays objects and records of African-

American history in the region, as well as special exhibits. There is also a research library on the premises. The center is open Tuesday through Saturday from 10:00 A.M. to 4:00 P.M.

Getting There

By car take the Arlington Memorial or 14th Street Bridge to the George Washington Memorial Parkway south, which becomes Washington Street in Old Town Alexandria. If you go to the Visitors' Bureau, they will give you an all-day parking pass, or you can park in metered spaces on the street.

Alexandria is also surprisingly easy to reach by Metro (whereas Georgetown is not). Take the Yellow line to the King Street station, and catch an eastbound AT2 or AT5 to the Visitors' Bureau.

RAINY DAY FUN

Visit Fredericksburg, Virginia, where you can find Kenmore Plantation and Gardens, the former home of George Washington's sister and brother-in-law, Betty Washington Lewis and Colonel Fielding Lewis. This stately mansion, built in 1755, is noted for its fine plaster ceilings. Located at ✉1201 Washington Ave., off I-95, the home is open to visitors Monday through Saturday from 10:00 A.M. to 5:00 P.M. and on Sunday from noon to 4:00 P.M. Admission is $6 for adults and $3 for children. There is a gift shop on the premises. Call ✆540-373-3381 for more information.

Fort Ward Museum and Historic Site

✉4301 W. Braddock Rd., Alexandria, Virginia
✆703-838-4848
🖱www.fortward.org

Fort Ward was taken under the wing of the City of Alexandria in 1961, and it has since been both restored and preserved as befits an important Civil War site. Today, this fifth largest of 162 forts built by Union forces features a completely restored northwest bastion and over 95 percent of its original walls. Both the fort and accompanying museum occupy a forty-five-acre park setting just east of Route 395.

The museum is open to visitors from 9 A.M. to 5 P.M. Tuesdays through Saturdays and from 12 to 5 P.M. Sundays. You can browse through artifacts, a research library, and a range of educational programs here. One recent exhibition covered "Medical Care for the Civil War Soldier," full of the expected horrors of battlefield treatment; a gentler exhibit dealt with the "Art of the Artilleryman."

The historic site itself is open from 9 A.M. to sunset daily. A path runs along the earthwork walls and can take as long as forty-five minutes to walk. Admission to the fort, and the museum, is free.

College Park Aviation Museum

✉ 1985 Cpl. Frank Scott Drive, College Park, Maryland
✆ 301-864-6029
🖰 www.pgparks.com

Opened in 1998, the College Park Aviation Museum is a 27,000-square-foot state-of-the-art facility located on the grounds of College Park Airport—the world's oldest continuously operating airport. The museum includes an open, one-and-a-half-story exhibit area for full-sized aircraft, as well as display and exhibition areas, a library, preservation and collection rooms, a lobby, The Prop Shop Gift Shop, offices, and an auditorium. The deck off the second-floor gallery, which is available for workshops and special events, offers a clear view of the airfield.

The museum highlights many aviation achievements through its use of animatronics and interactive exhibits. Memorabilia, photographs, aviation-related books and manuscripts, oral histories, and information kiosks provide considerable information to visitors about College Park Airport's significance in aviation history. Architecturally, the facility combines brick and glass, and it has a curved roofline reminiscent of an early Wright aeroplane.

The facility is open to the public for self-guided tours and for a variety of special events, lectures, and fun activities. Group tours are scheduled by appointment, and combine fun and education in an exciting environment. The museum is open from 10 A.M. to 5 P.M. daily, except holidays.

NASA/Goddard Space Flight Center

✉Soil Conservation Rd., Greenbelt, Maryland
📞301-286-8981
🖱www.gsfc.nasa.gov

Named for the "Father of Modern Rocketry," the Goddard Space Flight Center was built by NASA back in 1959. Along with displays of rockets and spacecraft, the lab's visitor center has lots of fun hands-on stuff—like a gyro-chair that lets you experience the sensation of steering with no gravity, and a maneuvering unit that lets you try to retrieve a satellite in space.

Special events include model rocket launches, stargazing groups, lectures by scientists, and videos of new NASA projects. The visitor center is open daily from 9 A.M. to 4 P.M.; call for a schedule of special events.

🧳 TRAVEL TIP

In addition to the exhibits at the Goddard Space Flight Center, you can tour some of the actual laboratories—including stops at the Test and Evaluation Facility, NASA Communications Network, Flight Dynamics Facility, and satellite control centers for such spacecraft as the Hubble Space Telescope. Tours are offered Mondays through Saturdays.

Amusement Parks

If your kids are a little tired of art, history, and "old houses," you might be able to bribe them into touring through the Hirshhorn, Corcoran, or Phillips collections with the promise of a trip to one of the three amusement parks in neighboring Virginia and Maryland.

Busch Gardens & Water Country USA

✉One Busch Gardens Blvd. Williamsburg, Virginia

✆757-253-3584

🖳www.buschgardens.com

An Anheuser-Busch theme park with seventeenth-century flair, Busch Gardens boasts more than forty thrilling rides, dazzling shows, quaint shops, European cuisine, and a separate water park. There's a combo ticket for both parks. The park is open March through October. Group rates and meeting space are available; call for details.

King's Dominion

✉Doswell, Virginia

✆804-876-5000

🖳www.kingsdominion.com

An amusement park in the national Paramount Six Flags amusement park chain, King's Dominion is known for its four wooden roller coasters as well as the steel roller coaster, the Anaconda, and its newest roller coaster, the Volcano. It also features a sixteen-acre water park with Big Wave Bay, a 650,000-gallon wave pool; Surf City Splash, which has fifty water attractions; and many water slides.

King's Dominion is open from March through October (in March, April, May, September, and October the hours are limited to weekends, so check the schedule before you plan to visit), and hours vary. There are concerts and special events, so call for information. Adult admission is $33.99; for children ages 3 to 6 it's $24.99; and for those 55 and over, admission is $28.99. There are two-day tickets available. Parking is an additional $6 per vehicle. Take Interstate 95 south to exit 98 and follow the signs.

Six Flags America

✉P.O. Box 4210 Largo, Maryland
✆301-249-1500
✍www.sixflags.com

This family theme park offers 100 rides, shows, and attractions, including the new Batwing and Typhoon Sea Coasters and four roller coasters, like the New Roar Wooden Coaster and the world-famous Mind Eraser. There's also a variety of children's rides in the specially themed "A Day at the Circus." Enjoy the twenty-five-acre Paradise Island Water Park and Crocodile Cal's Outback Beach House, plus seven live shows, games, gift shops, restaurants, and more. Six Flags is open daily Memorial Day through Labor Day, and on weekends only in May, September, and October. The park is closed November through April. Admission for adults is $35, for children $25, and you'll pay $9 for parking. Call for group rates.

CHAPTER 20

Suggested Itineraries

WASHINGTON, D.C. could keep you and your family entertained for weeks. There is so much to see and do that you'll never feel you've seen it all, even if you spend a month there. It's impossible to cover everything—new museums and exhibits open in the nation's capital every year, and there's always more to see and do. This may be why Washington, D.C., is one of the leading family travel destinations in the country.

When you're traveling with children, you really have to plan your trip and cater your activities to their ages and interests—and your own interests as well. That means reading up ahead, going online to check schedules and timing, and making sure you have as many tickets in advance as possible so as not to waste a lot of time waiting in lines or disappointing your kids. It's also a good idea to make reservations at popular or trendy restaurants ahead of time.

If You Only Have One Day

One day is barely enough to get a feel for the city and see what it has to offer, but if you are only in town for one day, head straight to the National Mall and visit the Smithsonian museums that interest you and your family the most—the Air and Space, Museum of

Natural History, and the Museum of American History would be the usual suspects. Plan on eating in one of the cafeterias or museum food courts, and preorder a ticket for the Washington Monument online, so you can make sure to see the city from this vantage point and experience this grand architectural and historical monument.

JUST FOR PARENTS

Washington's art galleries have banded together, and they hold mutual gallery openings during which the galleries are open later so that you can see new works on one night. In the Dupont Circle area, on the first Friday of every month, the galleries along Connecticut Avenue hold opening-night receptions. In Georgetown, the Canal Street courtyard galleries are the place to be on the third Thursday of every month, while the galleries along Georgetown's main drag hold their opening night on the third Friday of every month.

If you have some time in the evening, race down to Union Station, or check with your hotel concierge to find out if you can take a nighttime tour of the city's monuments (by bus, Tourmobile, trolley, or van), which should include the Lincoln, Jefferson, Vietnam Veterans, Korean War, and Franklin Delano Roosevelt Memorials.

A Weekend in D.C.

If you and your family are in town for a weekend and have a full Saturday and Sunday, check the museum and federal building schedules to make sure that they are open on the weekends—most museums are. If you have White House tickets, they would be for early Saturday morning, and that would be your first stop.

⬛ TRAVEL TIP

The only weekend day White House tours are given is Saturday from 7:30 A.M. until 11:00 A.M. Do not be late, and don't forget to have breakfast before the tour, as no food or drinks are allowed inside the White House. Also make sure you and the family have all gone to the bathroom in the visitors' center, because there are no bathrooms open to the public inside the White House.

If possible, try to find a hotel downtown or near the national Mall (Loews L'Enfant Plaza, Holiday Inn Downtown, Red Roof Inn, or the Hotel Monaco), so you can do as much as possible in a short amount of time, and if your kids get tired, you can race back to the hotel for a nap.

Saturday

Once you check into your hotel, either head toward Union Station and take the D.C. Ducks or Old Town Trolley tour of the city, or head to the Mall and hop on the Tourmobile. Sit with the kids and let the wise and entertaining tour operators give you and your family a grand overview of the sites. Then you can get your kids to help you decide what you'll see over the rest of the weekend. You may not be able to fit everything into the schedule, but it's nice to see what's out there, and how close some of the places are to each other.

If you take the Tourmobile or Old Town Trolley, you can hop on and off, and you might want to make that your day, visiting some of the museums on the Mall and some of the sites. D.C. Ducks is a three-hour tour that goes on both land and sea in those wonderful amphibious vehicles from World War II. They hand out duck noise-makers, which are charmers for kids, and the kids can keep them as mementos (and annoy you in the car on your way back home).

If you have not elected to hop on and off, you might want to spend an afternoon in one of the Mall museums until it closes. You can have dinner at Jordan's (Michael Jordan's fancy new celebrity restaurant) right off the Mall, or at Planet Hollywood, the Hard Rock Cafe, or TGI Friday's. If you have older kids who would enjoy French food, Les Halles is always excellent.

Then either go on a nighttime exploration of the Washington Monument (if you have a ticket and it's summertime) or catch a movie at Union Station—there are nine theaters—or even in your hotel room on pay-per-view.

Sunday

Eat breakfast in your hotel, and then head to the National Zoo. It is a must-see for families with children. Get there early so you can catch a museum later in the afternoon. If it is Sunday, and you are so inclined, you might want to catch a morning service at the National Cathedral, where you can see the Darth Vader gargoyle and the moon-rock stained-glass window (or just pop in there to take a look). They are very close to the zoo.

The zoo will take about three or four hours to see. Plan on eating lunch there. Then you can take a cab downtown and do a late afternoon walk-through of the International Spy Museum. If there's some time left, you can quickly pop into Ford's Theatre (where President Lincoln was shot) and then cross the street to look at the Petersen House, where Lincoln died. You can have dinner at Zola or Zaytinya, or even Poste in the nearby Hotel Monaco, or try one of the fabulous restaurants in nearby Chinatown.

TRAVEL TIP

After a hard day of sightseeing the monuments and the museums, your kids may not be ready to call it a night, but you might be tired. An easy dinner and a movie can be found at Union Station, where there's a nine-theater multiplex and a food court that offers everything from 1950s-style diner burgers to quiche Lorraine to cannolis for dessert.

In the evening, check with your hotel concierge or head to Union Station, and take a bus tour of the memorials at night— Lincoln and Jefferson are spectacular all lit up, and the Vietnam Wall has a unique power after dark.

Three-Day Weekend in the Capital

If you're visiting D.C. over a Monday-holiday weekend, expect many other families to do the same. Book hotels early, and do make reservations at the restaurants you and your family really want to go to.

☂ RAINY DAY FUN

If you are traveling with toddlers, make sure you include D.C. Ducks Tour, the Children's Museum, the Smithsonian Carousel at the Mall, the Orkin Insect Zoo at the Museum of Natural History, and the Washington Dolls' House and Toy Museum in your itinerary.

Day One

If it's not a federal holiday, and you've opted for a Friday/ Saturday/Sunday visit, try to get the White House tour for Friday morning. It should be a little easier to get and less hectic and crowded. Eat a quick lunch at Old Ebbitts Grill or Ollie's Trolley, which has great burgers and hotdogs. Then head to the U.S. Mint to see paper money being printed and shredded.

In the early afternoon, you can catch a tour—the last one is usually at 2:00 P.M., but they sometimes add later tours in the summer. They're closed on the weekend, but you could visit Monday morning, if you have a Saturday/Sunday/Monday visit.

If you have energy left, head to the Mall and do as much of the Museum of American History as you can. Pause for an ice cream in the re-created old ice cream parlor in the museum, and let the younger kids take a ride on the carousel outside the museum. In the evening, take one of the night bus tours.

Day Two

After a quick breakfast in your hotel, head straight to the Mall, and finish Air and Space and Natural History. Eat lunch in either Wright Court in Air & Space, where you can choose burgers, pizza, or a chicken meal, or the restaurant in Natural History, where they feature soups and sandwiches. If you've got time, stop in at the National Aquarium around 2:30 P.M., when you can catch them feeding the sharks, piranhas, or alligators—always a kid-pleaser.

If you're planning on heading to the Kennedy Center for the free daily 6:00 P.M. concert, you can have dinner in or around the Center and then enjoy the show.

▐▐▌ TRAVEL TIP

D.C. is a tourist town, and many tourists are too exhausted to go out at night. This means you can usually catch a good theater performance. Many Broadway shows make their way to Washington, and you can often catch some really good theater on tour, often for half price by calling ✆202-TICKETS, which offers half-price tickets the day of the show. If there is a production at Ford's Theatre, it might be interesting to see a play in the same theater where Lincoln was assassinated.

Day Three

Start with breakfast at the National Cathedral or at one of those terrific D.C. Sunday brunches, then visit the zoo and the International Spy Museum. If you get hungry, the Waffle Shop right next to the Petersen House is an authentic D.C. lunch counter, where you can get crab cakes or steak sandwiches with great onion rings for under $5.

In the evening, visit the MCI Center for a sporting event. Tickets are pretty easy to come by.

A Five-Day Getaway

Follow the three-day weekend plan, and add the following activities. Unless your kids are very young (and therefore don't have the attention span for this), you can dedicate a day to learning about how our government works and touring government sites (see Chapter 8). This is best done during the week, as you might be able to catch the U.S. Supreme Court and/or Congress in session. Write ahead of time, and see if it's possible to meet with your representative or senator while you're in town. It will be a memorable family event, and one that you should definitely bring the camera to record (even if you didn't vote for him/her).

Day Four

Begin with a hearty breakfast at Eastern Market. Perhaps one of the adults can run over to the line for free tickets to the Capital while the other waits with the kids for a seat for breakfast of blueberry buckwheat pancakes or the breakfast "brick"—eggs, sausage, and a roll. If there's time, explore the marketplace.

Try to get a morning tour of the Capitol, the legislative seat of our government. The guided tour will take forty-five minutes, and you'll probably want to walk around a bit. Make sure you let the kids try the whisper that can be heard across the room. Then tour the U.S. Supreme Court.

You might want to head to Union Station for lunch at either the food court (with forty kiosks to choose from, there's bound to be something for everyone), or a sit-down meal at Pizzeria Uno or America. If the kids are feeling rambunctious, let them run through the National Postal Museum across the street from Union Station. It will take less than an hour, and will be surprisingly entertaining for everyone.

Then head to the Library of Congress, the world's largest library with 26 million items, and follow it up with a trip to the National Archives, where the kids will see the Declaration of Independence and the Bill of Rights.

Everyone will be pretty tired, so a nice leisurely dinner is probably in order. You can head to Georgetown and eat in a historic restaurant like 1879 (pricey, but memorable) or take the kids to the Jefferson Hotel, where they can eat amongst genuine antiques, or enjoy a relaxing dinner at Firefly downtown in the Hotel Madera.

💼 TRAVEL TIP

If you want to just walk through the streets of the city and window shop (or even buy something), Georgetown is Washington's late-night shopping area, where many of the stores are open until 11:00 P.M. From college gear such as The Gap and Banana Republic to fun youth-oriented clothing and housewares in a funky store like Urban Outfitters and Betsy Johnson, Georgetown has an eclectic mix of stores and late-night eateries too. The Shops at Georgetown, the three-story mall, are open until 9:00 P.M.

Day Five

If you've brought the car, drive out to the new Udvar-Hazy Center near Dulles, where you can see even more aviation artifacts and specimens. The museum has the *Enola Gay*, the plane that dropped the bomb on Hiroshima, as well as the space shuttle *Enterprise* and an Air France Concorde. You can have lunch at the center or drive to the nearby Westfields Marriott, where you can have a spectacular Sunday brunch or a delightful afternoon tea. In the afternoon, drive to Tyson's Corner, one of the outlet staples of the city, and shop until you drop. You can have dinner at one of the many restaurants in the outlet center or neighboring malls, or head back to the city for a meal at one of the many Ethiopian restaurants, where kids get to eat with their hands.

Make It a Full Week

You should plan on spending a full day at Mount Vernon/Woodlawn Plantation (make sure you explore the Pope-Leighey House, designed by Frank Lloyd Wright, which is also on the grounds) and then have dinner in Alexandria, Virginia. It's a delightful way to explore the past and present, and there's so much for both kids and adults.

You might also want to consider spending a day at one of the nearby amusement parks—Busch Gardens, King's Dominion, or Six Flags. It's a great way to let your hair down after an educational vacation.

RAINY DAY FUN

Preteens and teens might be interested in the Washington Walks Tours, shopping at Georgetown and the outlets, and visiting the National Museum of Health and Medicine, which has some of the grossest medical exhibits in the country. If your kids are over 12 and mature enough, the Holocaust Museum is a good family event, although very difficult to experience.

Washington's Annual Events

January

Restaurant Week

One week during the year, to be announced. Visit ✎*www. washington.org/restaurantwk* for more information. During Restaurant Week, the city's most famous restaurants offer patrons a three-course *prix fixe* meal for the price of the year, such as $20.04 for 2004. Dinner is usually $10 more. This is a wonderful opportunity to sample the very best cuisine the city has to offer at a fraction of the price.

Presidential Inauguration

January 20 after a presidential election is the day of presidential inauguration. This is always a major production in D.C. The swearing-in ceremony takes place in front of the Capitol, and crowds line the sidewalks. Afterwards, the new president and his entourage head toward the White House on Pennsylvania Avenue. The entire day features free public events, such as concerts and parades, as well as many semi-private parties.

Martin Luther King Jr. Day

Every third Monday of January the city hosts a variety of activities such as speeches by civil rights leaders, lectures, readings, theatrical performances, and concerts. There's also the laying of a wreath at the Lincoln Memorial and the playing of King's "I Have a Dream" speech. The Martin Luther King Jr. Memorial Library usually hosts some commemorative events. Call ✆202-727-1186 for more information.

February

Chinese New Year Celebrations

The Chinese follow a lunar calendar, so the exact dates vary from year to year; generally the Chinese New Year falls in late January or early February. D.C.'s Chinese neighborhood is centered in the area around 7th Street and H, marked by the brightly colored arch given by its sister city of Beijing. From the day of the Chinese New Year and the ten days following there are parades, fireworks, and celebrations. Area restaurants feature special menus. Check the *Washington Post* for listings.

Black History Month

The city offers a wealth of special exhibits, concerts, and performances all month long. Call the Smithsonian's Anacostia Museum for its events (✆202-287-3382) as well as the Frederick Douglass Historic Site (✆202-426-5960), the Mary McLeod Bethune House (✆202-673-2402), and the Martin Luther King Jr. Memorial Library (✆202-727-0321). Also check the *Washington Post* listings.

Lincoln's Birthday

Every February 12, there is an annual laying-of-a-wreath ceremony at the Lincoln Memorial and a reading of the Gettysburg Address at noon in commemoration of Lincoln's birthday. Call ✆202-619-7222 for more information.

Frederick Douglass's Birthday

February 12 also marks the birthday of Frederick Douglass, an African-American abolitionist and writer. A wreath-laying ceremony, performances, and activities are held all day long at his historic home, ✉Cedar Hill, 1411 W Street. For more information, call ✆202-426-5961.

Washington's Birthday

George Washington was born on February 22, and his birthday is marked with a celebration similar to other birthday events, plus a parade. Mount Vernon celebrates Washington's birthday with free admission all day, as well as activities and fanfare on the bowling green. Call ✆703-780-2000 for more information.

A Black History Month Masquerade Ball

In late February, a carnival is held at the Smithsonian Castle (✉100 Jefferson Drive). Tickets are expensive. Call ✆202-287-2061 for dates and information.

March

St. Patrick's Day

On the Sunday before March 17 (St. Patrick's Day), parades are held in D.C. (on Constitution Avenue, from 7th to 17th Streets) and Alexandria's Old Town.

Annual Flower Show

March is also when the U.S. Botanic Garden hosts its annual flower show. Call ✆202-225-8333 for more information.

Ringling Brothers and Barnum & Bailey Circus

The circus comes to town at the D.C. Armory, ✉2001 E. Capital Street, and the MCI Center. Call ✆202-432-7328 for tickets and dates (generally March and April).

National Cherry Blossom Festival

Late March and early April is when the Japanese cherry trees along the Tidal Basin are in bloom. National news media monitor the cherry trees' budding, and the festivities are timed to coincide with the two weeks of blooming. Activities include a parade, which marks the end of the season. For parade information or tickets for seats along the parade route, call ☎ 202-728-1137. The National Park Service offers guided tours of the trees in bloom, leaving from the Jefferson Memorial. For more information, visit them on the Web at ✎ *www.nationalcherryblossomfestival.org.*

Seal Days

In late March, the National Zoo (3001 Connecticut Avenue) hosts its Seal Days. There are seal feeding and performances, as well as face painting for children. Call ☎ 202-673-4717 for more information.

Smithsonian Kite Festival

Held on the last weekend in March, the festival allows kite flyers and makers from all over the country to come to the parkland around the Washington Monument to show their stuff and compete for juried prizes and ribbons. For more information and rules call ☎ 202-357-2700.

April

Easter

Easter in the capital is a special time. Events include sunrise services at Arlington National Cemetery at the Memorial Amphitheater (☎ 202-789-7000) as well as various services at the National Cathedral (☎ 202-537-6200).

White House Easter-Egg Roll

This fantastic hunt for more than 1,000 wooden Easter eggs for kids between the ages of 3 and 6 takes place on Monday after Easter Sunday. Entertainment is also provided for the parents and siblings who accompany them. The hunt and entertainment takes place between 10:00 A.M. and 2:00 P.M., but entry is by timed tickets, which are issued at the National Park Service Ellipse Visitors' Center (just behind the White House at 15th and E Streets) beginning at 7:00 A.M. If you're planning on attending, you might want to ask your representative or senator about getting tickets way ahead of time. There is also an Easter Celebration at the Ellipse, which includes entertainment, music, storytelling, and food giveaways for the whole family.

African-American Family Celebration

This annual festival of music, dance, and art is held every Easter Monday at the National Zoo, at 3001 Connecticut Avenue. For more information, call ☎ 202-673-4717.

Capital Classic Game

Some time in early April, high school basketball players from all over the country play in this all-star game at the MCI Center. Call ☎ 202-432-7328 for tickets and dates.

Thomas Jefferson's Birthday

April 13, Jefferson's birthday, is celebrated with wreath-laying, speeches, and a military ceremony, all of which take place at the Jefferson Memorial. Call ☎ 202-619-7222.

White House Garden Tours

Every year, for two afternoons in mid-April, the White House opens its beautiful gardens and terrific outdoor sculpture to the public. Call ☎ 202-456-2200 for more information. Again, this might be something you ask your representative or senator to see about getting tickets for.

Shakespeare's Birthday

In mid-April, the Folger Shakespeare Library hosts an afternoon party in honor of the Bard's birthday. The party includes performances for kids and adults, music, and food. Call ☎ 202-544-7077.

Washington International Film Festival

The festival is held for two weeks in middle or late April. Films are screened at various locations including theaters and embassies. Call ☏202-628-FILM for schedule and location, or visit the Web site at ✎*www.filmfestdc.org*.

Taste of the Nation

As part of a national fundraiser to feed the hungry, nearly 100 D.C. restaurants offer tastings of their cuisines at Union Station on the Taste of the Nation Day, held in late April. Tickets run about $75, and there is an auction afterwards. Call ☏1-800-955-8278 for information and tickets.

Smithsonian Craft Festival

A juried craft fair in the National Building Museum on the Mall, held in late April, features about 100 artists and artisans offering beautiful one-of-a-kind crafts. There is an entry fee per person. Call ☏202-357-2700 for more information.

May

Annual School Safety Patrol Parade

On May 1 local schools honor their safety patrol members with a parade of marching bands and cheerleaders on Constitution Avenue from 7th to 17th Street. The parade begins at 10:00 A.M.

National Cathedral Annual Flower Mart

This May festival and flower sale takes place on the first Friday and Saturday in May. There are activities for children and adults, as well as food. Call ☏202-537-6200 for more information.

Georgetown Garden Tour

The annual tour, which takes place on the second Saturday in May, offers a glimpse into the private gardens of D.C.'s oldest homes. Light fare is usually provided with the cost of the ticket (about $20). Call ☎202-333-6896 for more information.

Annual Goodwill Embassy Tour

The second Saturday in May is also the day of the Annual Goodwill Embassy Tour. As you drive around Cleveland Park on your way to and from the National Cathedral, you will pass nearly 200 embassy buildings and the residences of the ambassadors. This tour is your chance to see the inside of these fabulous old homes, now the property of other countries, as well as the incredible art that hangs on many of the embassy walls. For a $30 fee, you board a bus that stops at ten or so embassies where there will be a tour guide, as well as music or performances from that country. Tours run from 10:00 A.M. to 5:00 P.M. Call ☎202-636-4225 for information and tickets.

Candlelight Vigil

This memorial service, held in mid-May, honors the nation's law enforcement personnel who have died in the line of duty. Services begin at 8:00 P.M. at the National Law Enforcement Officers Memorial, at 4th and E Streets. Call ☎202-737-3400 for more information.

Annual Mount Vernon Wine Festival

Wines of Virginia and modern-day versions of those made at the Washington estate are presented at this festival; arts and crafts of the Colonial period are on sale as well. The festival takes place in mid-May. Call ☎703-799-8604 for more information and tickets.

Andrews Air Force Base Annual Air Show

Another option for travelers to D.C. in mid-May is the Andrews Air Force Base Annual Air Show, your opportunity to watch the flying feats, parachute jumps, and an open house at the Andrews Air Force base, at Route 5 and Allentown Road. This is a crowded event, so get there early. Attendance is free of charge. Call ☏301-981-1110 for more information.

Welcome Summer Concert

The National Symphony Orchestra performs a free concert to welcome summer on the West Lawn of the Capitol. The event is held on the Sunday before Memorial Day. Call ☏202-619-7222 for more information.

Memorial Day

The last Monday in May is Memorial Day. In D.C., this national holiday is celebrated with a wreath-laying ceremony at the Tomb of the Unknown Soldier in Arlington National Cemetery, followed by a service and speeches by officials (sometimes the president), as well as a performance by a military band. Call ☏202-685-2851 for more information.

Wreath-laying ceremony, speeches, and the playing of taps takes place at the Vietnam Veterans Memorial at 1:00 P.M. The U.S. Navy Memorial (⊠701 Pennsylvania Avenue NW) commemorates the navy veterans with performances and speeches all day. Call ☏202-619-7222 for more information.

June

Capital Pride

Held on the first week of June, Capital Pride is the fourth largest gay-pride event in the country and is a nine-day diversity festival with varied events and an annual parade and street festival. For more information, visit ✍*www.capitalpride.org.*

Annual Dupont-Kalorama Museum Walk

An all-day event held in early June along Dupont Circle and the Kalorama district, this walk includes open houses of six museums and historic sites featuring food and performances. Call ☏202-667-0441 for more information.

Shakespeare Theater Free for All

In mid-June, a two-week run of evening performances of a free Shakespeare play are offered at the Carter Barton Amphitheater. Call ✆202-547-3230 for information and dates.

Juneteenth

On June 19, the Anacostia Museum (✉1901 Fort Place SE) observes Juneteenth, a celebration of the day when Texas slaves finally learned of their freedom, with music, food, and performances from noon to 6:00 P.M. Call ✆202-287-2061 for more information.

Barbeque Battle

For the past decade, the annual barbeque battle has seen the nation's leading barbeque chefs and restaurants compete for a prize of $15,000. The event features lots of free food and interactive cooking demonstrations, as well as children's activities. The battle takes place on the third weekend in June. For more information, visit ✍*www.barbequebattle.com.*

D.C. Caribbean Carnival

The last week of June presents a week-long celebration of Caribbean culture and food, culminating in an eight-hour parade down Constitution Avenue, starting at 14th Street and ending on Pennsylvania Ave. There is a three-block area on Pennsylvania Avenue with crafts, food, and art for the general public. For more information, visit ✍*www.dccaribbeancarnival.com.*

Cadillac Grand Prix of Washington, D.C.

Held on the last weekend of June, the Grand Prix is an international car show with concerts and celebrity appearances, as well as racing on the grounds of the Robert F. Kennedy Memorial Stadium. For more information, visit ✍*www.nationalgrandprix.com.*

Smithsonian American Folklife Festival

This ten-day event begins in late June and lasts through the Independence Day weekend. The festival features crafts, performances, music, and food from all fifty states, highlighting one region or state in particular. Most performances and demonstrations are free, and food is available for purchase. Call ✆202-357-2700 or visit ✍*www.folklife.si.edu* for dates and featured states.

July

Fourth of July Weekend

Millions of tourists visit D.C. for the Fourth of July, and the city hosts a number of free family activities. There is a huge Independence Day parade down Constitution Avenue at noon, with floats and 100 marching bands. At the National Archives, there is a morning reading of the Declaration of Independence, as well as performances by military bands. There is free entertainment at the Sylvan Theater on the grounds of the Washington Monument all day long.

In the evening, the National Symphony holds an annual free concert on the west steps of the Capitol building at 8:00 P.M. Fireworks over the Washington Monument begin at sunset (around 9:20 P.M.).

Mary McLeod Bethune Annual Celebration

Each July 9, an annual celebration is held at the Bethune statue in Lincoln Park, at 11th and East Capital Streets NW. There are gospel choir performances, guest speakers, and a wreath laying.

Annual Soapbox Derby

On July 10, homemade and professional soapbox cars drive down Constitution Avenue, between New Jersey and Louisiana Avenues, from 10:00 A.M. to 6:00 P.M. Call ✆301-670-1110 for more information and entry rules.

Bastille Day

Hosted by the French restaurant Les Halles (1201 Constitution Avenue) on July 14, this celebration of French Independence Day features a tray-balancing competition by the establishment's wait staff from the restaurant to the U.S. Capitol and back, as well as live entertainment. Call ☎202-347-8648 for more information.

Latino Festival

In late July, Latin bands from all over the United States play music on Pennsylvania Avenue between 9th and 14th Streets. Food is available for purchase.

Legg Mason Tennis Classic

Tennis champions including Andre Agassi are present for this prestigious tournament at the William H.G. Fitzgerald Center, held on the last week of July and the first week of August. For more information, visit ✍*www.leggmasontennisclassic.com.*

Screen on the Green Film Festival

On Monday nights during July and August, you and your family can attend free showings of American movie classics on a twenty-by-forty-foot screen on the grounds of the National Mall. Past films include *The Wizard of Oz* and *King Kong.* Bring a blanket to sit on and get there early to stake your claim on the lawn. Films start at sunset. Call ☎877-262-5866 for schedule.

September

Kennedy Center Prelude Festival

Each September, the Kennedy Center gears up for its fall season with a two-week festival of free performances and events designed to celebrate the performing arts in D.C. In the past, the festival has included performances by the Washington Ballet and The National Symphony Orchestra.

For more information, visit ✍*www.kennedy-center.org.*

Labor Day Concert by the National Symphony Orchestra

On the first Monday of September, Labor Day, the National Symphony Orchestra offers a free concert that begins at 8:00 P.M. on the West Lawn of the Capitol.

National Frisbee Festival

Over the Labor Day Weekend, an annual gathering for Frisbee lovers (and their dogs) is held on the grounds of the Washington Monument. Call ☎301-645-5043 for more information.

National Black Family Reunion

This national celebration of black families in America, held in mid-September, features performances, food, and entertainment on the grounds of the Washington Monument. All events are free, except for the opening prayer and breakfast ceremony (tickets are $35). Call ☎202-737-0120 for more information. *www.ncnw.org*.

Kalorama House and Embassy Tour

Held in mid-September, this is another opportunity to take an all-day tour of the historic homes and embassies of D.C. Call ☎202-387-4062 for more information.

Annual Children's Festival at the Wolf Trap Theater in Vienna

The festival is held in mid-September. Featured are paid performances, as well as clowns and puppet shows. Call ☎703-642-0862 for information on performers.

Wildlife Art Festival at the Smithsonian National Zoo

This two-day art festival and fair held in mid-September features eighty artists, craftspeople, and photographers, with art and animal demonstrations and a kid's creation station. The art festival is free, but the patron preview party costs $25. Call ☎202-673-4613 for more information and tickets.

Fiesta Festival

This two-day celebration of Hispanic heritage is held in late September at the National Zoo (3001 Connecticut Avenue). Call ☎202-673-4717 for more information.

National Cathedral Open House

In late September, there are demonstrations by master stone-carvers, activities, and food from 10:00 A.M. to 5:00 P.M. The *Washington Post* claims that this is the only opportunity to climb the central tower stairway and see the bells and a spectacular view. Call ☎202-537-6200 for more information.

October

Dupont Circle Historic Homes Tour

The tour is offered sometime in mid-October, from noon to 5:00 P.M. Call ☎202-265-3222 for tickets and information.

Goodwill's Giant Used Book Sale

Everything but the kitchen sink is on sale for five days in mid-October, from books to CDs and artwork, at the Washington Convention Center (9th and H Streets). Call ☎202-636-4225, ext. 1257, for more information.

White House Fall Garden Tours

In mid-October, the White House opens its private gardens to visitors for two days, with musical entertainment. Call ☎202-456-2200 for more information.

Taste of D.C. Festival

On Columbus Day weekend, many of Washington's best restaurants along Pennsylvania Avenue from 9th to 14th Streets offer samples of their fare, as well as performances and entertainment. The festival is free, but the tasting requires tickets. Call ☎202-724-5430 for more information. *www.tasteofdc.org*.

Marine Corps Marathon

In late October, thousands of runners race from the Iwo Jima Memorial in Arlington through the city and end at the Mall, a 26.2-mile run that passes by most of the city's most famous attractions and has been nicknamed "Marathon of the Monuments." The race starts at 8:30 A.M. Call ✆703-784-2225 or visit ✍*www.marine marathon.com* for more information.

The Annual Boo at the Zoo

Over a Halloween weekend, usually the Friday and Saturday before Halloween, the National Zoo stays open late and offers night tours of the bat cave, haunted trails, and trick-or-treat stations for kids where costumed volunteers hand out treats. There's also a goodie bag for all grownups, from 5:30 P.M. to 8:30 P.M. Children under 2 free, members $10, nonmembers $20. Call ✆202-673-4717 for more information.

November

Veterans Day

Memorial ceremonies are held at Arlington National Cemetery at the Tomb of the Unknown Soldier at 11:00 A.M. and at the Vietnam Veterans Memorial at 1:00 P.M.

Kennedy Center Holiday Performances

Holiday concerts and free performances run at the Kennedy Center from late November through New Year's Eve. Call ✆202-467-4600 for more information.

December

Pageant of Peace

The pageant begins on a Wednesday or Thursday in early December, when the president lights the national Christmas tree on the Ellipse south of the White House. The pageant lasts for three weeks, with seasonal music, caroling, a nativity, and a display of fifty state trees. Call ✆202-619-7222 or visit ✍*www.pageantofpeace.org* for more information.

Tree Lighting Ceremony

In early December the National Museum of Women in the Arts (✉1250 New York Avenue) hosts a tree-lighting ceremony from 11:30 A.M. to 2:00 P.M. The tree remains on display all month, with handmade ornaments by female artists. Call ☏202-783-5000 for information on submitting ornaments for display.

Charles Dickens's *A Christmas Carol*

The play has a two-week run at Ford's Theatre in late December. Call ☏202-347-4833 for tickets and information.

White House Candlelight Tours

Evening viewing of the decorated interior of the White House by candlelight is available from 5:00 to 7:00 P.M. on December 26 through 28. Lines are long for this special holiday event, so get there early or ask your representative or senator to put you on the list. Call ☏202-456-2200 to make sure that the tour is offered this year.

A Frank Lloyd Wright Christmas

All December long, the Pope-Leighey House on the grounds of Woodlawn Plantation near Mount Vernon offers a Frank Lloyd Wright Christmas event. Decorations from the 1940s, when the house was built, adorn the Christmas tree. Call ☏202-703-4000 for more information.

Trees of Christmas Exhibition

Another month-long event, the exhibition takes place at the Smithsonian's National Museum of Natural History. A number of Christmas trees and their decorations are on view in the museum.

New Year's Eve

The Postal Service's giant "LOVE" stamp is lowered to ring in the New Year at the Old Post Office Pavilion (✉1100 Pennsylvania Avenue). Call ☏202-289-4224 for more information.

Additional Resources

Washington, D.C., Convention and Tourism Corporation
www.washington.org

This is the essential Web address for planning your trip. This site will give you hotel and restaurant suggestions and discounts, a local calendar of events, as well as suggested itineraries and ways to plan and save money.

AlexandriaCity.com
www.alexandriacity.com

This is a good resource for tourist information in Alexandria, Virginia.

Washington Post
www.washingtonpost.com

In addition to news, the *Post* covers just about everything you need to orient yourself to the city, from a neighborhood guide calendar of events to a tourism site where a *Post* reporter plays tour guide for your benefit. The site also offers a trip planner: type in the days you will be visiting, and it gives you a listing of what will be taking place while you're there. Other resources include a weather forecast, tours of the town, Metro maps, restaurant listings, Weekend Best Bets, and an archive.

DCPages.com
≪www.dcpages.com

This site offers a fairly comprehensive overview of Washington, D.C., with weather forecasts, events listings, and a search of entertainment topics.

The Washingtonian
≪www.washingtonian.com

The Washingtonian is the regional magazine for the city, sold on newsstands. Its Web site will give you sample articles about the city from the recent issue, as well as listings for 100 Cheap Eats and the top 100 restaurants in the city.

Washington Free Weekly
≪www.washingtoncitypaper.com

This is the Web site for the capital's alternative newspaper, which is published on Wednesdays and is available free of charge at most coffee shops and bookstores. It features a lively and opinionated listing of events, as well as an archive of past articles.

Suggested Reading

The following is a brief list of books you might want to read before or after your visit, if you found any history or lore of the capital particularly fascinating:

Alexander, John. *Ghosts: Washington Revisited.* (1998, Schiffer Publishers Ltd.). This is a great guide to capital-city hauntings.

Berman, Richard. *Natural Washington: A Guide for Hikers, Bikers, Birders and Other Lovers of Nature in the Greater Capital Area.* (EPM Publishers, 1994, 3rd edition). You'll find this a good guide to outdoor recreation.

Carey Francine Curro. *Washington Odyssey: a Multi-Cultural History of the Nation's Capital.* (2003, Smithsonian Institution Press). Check out this wonderful history of D.C.'s immigrant communities.

Graham, Katherine. *Personal History.* (1998, Vintage Books USA). You'll find this memoir by the former owner of the *Washington Post* both interesting and informative.

Moore, John L. *Speaking of Washington: Facts, Firsts and Folklore.* (1993, CQ Press). You'll enjoy this, a good guide for fun facts and trivia.

Whitman, William B. *Washington, D.C.: Off the Beaten Path, A Guide to Unique Places, 2nd Edition.* (2003, Globe Pequot). This great guide points out unique places of interest.

APPENDIX C

Maps

The Mall

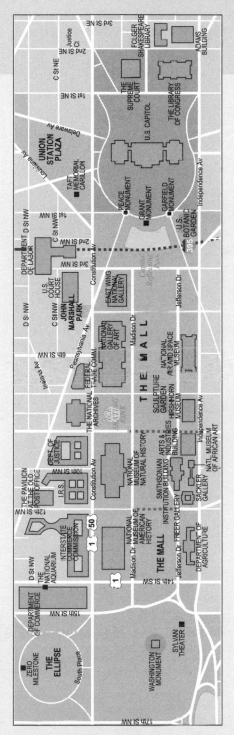

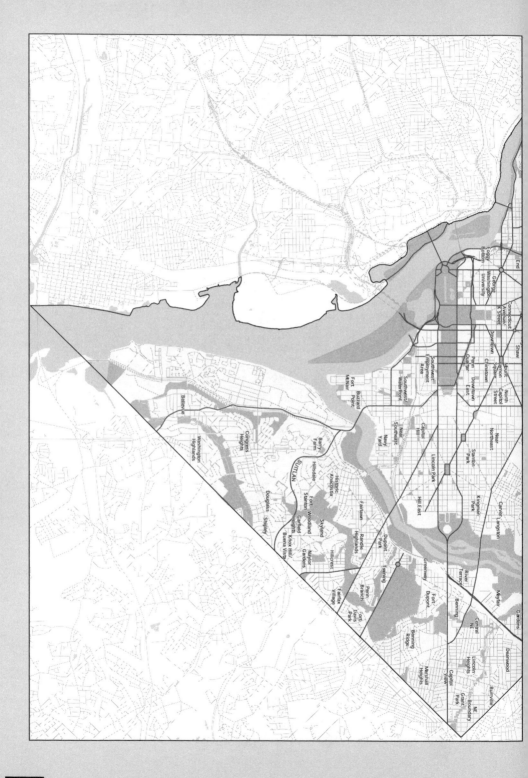

D.C. Neighborhood Map

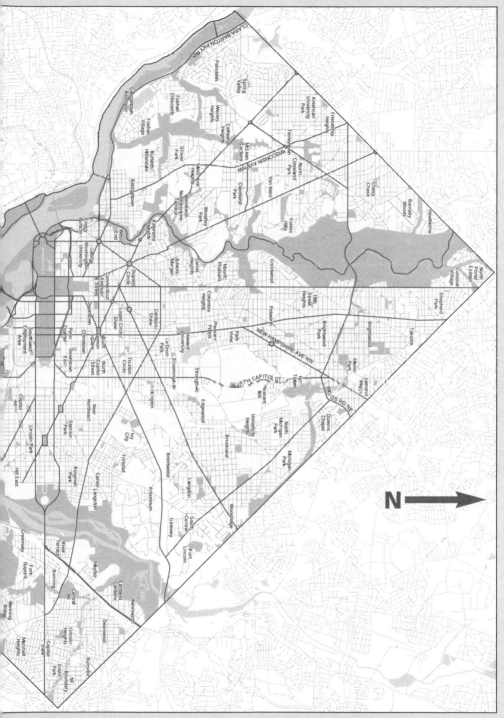

D.C. neighborhood map used with permission of the D.C. Office of Planning, the National Park Service, the D.C. Department of Parks and Recreation, and the District Department of Transportation.

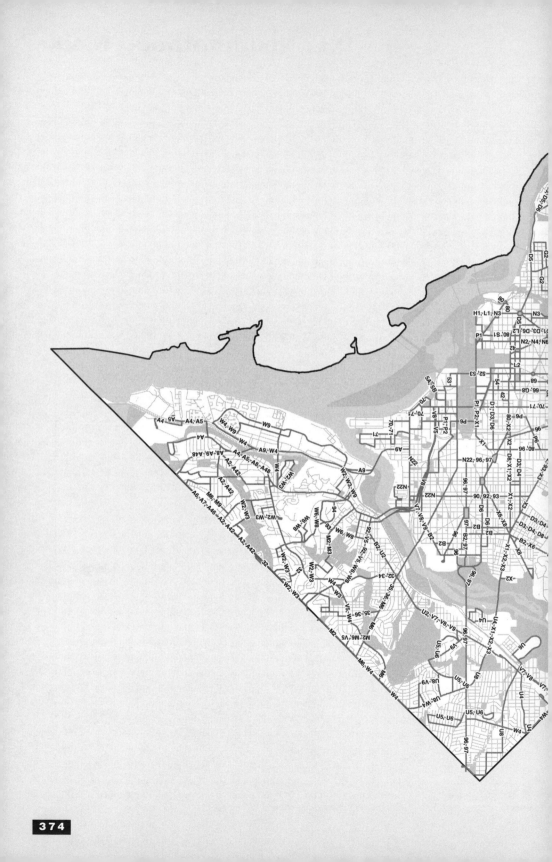

Washington, D.C., City Bus Routes

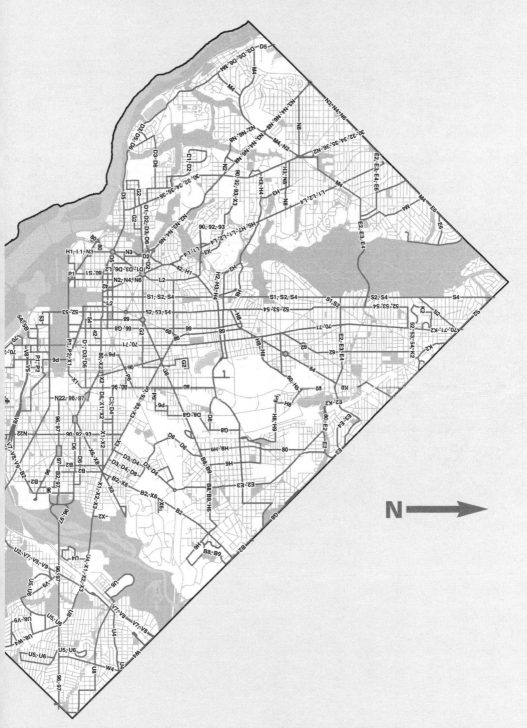

N →

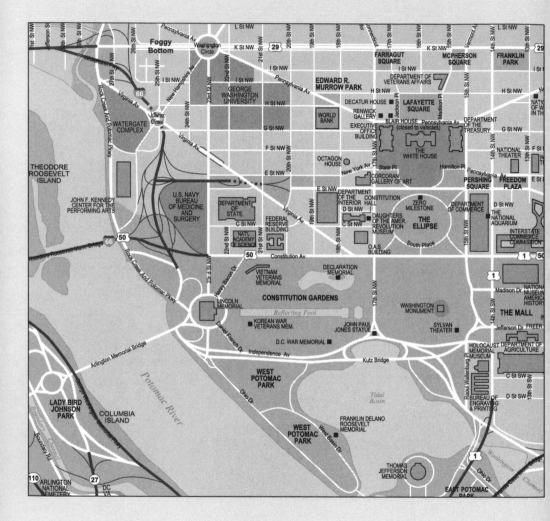

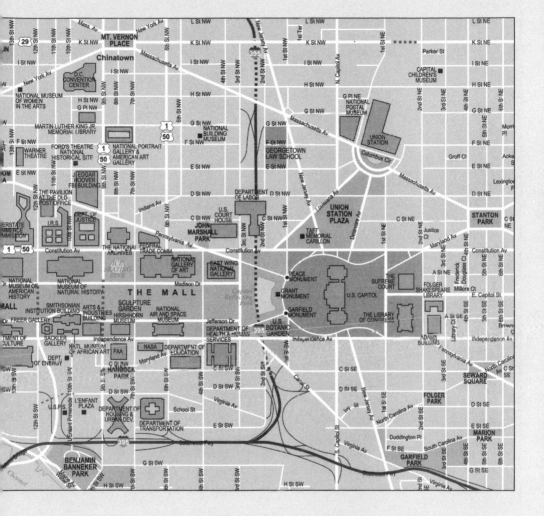

Index

For Travel!

The Everything® Family Guide to Hawaii
Donald P. Ryan, Ph.D.

The Hawaiian islands have long been known as a premier travel destination. This island paradise is also gaining recognition for its family-friendly sites, high-quality accommodations, and exciting activities. *The Everything® Family Guide to Hawaii* provides readers with an easy-to-use guide to all the best hotels, shops, restaurants, and attractions in the Aloha State. This book features tips for finding the cheapest fares, traveling between islands, avoiding the tourist traps, and enjoying the unique culture and heritage of the Hawaiian people.

1-59337-054-7,
$14.95($22.95 CAN)

1-59337-136-5,
$14.95 ($22.95 CAN)

The Everything® Guide to New York City, 2nd Edition
Lori Perkins

The Everything® Guide to New York City, 2nd Ed. features all of New York's best-loved attractions, from Battery Park to Museum Mile. Starting with the must-see landmarks—the Statue of Liberty and Empire State Building—to surprising secret treasures that are off the beaten path, this book includes information on where to stay and eat, neighborhood explorations, shows and attractions, New York after dark, and more.

To order, call **800-872-5627** or visit *www.everything.com*

1-58062-742-0,
$14.95 ($22.95 CAN)

The Everything® Travel Guide to The Disneyland Resort®, California Adventure®, Universal Studios®, and the Anaheim Area

Jason Rich

With millions of visitors each year, it's easy to see why Disneyland® is one of America's favorite vacation spots for families. Containing the most up-to-date information, this brand new expansive travel guide contains everything needed to plan the perfect getaway without missing any of the great new attractions. This book rates all the rides, shows, and attractions for each member of the family, allowing readers to plan the perfect itinerary for their trip.

The Everything® Family Guide to The Walt Disney World Resort®, Universal Studios®, and Greater Orlando, 4th Edition

Jason Rich

Packed with fun things to see and do, the Orlando area is the number one family vacation destination in the country. In this newest edition, travel expert Jason Rich shares his latest tips on how the whole family can have a great time—without breaking the bank. In addition to the helpful ride, show, and attractions rating system, the revised fourth edition contains a fully updated hotel/motel resource guide, rated restaurant listings, and the inside scoop on all the new additions.

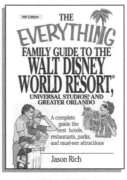

1-59337-179-9,
$14.95 ($22.95 CAN)